PENGUIN BOOKS

THE PEENEMÜNDE RAID

On a visit to France and Belgium in 1967 Martin Middlebrook was so impressed by the military cemeteries on the 1914–18 battlefields that he decided to write a book describing just one day in that war through the eyes of the ordinary men who took part. The book, *The First Day on the Somme*, was published by Allen Lane in 1971 and received international acclaim. Martin Middlebrook has since written other books that deal with important turning-points in the two world wars: these are *The Kaiser's Battle*, *Convoy*, *The Battle of Hamburg*, *Battleship* (with Patrick Mahoney), *The Schweinfurt-Regensburg Mission*, *The Nuremburg Raid*, *The Bomber Command War Diaries* (with Chris Everitt), *Task Force: The Falklands War, 1982*, *The Fight for the 'Malvinas'*, *The Berlin Raids* and *The Somme Battlefields* (with Mary Middlebrook). Many of his books have been published in the United States and West Germany and three of them in Japan, Yugoslavia and Poland.

Martin Middlebrook is a Fellow of the Royal Historical Society. Each summer he takes parties of visitors on conducted tours of the First World War battlefields.

D1434545

Martin Middlebrook

THE
PEENEMÜNDE
RAID

The Night of 17–18 August 1943

PENGUIN BOOKS

PENGUIN BOOKS

Published by the Penguin Group
Penguin Books Ltd, 27 Wrights Lane, London W8 5TZ, England
Penguin Books USA Inc., 375 Hudson Street, New York, New York 10014, USA
Penguin Books Australia Ltd, Ringwood, Victoria, Australia
Penguin Books Canada Ltd, 10 Alcorn Avenue, Toronto, Ontario, Canada M4V 3B2
Penguin Books (NZ) Ltd, 182–190 Wairau Road, Auckland 10, New Zealand

Penguin Books Ltd, Registered Offices: Harmondsworth, Middlesex, England

First published by Allen Lane 1982
Published in Penguin Books 1988
10 9 8 7 6 5 4 3

Printed in England by Clays Ltd, St Ives plc
Filmset in Baskerville

Contents

List of Plates

(The Deutsches Museum is in Munich.)

List of Maps

Maps by Reginald Piggott from preliminary drawings
by Mary Middlebrook

Introduction

In the early evening of Friday 8 September 1944 – three months after the Allied invasion of Normandy – there was a violent explosion outside No. 13 Staveley Road, Chiswick, in west London. When the dust and debris had subsided, there was found in the roadway a crater thirty feet across and twenty feet deep. Three people who lived nearby were killed and seventeen more were injured.

The people of London had become used to German bombs and recently to flying bombs (sometimes called V-1s or 'Doodle Bugs'), but this explosion had not been preceded by a warning siren and no one had heard either the sound of German bombers or the distinctive noise of a flying-bomb engine, for which all London ears listened intently at this period of the war. Many people had heard, however, an unusual, reverberating double 'boom' immediately after the explosion at Chiswick and, a little later, a peculiar 'whooshing' sound. Within a minute, there was a repetition of these strange events near Epping in Essex, twenty-five miles to the north-east of Chiswick, this time in open country, so that there were no casualties. The Epping explosion caused little comment and the Chiswick phenomenon was attributed to a faulty gas main. The authorities made little attempt to deny this explanation.

But the Chiswick explosion had been caused by three quarters of a ton of high explosive contained in the nose of a large rocket launched by a German artillery unit from a position in Holland, 200 miles away. The double 'boom' heard after the explosion was the noise of the rocket breaking the sound barrier, and the 'whoosh' that followed was created when the plunging missile – travelling at over 2,000 miles per hour – pushed its way through the denser air encountered as it approached the ground from a height of more than fifty miles. This event was a turning point in the history of warfare; the three people killed at Chiswick – sixty-three-year-old Mrs Ada Harrison, three-year-old Rosemary Clarke, and Sapper Bernard Browning who had been on leave from the Royal Engineers – were the first British victims of the operational use of military rockets. The Chiswick rocket was not the first to be fired in anger, however; at 7.28 that morning a similar rocket, dispatched from Holland in the direction of Paris, had exploded in a suburb, the name of which is not recorded in any Paris archive. *Le Figaro* states that six people died and forty-five were injured and that forty houses over a radius of 300 yards were damaged. The Paris press attributed the explosion to a V-1 flying bomb. The rockets continued to fall for the next seven months. They always arrived without warning. There never was any defence.

Their introduction did not come as a surprise to the Allied authorities, who had been making strenuous efforts to delay and frustrate the German rocket programme. Without these efforts, the terrible weapons would have struck many weeks earlier, and the ensuing campaign would have been longer and of greater intensity. It was not only civilians in London and other cities who benefited; even the success of the invasion of Normandy might have been imperilled had the German rockets come into operation at the time and in the numbers planned and if they had been fired against the Channel ports being used for the invasion.

The main Allied countermove against the rocket had been a raid by the Royal Air Force on a hitherto unbombed target on the Baltic coast of Germany. This target, Peenemünde, was the site of the experimental and development work carried out by the German rocket designers, and it was attacked at very great risk to the bomber crews in the early hours of 18 August 1943. This book is the story of that air operation. In preparing it, I have attempted to identify each major element in the story, proceeded to collect as much documentation as possible to provide a firm background, and, finally, searched for as many people as I could find who were participants in the raid.

The identification of the main groups of participants was easy: first the R.A.F. bomber crews who carried out the raid together with their commanders and the planning staffs; then their counterparts in the Luftwaffe's defending fighter forces; and finally the many and diverse people whose work and homes were at Peenemünde. The documentary research for the R.A.F. side of the operation was also easy; but it was soon found that original documents both from Peenemünde itself and from the Luftwaffe units defending it are scarce. A framework for the Luftwaffe side can be constructed, however, from various scattered documents, and for Peenemünde itself one is lucky to have two books that are almost as valuable as prime sources: General Dornberger, the German military commander at Peenemünde, survived the war to write his memoirs, *V-2, Der Schuss ins Weltall*; and the English historian David Irving, after a classic research effort, produced his history of the German V-weapon programme, *The Mare's Nest*, in 1964.[1] I willingly acknowledge the use I made of these two books.

For me, however, the most interesting part of my preparation is always the contact made with those who took part in the events I wish to describe, and this book has been as fruitful as any. Suffice it at this point to say that it has been my pleasure to have met many representatives of every group of people involved and to have corresponded with many more: the reader will in turn meet many of them in the following pages. There are, I believe, no major gaps in the coverage of the main elements of the Peenemünde story.

The central theme of the book is the R.A.F. raid on Peenemünde on the night of 17/18 August 1943, the Luftwaffe defence of that target, and the events on the ground during the raid and immediately afterwards.

The Peenemünde operation was as unique as was the nature of the target. Two of my earlier books – *The Nuremberg Raid* and *The Battle of Hamburg* – described R.A.F. raids which resulted in extremes of good and bad fortune for both sides, but the tactics employed at Nuremberg and Hamburg were the routine ones for Bomber Command during the relevant periods of the war. The targets were large German cities, the methods the standard ones employed to ensure that, despite the difficulties of night bombing, some useful part of the target city was always hit. Peenemünde was different. Compared to Nuremberg and Hamburg, this was a minute target: nevertheless the normal, front-line units of Bomber Command, mostly without any special training, all with no more than twelve hours' notice before their take-off time, were dispatched on what was, as far as I am aware, the only purely precision raid carried out at night by the full strength of Bomber Command during the war.

Further research has been devoted to a secondary theme: a description of the unique community of Peenemünde before the attack. Two other subsidiary subjects – the Allied intelligence effort to discover what work was being carried out at Peenemünde and the story of German rocket development – have already been described in excellent books; I have nothing new to offer, and have therefore dealt with these aspects in no more detail than is necessary to provide a background for the main story.

NOTE

1. Dornberger's book, published by Bechtle Verlag, Esslingen, in 1952, was translated into English and published as *V-2* by Viking Press, New York, in 1954. *The Mare's Nest* was published by Kimber of London.

CHAPTER I

Peenemünde – The Sleeping Beauty

The rocket men had come to Peenemünde in 1937.

It has been said that Peenemünde was one of the offspring of the frustrations of the Treaty of Versailles which, after the defeat of 1918, imposed severe limitations on Germany's use of conventional weapons. It is probably true that the German armed forces looked to rocketry as a means of developing weapons not subject to the treaty restrictions; but it is equally possible that, even without Versailles, German initiative and ingenuity would still have led to the adoption of rocketry for military purposes. Whatever the reason, the German Army – the Wehrmacht – was prepared in the 1930s to devote manpower and resources to the development of what had, until then, been little more than an amateur interest for civilian scientists and engineers. The vision of some of those early German space enthusiasts was astounding; they planned to send postal rockets from Berlin to New York, and even to visit the moon! In 1931 the Wehrmacht built an experimental centre in remote woodland near the village of Kummersdorf, south of Berlin, but the work soon outgrew the accommodation, and the search for a new location led to Peenemünde.

Peenemünde was then a small fishing village on the right bank of the river Peene where it flows into the Baltic; the name in fact means 'the mouth of the Peene'. It is often described as being 'on the island of Usedom', but that is a misleading technicality: the ragged-shaped area of land called Usedom, more than twenty-five miles long, is an 'island' only because it is separated from the mainland at its southern end by another small river, the Swine, at Swinemünde. For practical purposes, it will be a better to regard Peenemünde as being at the seaward end of a long peninsula which varied in width from fifteen miles to as little as 500 yards. The area had two advantages – its remoteness and the fact that the east coast of the peninsula looked out over an uninterrupted stretch of German-controlled sea 300 miles in length. That stretch of the Baltic would provide a safe firing range for German rockets for as long as Peenemünde was destined to hold a place in the history of rocket research.

In a complicated arrangement between the Wehrmacht and the Luftwaffe, it was decided to share the cost of building a joint experimental establishment, together with the necessary living quarters for families. The Luftwaffe's construction department, which had a reputation for producing elegant yet functional buildings of the type and scale required, would actually carry out the work. But the 'joint-service' aspect of the plan did not survive the test of time, and the Luftwaffe eventually drew off most of its activities to other places and to the airfield being built nearby. This was the genesis of the *Heeres-Versuchsanstalt, Peenemünde* – the Military Experimental Station, Peenemünde. Building began in 1937, and the first scientists soon moved in.

The forerunners of the new community found themselves in one of the most beautiful – and healthy – parts of north Germany. The northern end of the peninsula, on which the experimental station was soon to be constructed, was a nature reserve, virtually untouched by man.

The place was far away from any large towns or traffic of any kind and consisted of dunes and marshland overgrown with ancient oaks and pines, nestling in untroubled solitude behind a reedy foreland reaching far out into smooth water. Big Pomeranian deer with dark antlers roamed through the heather and among the bilberry bushes of the woods right to the sands of the low-lying coast. Swarms of ducks, crested grebes, coots and swans inhabited this beautiful spot, undisturbed for years by the report of the huntsman's shotgun.

So was later to write the army officer who commanded the Peene-münde establishment.[1] The people who arrived then have the fondest memories of that beautiful forest and those superb dunes and beaches. The climate is semi-continental and the summers are warm, much warmer than on Germany's North Sea coast; everyone became well tanned. The winters on the other hand are crisp and cold, and the sea often freezes over: people have walked across the ice to the island of Greifswalder Oie, seven miles away.

It was lonely, too, in those early days. The nearest branch railway line was seven miles away, and only one narrow lane ran up the peninsula and through the woods to Peenemünde village. To the south and across the river Peene were some small towns, but the nearest cities were Rostock and Stettin, each nearly seventy miles away; Berlin was 110 miles to the south. The loneliness and inaccessibility were not to last for long. The builders moved in.

The heart of the new Peenemünde was constructed among the dense woods near the north-eastern corner of the peninsula; here were the experimental, research and development laboratories and work-shops for the rocket programme and the headquarters office block. A

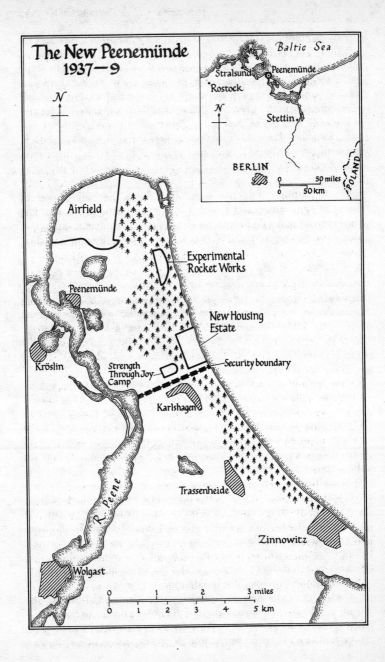

The New Peenemünde 1937–9

N

Baltic Sea

Stralsund
Rostock
Peenemünde

Stettin

BERLIN

POLAND

50 miles
50 km

N

Airfield

Experimental Rocket Works

Peenemünde

New Housing Estate

Kröslin

Strength Through Joy Camp

Security boundary

Karlshagen

R. Peene

Trassenheide

Zinnowitz

Wolgast

0   1   2   3 miles
0   1   2   3   4   5 km

host of small buildings soon sprang up among the pines. As few trees as possible were cut down, in order to leave some cover from inquisitive eyes; the new work was thus concealed at ground or sea level, but, as R.A.F. photographic reconnaissance pilots would find a few years later, every building was clearly visible from the air. This part of the new establishment – the *Entwicklungswerk* or Experimental Works – became known officially as 'Peenemünde East'. To the north, in a long line on the boundary between the forest and the sandy meadows which ringed the northern tip of the peninsula, would eventually be constructed no less than ten launching stands for the test firing of rockets. These stands now hold a privileged place in the history of space exploration.

On the more extensive sand meadows on the west of the peninsula, where only a small area of trees had to be cleared, the Luftwaffe built an airfield, known as Peenemünde West, which would prove very useful for time-saving communications flights for senior personnel of the army rocket establishment and for their visitors. But the airfield also had an important Luftwaffe function: it became a centre for the test flying of secret types of aircraft, and the new population of Peenemünde would see much interesting air activity in ensuing years. In turn, the Luftwaffe men would be fascinated witnesses to the test firings of the military rockets. There was, naturally, some rivalry, and a growing envy among the Luftwaffe of the seemingly limitless resources devoted to the rockets.

In the remaining south-west corner of the peninsula little expansion took place. This less wooded area was in clear view of the civilians in the villages across the river Peene. A new coal-fired, steam-turbine power station provided 20,000 kilowatts of electricity; later, a factory was built to produce the liquid oxygen which was to be the chief rocket fuel. These two plants were close to the original Peenemünde village and harbour.

I have been given conflicting versions of what became of the original Peenemünde village and its inhabitants. The community was certainly not allowed to remain as it was. One report says that many of the local men became security guards in the army establishment and their wives became domestic servants for the families of the incoming scientists in their new housing area. Another contributor says that the 300 or so inhabitants were evacuated and most of the smaller buildings in the village demolished, but this may not have happened until after the outbreak of war. Whichever version is correct, it is certain that Peenemünde village became a victim of the scientific invasion. The customs house, the harbourmaster's office and the large home of the manager of a nearby state-owned farm were allowed to remain intact, as were some of the more useful buildings in the village such as several small hotels and inns. The existing harbour was deepened and improved. It is said that the only original inhabitants to remain in their homes were the farm manager and his dairyman and their families and one old lady who refused to move. Despite what had happened to her former neighbours, this old lady is said to have shown the most friendly attitude to the people who now moved in – the new harbourmaster, the power station manager and one or two of the other new families. When most of the women and children were evacuated after the R.A.F. raid, this lady apparently still refused to budge. The old Peenemünde village was destined to be one of the smallest and quietest parts of the new community.

On the east coast of the peninsula, south of the region being taken over so thoroughly by the Wehrmacht and the Luftwaffe, stood the holiday and farming village of Karlshagen, the first of many strung out to the east along the sweeping coast facing the Baltic. Just north of the old Karlshagen, the planners decided to build a new housing area for the families of the builders, scientists, engineers, administrators, and all the others needed to construct and staff the new establishment. The forest was cleared and the new homes were built – and in the most elegant of styles, too. Photographs show the high quality of design and construction, particularly of the houses of the senior men who brought their families. The new settlement was complete with shops and a school; a sports field was laid out, and an existing modern hotel on the edge of the sea became the *Kameradschaftsheim* – the local club. All around were beautiful pine forests and, only a short walk away, always the dunes and the beach.

(The Germans called this new housing the 'Karlshagen Siedlung'. The word *Siedlung*, translated literally, means 'settlement', 'colony' or 'housing estate'; because what happened in this area will form an important part of later chapters, it is necessary to choose the best term when referring to it. The 'scientists' living quarters' of some books is not apt because it was essentially a family area, although father came home most nights, and because scientists formed only a small part of the male community; a better phrase is 'housing estate'. It should also be stated here that the term 'Peenemünde' will often be used for the whole research establishment even though the establishment included Karlshagen and, later, other villages.)

So was built Germany's new rocket research centre. The different parts were linked by a new road system and by a fast new electric railway line which started at the old station at Zinnowitz, four miles south of Karlshagen. This new railway, its track and rolling stock based on the modern *Schnellbahn*, or overhead railway, at Berlin, was one of the minor wonders of the new Peenemünde. It brought to work each day those who had to live outside the official encampment. When they reached the boundary fence across the peninsula at the southern limit of the secret area, they had to show their special passes; indeed, security was to be an integral aspect of Peenemünde life from first to last. Each part had its guards, and only those who had the pass required for that area were ever allowed into it.

Much fascinating work would be done by the scientists, engineers and technicians who came to the establishment, but it must be stressed that one project alone would dominate all life there from beginning to end. Peenemünde had been created in order to develop a liquid-fuelled rocket capable of carrying a warhead of high explosive for the purposes of military bombardment. The performance specifications had already been set down on paper by Peenemünde's leading scientist in 1937, the year in which the new establishment started work and two years before the war. It was hoped that this weapon would develop a thrust of 45,000 lb. and carry a one-ton warhead to a target 160 miles away.[2] In fact, the rocket eventually produced developed a greater thrust and range – 55,000 lb. and 200 miles – but its warhead was to be smaller by a quarter. The potential of this weapon, if it could be made to work and if it could be mass-produced, was breathtaking. There could be no conceivable defence against it.

To prepare for this exciting venture, the German team first produced a series of three small-scale test rockets, giving them the deliberately vague cover name *Aggregat*, which means nothing more than 'machine unit' or 'assembly of machine parts'. The '*Aggregat*' was quickly abbreviated to its capital letter, and so these early test rockets became simply the A-1, A-2 and A-3. The big military rocket which was to follow would thus carry the prosaic title 'A-4'. This book does not intend to cover the interesting but often frustrating work carried out by the Germans in the preparatory stages. It is sufficient to say that the A-3, in particular, ran into so many difficulties that a further experimental rocket, the A-5, had to be produced, and that on the outbreak of war in September 1939, the A-4 was still little more than a dream.

The officer entrusted by the Wehrmacht with establishing Peenemünde and pushing the A-4 project forward was Walter Dornberger, whose home town was Giessen. A First World War artillery officer, in the late 1920s he had completed with distinction an engineering course at the Berlin Technical Institute. The Wehrmacht had then posted him straight to the rocket work which would establish his place in history. There is no doubt that Dornberger was the ideal man for this challenging task. One of his wartime adjutants at Peenemünde, Werner Magirius, has described him thus:

> As good an officer as he was an engineer, with a strong personality and a direct manner of command. It was difficult to find one person who combined the necessary qualities of a military commander and an engineer with an understanding of the engineer's language and that third quality, that of what we would now call a project manager. He represented Peenemünde very well against any military department or industrial concern or anyone else who threatened Peenemünde's interests.

Dornberger undoubtedly deserves his position in history, but he is forced to give pride of place in the popular conception of space research to his chief scientist. The legendary Wernher von Braun worked on Peenemünde's military rocket programme from the very beginning, coming straight to Dornberger's staff as a nineteen-year-old student. The partnership between the army officer and the scientist seventeen years his junior was an ideal one and, if there was ever a period when co-operation was less than perfect, it never became public knowledge.

Von Braun came from a Prussian *Junker* family and his traditional, landowning father could never understand how he had fathered a scientific genius. Tall, fair-haired, handsome and vigorous, a bachelor with a succession of girlfriends which kept Peenemünde's gossips busy, Wernher von Braun worked extremely hard; it is said that he sometimes needed three secretaries, working in shifts, to cope with his paperwork. He relaxed by sailing on the Baltic, as did many others, and by riding in the woods on one of the beautiful horses from the stables reserved for Peenemünde's leading figures. He was also a qualified pilot and often used the nearby airfield for private or business flights in his single-engined Messerschmitt *Taifun*. He and a few other bachelor or unaccompanied members of Peenemünde's senior ranks lived 'on the job' in a small dwelling block near the headquarters office building (where Dornberger also lived; his wife had remained in Berlin). Von Braun was a well-known, popular and respected figure in the community. There were of course many other brilliant men there, but it was he who was the acknowledged genius and leader of the scientific team.

Much has been made by the surviving members of the team of the idealism of the early rocket scientists, and attempts are made, particularly in the case of von Braun, to present them as men whose real aim was that of peaceful space research, their work on military rockets being no more than a temporary, if unfortunately necessary, phase.

There is some truth in these claims. Von Braun undoubtedly had his eye on the moon as the eventual destination for his rockets, and he was sometimes heard to say that, if he lived to be seventy, he would be the first man to stand on the moon. The early A-4 rockets all had painted on them the motif of a rocket alongside a crescent moon upon which sat a beautiful girl. In the later stages of the war, von Braun's grumbling about the wartime use to which his rockets were being put and Germany's fading chance of victory led to his arrest by the Gestapo together with two of his colleagues. They were imprisoned at Stettin, and it was only the rocket programme's continuing need of them that enabled Dornberger to secure their release.

These later events do not alter the fact that, even when first established, Peenemünde existed as part of Germany's plans for war. The research centre may have been the most exciting and interesting place for young scientists and engineers to be at that time, and the work there certainly did lead to a man one day standing on the moon, but all the resources allocated to this place had one purpose – to produce that A-4 military bombardment rocket.

In the last few months of peace, Albert Speer, Hitler's gifted architect, was given the task of completing the plans for Peenemünde, and there was a brief phase of glorious expectation for the scientists when Speer announced that the establishment would not be concerned solely with military rockets but would also be a prestigious centre for lunar and space research. The coming of war swiftly ended these dreams, and Peenemünde had to get down to the serious work of developing the A-4 for military use. During the next three and a half years financial support was erratic, waxing and waning according to Germany's military fortunes on her various fighting fronts, her declining expectations of victory, and her increasing desperation. Peenemünde also suffered severely from the rivalries of various ministers and ministries in Berlin, all struggling for allocations of scarce resources.

Peenemünde survived these tribulations, and we can pass swiftly on to the beginning of 1943. The establishment was at that time enjoying strong support. Germany had seen her Luftwaffe fail to knock out Britain in 1940, was watching the destruction of her own cities by Allied bombing, and was in the process of suffering the crushing defeat of Stalingrad. Where conventional arms were failing, Germany now had the greatest need for new weapons such as the A-4 rocket. Money and manpower were pouring into Peenemünde.

Great strides had been made in the development of the A-4, and test firings had commenced from the now famous Test Stand VII in June 1942. The first had been a failure and a second, in August, performed no better; but the third attempt, on 3 October, was a complete success. Defying the forces of gravity, the rocket thrust its way into the stratosphere, broke through the sound barrier unscathed, tilted to a near horizontal trajectory exactly as planned, and flew on to come down in the Baltic in the correct position 120 miles from Peenemünde. Dornberger is reputed to have said to von Braun, 'Today, the spaceship was born!' The test firings continued; problems were gradually eliminated, reliability increased, the range extended. There was no technical reason why the rocket should not become an operational reality. With Germany now controlling the whole of the Channel coast of France, Belgium and Holland, London and south-east England were within easy range and the bombing of German cities could be avenged. It was at this time that the A-4 came increasingly to be known as the V-2. The 'V' originally stood for *Versuchs-muster* (experimental type). Later, in the hope of boosting morale in bombed cities, German propaganda declared that it meant *Vergel-tungswaffen* (weapons of revenge); the exact nature of these weapons was not however revealed. In this way, the A-4 rocket became the more popularly known and remembered V-2, which is what I shall call it from now on.

The whole establishment basked in the glory of the successful tests. Dornberger had been steadily promoted, becoming a major general in May 1943. Von Braun was awarded the honorary title of professor, as well as the honorary rank of *Sturmbannführer* in the S.S. – a dignity he probably found embarrassing; he wore his black S.S. uniform only when required to do so.

As the experimental work on the V-2 neared its end, plans were being made for a second generation of rockets, in particular for an A-9, probably the world's first planned multi-stage rocket, with an ordinary A-4 (V-2) mounted on top of a larger first-stage rocket to extend the range to more than 400 miles. This would be able to bombard any part of England and Wales and reach into Scotland as far as Glasgow. Other projects were also in hand, of which the *Wasserfall* and *Rheintochter*, both ground-to-air anti-aircraft missiles, and the *Taifun*, an anti-aircraft rocket, were the most prominent. But the V-2 still claimed the greater part of Peenemünde's attention.

For the V-2, the emphasis was changing from development to production. The first, almost hand-made, V-2s had been assembled in a large workshop in the middle of a one-mile-long area of virgin woodland between the Experimental Works Peenemünde East and the housing estate. A second, larger workshop, reputedly based on the design of the modern Volkswagen motor-car assembly buildings at Wolfsburg, was now being constructed nearby and fitted with equipment to enable V-2s to be mass-produced from the hundreds of parts being made in factories all over Germany. The first trial runs of this assembly-line were being made by the midsummer of 1943. The resulting rockets were to be used in further test firings and also for the working up of the first Wehrmacht field units being formed and trained at Zempin, just south of Peenemünde. The next phase, to follow very shortly, would be the production of rockets for operational use.

The two assembly halls in the pine woods became known as *Werke Sud* or Peenemünde South; the English term 'Production Works' is a suitable one. It was only one of three places where V-2s were to be assembled; the others were at the Zeppelin plant at Friedrichshafen in southern Germany and at a factory at Wiener Neustadt in Austria. When this plan was first mooted, all three were considered to be reasonably remote and safe from serious Allied air attack. Speer, now in charge of German war industry, appointed a special overseeing committee headed by a man called Gerhard Degenkolb, and in April 1943 the Degenkolb Committee in Berlin produced a programme for the increasing production of V-2s at Peenemünde and the other two factories which aimed at reaching a peak of 950 rockets per month by the end of the year!

The V-2 was not the only secret weapon to be seen at Peenemünde. On the other side of the peninsula, at the airfield of Peenemünde West, Luftwaffe scientists were hard at work on their projects. The most important of these – the *Fi. 103* ('*Fi*' for Fieseler, the aircraft company concerned), which later became so well known as the V-1 – was a pilotless flying bomb which was simply aimed at its target, launched from a ramp on the ground, and flew on until the measured amount of fuel for its small jet engine was expended, whereupon it dived to the ground and exploded. The advantage of the V-1 when it came into service would be that it was cheap and easy to produce; its main disadvantage was that it would fly only on a constant course and altitude and at only a modest speed – just over 300 miles per hour – enabling it to be tracked by radar and attacked by Allied anti-aircraft guns and fighters.

The V-1 was the Luftwaffe's main hope of securing a major place in Germany's secret weapons programme, and the direct competitor of the Wehrmacht's V-2 rocket. Although the V-1 was a late starter – serious work began only in 1942 – and although early tests had been disappointing, it was making rapid progress by the summer of 1943, and plans were in hand for the production of 2,000 V-1s per month by the end of the year and no less than 5,000 per month by the middle of 1944. As far as the story of Peenemünde is concerned, however, it must be stressed that the V-1 was conceived and developed elsewhere in Germany; Peenemünde West airfield was merely the location of its test flying programme, where these strange little aircraft were launched, like the V-2s, out over the Baltic.

The Luftwaffe team was testing other secret projects such as the Messerschmitt 163 rocket-propelled aircraft, which had exceeded the official world speed record of 624 m.p.h. in May 1941, and a radio-controlled glider-bomb which the Luftwaffe would use later in the war to attack Allied shipping. There was often other test flying at Peenemünde airfield, but compared with the Wehrmacht's large and sophisticated establishment on the other side of the peninsula, the Luftwaffe base was modest. The two services worked in friendly rivalry despite one V-2 test firing which went astray and fell on the airfield, destroying four of the Luftwaffe's aircraft and leaving a large hole in the ground.

To perform its wartime function, the unusual community at Peenemünde had increased its numbers several times over, and many thousands of people of both sexes and of all ages now worked and lived there, wearing an array of different uniforms or a range of civilian clothes contrasting from the smartest of business suits to the most ragged of labourer's clothes, and often speaking the strange languages of the distant countries in which they had been born. It is unlikely that anyone will ever be able to identify and catalogue every single element of Peenemünde society at that time. It must have been one of the most interesting, varied and – in parts – talented communities in Germany.

The original body of scientists and engineers and their families remained almost intact; no part of Germany's war effort had a greater call on their services. Indeed they received strong reinforcements, for the whole of Germany and its armed forces were combed out for technical men, who arrived in increasing numbers as the war progressed. The principals of German universities and technical high schools were asked to name their best graduates of recent years, and these men were then tracked down. Many men were thus suddenly plucked from military service or other civilian employment and found themselves at Peenemünde.

Such transfers were accepted with the greatest of pleasure by men taken from military units. At a stroke they were virtually freed from normal military discipline and were able to practise their hard-learned civilian qualifications in this quiet, pleasant, and seemingly safe part of Germany. Typical of many was one of my contacts who had been serving in a Wehrmacht signals unit in France and was sent to work for '*Elektromechanische Werke GmbH, Karlshagen*' which he discovered was one of several cover names for the Peenemünde research establishment. His pay increased six times over! Once there, even the youngest and most able-bodied were safe from routine military conscription. Another man, a civilian engineer recently sent to Peenemünde, who received calling-up papers for the S.S. which his wife had posted on from his home, handed them to his departmental chief at Peenemünde and heard no more of them. '*Peenemünde war stärker als die S.S.*,' he says. 'Peenemünde was more powerful than the S.S.'

Peenemünde's original accommodation soon proved inadequate; the housing estate expanded a little to take in the families of the more prominent newcomers, but most had to look elsewhere. The expansion was a boon for the owners of the numerous hotels and guest houses in the string of pre-war holiday resorts along the coast to the southeast. In this way the nearby villages of Zinnowitz, Zempin and Koserow, and other places as far afield as the larger town of Heringsdorf, twenty miles away, were filled up with Peenemünde's overflow. Some men managed to move their families into the new homes, but most were forced to live in little bachelor communities in the holiday resorts, travelling to work each day by the coastal railway and changing to Peenemünde's electric railway system at Zinnowitz station, the great meeting place for arrivals and departures. Others lived in the inland villages, but not many, for there was little spare accommodation there.

Peenemünde gradually became more militarized as the war progressed, and a formal military unit, *Versuchskommando Nord* (Experimental Detachment, North), was established there late in 1942. I would not be the first to describe this as one of the strangest units in the German Army. The successive waves of technical men remained in uniform, but rank meant little, and orders were usually given by the man with the highest technical qualification regardless of the insignia of rank, or lack of it, on his arm. Civilians often ran supposedly military departments. The result of this military expansion, however, was that an increasing number of Peenemünde's inhabitants had to be housed in army barracks. The first was created at Karlshagen in a convenient pre-war holiday camp belonging to *Kraft durch Freude* (Strength through Joy), an organization founded by the Nazi Party after the German trade unions had been disbanded in 1933 which owned hotels, holiday camps and even cruise liners for workers and their families. The distinctive horseshoe-shaped camp at Karlshagen would later show up well on R.A.F. aerial reconnaissance photographs. I have been given figures of the number of men who lived there ranging from 700 to 3,000, but 1,000 is believed to be the best estimate of its capacity. More barrack blocks were built to the south and further detachments of soldiers established at other coastal villages. Peenemünde always expanded to the south.

Uniforms, besides the Wehrmacht's, included those of the Luftwaffe from the airfield and the local Flak units, S.S. detachments whose purpose will be described later, and sailors from Flak ships and patrol vessels operating from the naval base now established at the former fishing harbour of the old Peenemünde village. A significant recent addition to the military garrison, however, was *Lehr und Versuchs Batterie 444* (Training and Experimental Battery No. 444). The '444' was irrelevant; this was the first unit to train the soldiers who would eventually fire operational V-2s against England. They started work just before Peenemünde was bombed, operating from one of the test stands – not the main Test Stand VII. Gefreiter Werner Küsters was a member of the unit.

I had only been seventeen years old when I joined the army and was only twenty when I came to Peenemünde and, when I saw my first rocket test firing, my jaw dropped with astonishment. I had been in the artillery and had seen the biggest guns fired – including the famous 80-cm railway gun called '*Dora*'. Its shell had a muzzle velocity of 160 kilometres per hour. With the rocket, however, you just heard '*Zero*' and then watched the flames start under the rocket, the electrical connecting leads fall away and the rocket went up with only the slowest of movement to start with. It was this contrast that astonished me.[3]

Peenemünde was by no means an all-male establishment. No women scientists are believed to have worked in the top rocket team, although the famous test pilot Hanna Reitsch frequently flew from the Luftwaffe airfield; but a large number of mostly single girls were employed as secretaries, clerks and typists. Some had received technical training and were able to process much of the scientific data connected with the rocket experiments. A few were the daughters of the earlier established families of scientists and officials, but most had been directed more recently to Peenemünde. These unattached girls now lived between the housing estate and the beach, one of the best spots in Peenemünde, in a group of buildings the largest of which was the *Kameradschaftsheim*, once a hotel, more recently a club for the pre-war Peenemünde community. Many survivors of Peenemünde talk of the youth, the vivacity and the beauty of this band of young women, and their presence was undoubtedly one of the more attractive aspects of life.

It was a fine life inside Peenemünde, at least for the Germans there. Some of the technical men worked long hours but, for such men, there could be no better place in Germany to be at that time – working on the exciting rocket project far away from fighting and air raids. One man says that such was the interest of his work, amid surroundings of natural beauty and in such congenial company, that his time at Peenemünde was just like a long holiday. The secretary to one of the top scientists says that such men did not always work at high pressure; they preferred a more careful, academic approach. When she talked to him about a letter from her brother at the front and the enthusiasm of the soldiers for the new 'wonder weapons', the scientist replied, 'Rubbish, the A-4 needs ten years of careful work yet.'

I asked some of the Germans who were there in those last few weeks before the bombing what were the best and the worst aspects of life at that time. The men had hardly any complaints; the women only a few. Peenemünde could be remote and boring; some people felt cut off from the mainstream and longed for city life, big shops, museums, theatres. One person said that the 'class structure' was too rigid. The majority, however, were more than satisfied. There were home-made pleasures to be had; social evenings and film shows were held in the canteen of the military barracks at Karlshagen. For those who liked fresh air, solitude, a quiet life of reading or homely evenings with neighbours, Peenemünde was perfect. Many people tell of the great beauty of the local beaches and the pleasures of swimming and sunbathing during those idyllic midsummer weeks of 1943. Zinnowitz, four miles away along the electric railway, was the 'play town'. Female company was short, but there were several good inns where comradely singing could be heard on most evenings.

The following people were all at Peenemünde during these weeks:

I was an apprentice mechanic at Peenemünde East. We were, of course, subject to strict military discipline. Hoisting flags, singing and window cleaning were all part of our daily routine. This did not bother me at the time; we youngsters had already got used to all that in the Hitler Youth movement. Despite the tough training conditions, I liked the technical education and also our frequent sporting activities for which one received sports medals which were regarded as highly desirable. Comradeship, at that time, was not only writ large but it led to a feeling of human togetherness. This comradeship was prevalent at Peenemünde and was not confined to professional or social groups. Whether one travelled by train or was in a canteen or in an air-raid shelter or at a lathe, we all felt like one big family. Perhaps this spirit of togetherness was also due to the fact that we had all, from the youngest apprentice to the general in command, come to this lonely island from all parts of Germany to witness the building of the A-4 rocket ... You might even meet von Braun at the dentist's.

I tell you all this to explain the phenomenon of being 'a member of the Peenemünde team'. I thought it was a remarkable thing at the time and that was certainly the best part of Peenemünde. (Gerhard Rühr)

There was nothing wrong with Peenemünde at all. After Russia, it was just like a holiday. You met all the interesting people at Peenemünde and that place was certainly something special in my life. I would go back there now if the development work was still going on. (Edgar Heym)

I was immensely proud to be at Peenemünde and associated with that wonder weapon which we called the V-2. We knew all about the so-called V-1 flying bomb but it was our rocket that was the big hope. We realized that the enemy could shoot down the V-1 but they could have no defence against our rockets. (Gerhard Hufer)

We lived peacefully and contentedly at Peenemünde until just before the raid. It was a lovely time, so completely untroubled with the world's affairs and it seemed to us that we must be safe and out of danger there. Bathing in the beautiful Baltic was how we normally occupied our free time. (Lotti Priem)

At that time, before the R.A.F. raid, Peenemünde was like a 'Dornröschen' – a sleeping beauty. (Inge Holz)

NOTES

1. *V-2* by Walter Dornberger, p. 41 of the Bantam Books edition.
2. Letter from Werner von Braun to War Office, Berlin; Irving, *The Mare's Nest*, p. 17.
3. All personal quotations are from conversations or correspondence with participants unless other sources are noted. Ranks are those held in August 1943. Quotations by women will use the surnames that the women had in 1943. The Acknowledgements section shows any subsequent married names.

CHAPTER 2

The Foreigners

It should not be forgotten, however, that much of the work in the exciting rocket programme now relied on the unwilling sweat and some hardship of a veritable army of foreigners. While Peenemünde could claim as much technical manpower as it needed from the German economy and armed services, it had to take what labour it was sent for the vast amount of manual work associated with its projects. All the digging, fetching and carrying, pulling and pushing, all the unskilled heavy work, was now being done by foreign workers. There was nothing special about Peenemünde in this respect. Most unskilled and semi-skilled German workers were now serving in the armed forces; only the very young, the old, the sick and the crippled were left. The places of the fit were filled with thousands upon thousands of prisoners of war and civilians taken from the German-occupied countries of Europe. It has been estimated that 5,000,000 foreigners eventually worked in Germany of whom no more than 200,000 were genuine volunteers.[1] The successful test firings of the V-2 in the autumn of 1942 and Germany's deteriorating military position had resulted in a huge expansion of Peenemünde's foreign labour force. The story is not complete without the story of 10–12,000 foreigners who were there in mid-1943 and who almost certainly exceeded the number of Germans. Their presence will be particularly relevant to the description of the R.A.F. raid.

There were three distinct groups of foreigners at Peenemünde. By far the most numerous were the civilian forced workers, 'slave labourers' to those writers who have little love for wartime Germany, '*Fremdarbeiter*' – 'guest workers' – to those who would gloss over the subject. General Dornberger calls them only 'construction workers' in his book. The Germans had differing attitudes to the taking of such manpower from their subject countries. In the East – in Poland, the Ukraine and Russia, which had never had large reserves of skilled labour – men and women were simply scooped up in large numbers and sent to Germany to do the most unskilled and dirtiest of work. In the West, however, the Germans started with a voluntary recruitment policy, looking mainly for skilled workers; but the number of volunteers was negligible and the Germans soon resorted to coercion.

The Military Governors introduced the necessary regulations and the local German *Reichsarbeitsdienst* (Labour Service) offices allocated quotas to towns and even to individual factories. In these various ways, trainloads – called 'transports' – of men and women were delivered from both East and West to many parts of Germany. For reasons of convenience, the Germans often delivered a complete transport or part of a transport to one place, so that a group of workers who had left one home area often remained together at their new place of work.

The largest national group at Peenemünde was from Poland, probably because of the proximity of Peenemünde and because the need was mainly for unskilled labour. I experienced little difficulty in making contact with survivors, and cannot speak too highly of the enthusiasm with which they offered their help for this book.

The Poles had come to Peenemünde from many parts of their homeland, a particularly large proportion of them young, some as young as sixteen. Most had been conscripted in the following way:

> A note came from the local *Reichsarbeitsdienst* to the farm where I was working, saying that I was to report at a certain place with food for one day and one change of clothes. It said that I would be well looked after. Then it was '*auf Wiedersehen*' and you were on your way. That was it!

Others were arrested and sent to Germany for petty offences against regulations, or even on suspicion of such offences. Others, again, had simply been taken from the streets of Warsaw and other cities in random round-ups. The latest Polish arrivals at Peenemünde were the men of a transport between 100 and 200 strong from Zamosc, a town in the rich farming area of Lubelskiego which had been chosen for 'Germanization' – i.e. the Polish population was to be evicted to make way for an eventual all-German settlement. The Lubelskiego men arrived at Peenemünde about a week before the bombing.

It is less easy to be precise about the other foreign civilians, and the following details may not be complete. There were Russians and Ukrainians, of course; there were Russians and Ukrainians everywhere in Germany. The few Ukrainian girls who did domestic work were probably the only female foreigners inside the establishment. There are also many reports of Czechs and Italians, the Italians probably being voluntary labour. Other reports mentioning Dutchmen and Yugoslavs in small numbers may be less reliable. It is certain that there were no Danes, and unlikely that there were any civilians from Belgium or Luxembourg; those who had been at Peenemünde in 1942 had been moved away. The most exact information on the smaller national groups comes from a Frenchman. Jean Degert states that there was an early transport of ninety-nine of his countrymen, all from the Atlantic coast in the Occupied Zone of France. His own group, eighty men strong, brought more recently from the Landes, had been embarked on a ship at Stettin. He thought that they were bound for Norway, but instead they were landed at Swinemünde and sent on to Peenemünde by train. Naturally, they had never heard of the place before, but Monsieur Degert says that 'this land of lakes, of marshes, of isolated farms, of sand dunes planted with pines, all reminded me of my home on the Landes coast.'

The earlier foreign workers had been housed in a small, five-barrack camp at Karlshagen, not far from the German civilian housing estate and the army barracks. When it became full, probably in 1942, an enormous new camp was built in virgin forest one and a half miles to the south, between the railway line and the sea. Photographs show that there may have been as many as forty large wooden barrack buildings in use in August 1943, with more being built. At least 8,000 and possibly as many as 10,000 men had their homes here. (There is sometimes confusion over the name of this camp. It was near the one-street village of Trassenheide, but also near the pre-war railway station named 'Karlshagen-Trassenheide'; therefore it was often referred to as 'the Karlshagen camp'. Because of the existence of the earlier labour camp nearer to Karlshagen village, however, it will be better to call this 'the Trassenheide camp'. The locations of these labour camps and of the other wartime additions to Peenemünde can be found on Map 2, page 47.)

Life was dull and grinding. A ten-hour working day was normal. Food was poor; the younger men, particularly, say that their main memory of Peenemünde is one of everlasting hunger. There was no home leave, letters only twice a month, hardly any parcels. The Germans' attitude to their forced employees was not consistent. Some groups were paid; others not. Some had better food and more privileges. There does not seem to have been any reason for some of the differences in treatment, although it is generally agreed that it was worse the further East a man had come from. The camps were surrounded by chain-link fencing with watch towers. Some of the workers were allowed out for short periods of relaxation, but at Zinnowitz there was a sign which read: 'Poles and dogs not allowed on the beach.'

The workers made the best of their life in the camps. The Poles at Trassenheide formed a little dance band which performed in a barrack hut; when the Germans half-heartedly tried to put a stop to it, the Poles simply moved on to another hut. Polish and Russian girls working on farms nearby sometimes came to the dances. This, too, was against regulations but the Germans usually turned a blind eye. One Polish girl, Irena Ocipka, who had been sent to work in Germany when she was only fourteen, wasn't at all worried.

> I didn't care. I would have been willing to pay the fine of twenty marks to have had that opportunity to meet fellow Poles. I looked at every face to see if I could find someone I knew from Warsaw. I longed to meet someone I knew from my own home area.

There was a brothel at Trassenheide – a not unusual feature of German forced-labour camps, intended to keep local women safe from attack. At Trassenheide, 2 Reichsmarks bought a girl, a vodka and two cigarettes.

Men who were later directed to other places in Germany say that Peenemünde compared well; but most foreigners hated being forced to work on weapons for use against the very people who were fighting to liberate their countries.

The large numbers of prisoners of war referred to in some accounts as working at Peenemünde were in fact mainly forced labour; 'prisoners of war' was a German euphemism. There may have been a few French soldiers, but the largest military group were the 300 or so Russian officers in the camp at Wolgast, six miles from Peenemünde. They were all technical men. A hundred of them worked in a large drawing office, producing blueprints for rocket parts; eighty-five more were in the 'graphite shop', making the delicately shaped graphite blades needed in the V-2's control system. Others worked in electrical and mechanical workshops. One of the Russians describes their living and working conditions as good. A completely different group were the prisoner-of-war 'volunteers' who provided most of the manpower for the smoke-generator companies which formed an important part of Peenemünde's air-raid defence. Unteroffizier Franz Czekalla, a German soldier, describes the Russians at his little post.

> I can remember them well. They were volunteers but I can't tell how willingly they had come. We two Germans couldn't guard them all the time and they were allowed to go freely inside a limited area. There were other Russians in a nearby labour camp and they hated and abused my four men because they were serving in a German military unit.
>
> When I went on leave they gave me little boxes decorated with shells for my family. I don't know where they found the paint; they

were very resourceful. They had a good time in their little hut; we often heard them singing. For the period in which we lived, their conditions, for Russians, were very good.

By contrast, the bottom of the heap were the unfortunate concentration-camp men. The reader may be surprised to learn that it was they who performed the final assembly work on the increasing number of V-2s being built in the newest production hall. A reliable report says that there were 1,200 of them.[2] They, too, were carefully selected technical men. One group actually had their living quarters on the lower floor of the production hall. A German civilian administrator contends that the conditions here were good by concentration-camp standards. 'It must have been one of the best concentration-camp units in Germany.' The prisoners were guarded by their own S.S. detachment, commanded by a young officer to whom the German administrator gave a bottle of cognac each day from his 'air-raid reserve' to induce the guard unit not to ill-treat the workers too much. The remaining men had a small compound attached to the Trassenheide labour camp. For security reasons, the choice of concentration-camp men for this work was sound: none of them was ever going to go home on leave or be released, and they had no contact with the outside world.

Who were these unfortunate men in their striped 'pyjama-suit' uniforms, probably living under the harshest conditions of anyone at Peenemünde? One report says they were mostly Germans; another report contradicts this. Despite appeals in many countries, I failed to find a single member of this shadowy group to give his own account. It is probable that they were a cross-section of Germany's concentration-camp population, Germans and non-Germans, probably some Jews. It is unlikely that many survived the war.

The Germans who once worked at Peenemünde and members of their families are acutely embarrassed to be reminded that their scientific research was partly based on the labour of so many dragged from their homes for no serious crime and held in such inhospitable conditions. This attitude is understandable after so many years; but a true historical record cannot but take account of this large body of men and their privations. In favour of the Peenemünde authorities it can be said that what happened there was no different from the normal routine of life in Germany at that time. The large-scale movement of forced civilian labour had not been foreseen by the Geneva Convention of 1929, which Germany had signed, and was not specifically prohibited, although post-war trials at Nuremberg and other places decreed that such behaviour had been a war crime.

Dornberger and von Braun did not ask for forced workers to be sent to Peenemünde although, when they requested more manpower, they knew that such men would be sent. The middle and lower ranks of the establishment had no say in the matter at all. Finally (in the absence of testimony from the men in the concentration-camp unit), it can be said that, while accommodation and food for the foreigners was basic and sometimes poor, there was no actual starvation and no evidence of unnecessary hardship or brutality.

So the eve of the R.A.F. raid found the establishment at its peak, with the German staff, their families, and the growing army of foreigners possibly numbering 17–20,000 souls. The security cordon had been extended seven miles further south to an ideally narrow neck of sand dunes astride the road and railway leading to Peenemünde from the south. This new barrier was manned by S.S. men; a second checkpoint had been established at the drawbridge over the river Peene at Wolgast. Except for these two entrances, the new security zone was completely surrounded by water. The inhabitants of the dormitory coastal villages and the inland farming villages on the 'island' had not been evacuated, but the original inner security fence and checkpoint kept them out of the most secret area.

Security was so tight that one soldier had no idea what was being made at Peenemünde until he had been there for three days. All arriving servicemen had to take a second soldiers' oath, swearing to keep absolute secrecy about the establishment on his visits home. All letters were censored. Those people who lived just outside the cordon had only the vaguest idea of what was happening. A sailor at the naval Flak school at Ueckeritz, four miles from the boundary, says that security measures were encountered '*auf Schritt und Tritt*' – 'at every step'. Another man nearby said that, '*keine Maus kam rein und raus*' – 'not even a mouse came in and out.' The rest of Germany was now hearing a lot from Propaganda Minister Goebbels about the new 'wonder weapons' with which Germany was going to repay the Allies for the bombing of German cities and turn the tide of the war, but V-1s, V-2s and Peenemünde were never mentioned. One secretary says that, if she had told her parents at home in another part of Germany, 'they would never have believed me; they would have thought I was crazy!'

NOTES

1. Jozef Garlinski, *Hitler's Last Weapons*, p. 39.
2. *Studien zur Geschichte der Konzentrationslager*, Stuttgart, 1970, p. 159.

CHAPTER 3

The Intelligence Hunt

British Intelligence was too slow in discovering what was happening at Peenemünde.

This bald statement will cause anger in some quarters: I hasten to add that it is made only with all the benefits of hindsight which the post-war researcher enjoys. No criticism is intended of those who had to conduct intelligence affairs under the pressure of those wartime years; but the cold, dispassionate judgement must be that the success of the various intelligence agencies came dangerously late.

This chapter makes no claim to cover the entire V-weapons intelligence hunt but merely to present the background to the R.A.F. raid on Peenemünde. The story is unlikely to be complete. Certain participants in the search have published their stories, in quite proper manner, but the nature of intelligence work and of the people who take part in it often leads to the erratic release of information: the agencies – and sometimes the personnel involved – often lie low long after the strict needs of security have been satisfied. It is no detraction from the good work of those whose part has been publicized to suggest that there were probably other resourceful people in the background of whom little will ever be heard.

The story starts in Oslo immediately after the outbreak of war. The British Naval Attaché there received an anonymous letter which offered to supply German technical secrets. No money was requested; the British were only asked to signify their willingness to receive the information by making a small alteration in the presentation of the regular B.B.C. news broadcast to Germany. The change was made and a small packet was immediately dropped through the Attaché's letter box. The contents were in London by 4 November 1939. Scientific intelligence experts who examined the material found a bewildering array of information including brief details of large, long-range rockets being tested at Peenemünde, a place easily found on pre-war German maps.

So rich and varied was the information provided in what became known as 'The Oslo Report' that there were suspicions that it had been planted by the Germans to induce the British to waste valuable intelligence resources. It was several years before it was confirmed that most of the information was genuine, based on weapons definitely being developed in Germany at that time. The mysterious donor never reappeared. It has been suggested that he may have been Dr Hans-Heinrich Kummerow, a Communist anti-Nazi who was later arrested by the Gestapo and died in their hands in the autumn of 1943, but there has never been any proof.[1] Whoever it was, his idealism was wasted as far as the rocket information was concerned. No British intelligence agency attempted to follow up the report, and Peenemünde was not heard of again for more than three years.

In December 1942 further information arrived in London, this time from Stockholm. A Danish chemical engineer working in Berlin had overheard a professor from the Berlin Technical High School talking to a German engineer about a rocket being tested near Swinemünde which contained five tons of explosive and had a maximum range of 200 kilometres. The German professor's foolish gossip was followed a month later by a report from 'a reliable neutral source' referring to Peenemünde by name, to the test firing of rockets, and to a new factory for the production of secret weapons. Even this was not enough to trigger off a full-scale intelligence effort. It was not until late in March 1943, following the now-famous conversation, in a room wired for sound, between two senior German prisoners-of-war, Generals von Thoma and Cruewell, former colleagues in the North Africa campaigns, that British Intelligence finally woke up to the danger posed by Peenemünde and its rockets. The German generals had been reunited in a camp on the outskirts of London after a long separation, and von Thoma, who apparently knew something about the German rocket programme, expressed surprise that they had heard no explosions and that the rocket attack on London had not yet commenced.

It would be easy to criticize that delay of more than three years between the receipt of the Oslo Report and the all-out effort which now started on Peenemünde, but there are two mitigating factors: there were fears in those years of numerous secret weapons of a nature so technically advanced that their existence must have been considered improbable; and moreover, Britain's intelligence resources in these early years were limited and hard pressed. The academic judgement must consider, however, that the large establishment at Peenemünde had been working for nearly *five years* before close attention was finally directed to it in the spring of 1943, despite the specific mention of Peenemünde and rockets in the Oslo Report received in 1939. During this time, the V-2 had been designed and successfully test fired and was now being prepared for mass-production. Those responsible for keeping Germany's secrets had served Peenemünde well.

There now followed even further delays and an unfortunate example of inter-departmental jealousy. The earlier rocket reports had all been sent to the intelligence branches of both the Army and the R.A.F. There was an understandable difficulty over responsibility. Were rockets an aviation matter and the province of the R.A.F., or were they missiles, of concern to the Army? Whatever the answer, neither service seems to have realized the extreme danger until they read the transcript of the conversation between Generals von Thoma and Cruewell. It was the Army's intelligence branch which decided to take the initiative of reporting their fears to the highest authority. The warning thus travelled through the various levels of purely Army responsibility, then to the joint services staffs. It finally reached the Prime Minister twenty-three days from the date of the conversation between the two German generals.

The matter had come into the hands of the Joint Chiefs of Staff, the senior officers of Britain's three services. This body acted with commendable speed. After consultation with the War Cabinet Secretariat, they recommended – such was the danger and urgency of the matter – that a single person from outside the various existing intelligence bodies should be appointed to oversee and co-ordinate all the effort now being directed into the German rocket programme, reporting his findings direct to the War Cabinet for decision and action. The man they had in mind was Mr Duncan Sandys, M.P. Within the day, the Prime Minister had agreed. The date was 15 April 1943.

Duncan Sandys, thirty-five years old and a pre-war M.P., must have seemed the ideal person for the task. He had been the commander of Britain's first experimental anti-aircraft rocket unit until a motor accident severely injured his feet and he was invalided from the Army. He later returned to the House of Commons, and soon became Joint Parliamentary Secretary at the Ministry of Supply. The fact that he was also Winston Churchill's son-in-law did not detract from his personal ability. But the appointment did not meet with universal approval: Viscount Cherwell (Professor Lindemann), accepted at that time as being the top scientific adviser to the Prime Minister and to the War Cabinet, seems to have dissented. He is said not to have liked Sandys personally, and records clearly show that he did not believe the Germans were as far ahead in rocketry as to pose any serious danger to Britain. Another objector was Doctor (later Professor) R. V. Jones, the head of the scientific section of the Air Ministry's Intelligence branch. In his book, *Most Secret War*, Jones makes no secret of his intense disappointment that his department was not to be allowed to pursue the rocket investigation alone, claiming that he already had matters 'in hand' and that 'our qualifications were much better'. Also, he says, 'It didn't occur to the Chiefs of Staff that they already had a Scientific Intelligence component inside their organization'[2] – by which he means his other position as Head of the Scientific Intelligence of M.I. (Military Intelligence) 6. One can understand his disappointment; yet it must be remembered that, although his department had received all the rocket and Peenemünde intelligence mentioned in the early part of this chapter, there is no evidence in his own book that his department went into top gear until after the conversation between the two German generals alerted everyone. It should also be said that Jones was soon to prove that he had something equally valuable to offer as part of the wider Sandys organization.

Mr Sandys and his staff quickly got down to the task of collecting as much new information as possible about German rocket development as well as examining all previous reports.[3] Three German prisoners of war who were believed to be willing to talk about their country's secret weapons were interrogated thoroughly. The first two – a 'tank expert' captured in the Middle East who provided no less than fifty-nine paragraphs of material, and a Luftwaffe pilot – produced evidence which, with hindsight, seems to be little more than fantasy. But the third German prisoner, more senior, certainly mentioned a long-range, liquid-propelled projectile being developed in the Peenemünde area. On 23 June, a report arrived from 'a well placed official in a technical department of the German Army High Command' telling of 'a secret weapon to be used against London . . . an air mine with wings, long distance steering and a rocket drive', but the further information that the weapon was 'launched from a catapult' must have confused Mr Sandys. Two more reports from Germans – a 'Mr George, an A-One source', and a refugee engineer who had left Germany in 1938 – contained little useful information, although 'Mr George' again mentioned Peenemünde as the place where secret weapons were being developed. The truth is that security was so tight that little reliable rocket information ever came from purely German sources, although Peenemünde was constantly being mentioned as the location of secret work.

The Public Record Office document does not reveal the nationality of the informant who in March passed on the important fact that Peenemünde was a German Army establishment and gave accurate details of the V-2's dimensions and main features and of its 1942 test firings. It is noted only that the report came from 'a most reliable and expert source which has provided most valuable information over a long period' and that it emanated from the indiscretion of workers at

Peenemünde. The mystery rivals that of the identity of the earlier donor of the Oslo Report. What stories of wartime spying remain untold!

Further success was achieved by the many willing nationals of German-occupied countries who were able to send fragments of information to London. The Polish Resistance headquarters in Warsaw passed on several reports originating from compatriots in the labour camps at Peenemünde, and further information came from Danish fishermen in the Baltic. These reports were not very specific, but again they pointed the finger of suspicion at Peenemünde. It was another occupied country, however, that provided some of the best information. The Germans had decreed that the inhabitants of Luxembourg – a tiny country with distant German roots – were to revert to German citizenship and that the men were liable for conscription both for military service and for labour service just as though they were ordinary Germans. So it was that a party of Luxembourgers were sent to work at Peenemünde in 1942. When their normal term of civilian labour service was completed, the Germans, rather foolishly, allowed them to return home. Their reports, which eventually reached London, were among the most useful to pass through the hands of the Sandys investigation.

After the R.A.F. raid on Peenemünde had taken place, the Germans are believed to have held an inquiry and to have decided that some of the Frenchmen working there had been passing information out of the camp and somehow getting it to England. I have found no firm evidence for this German suspicion, but an interesting incident did occur in the early morning of 16 August 1943, less than forty-eight hours before the raid. An R.A.F. Lysander landed on a field fifty miles north-east of Paris and dropped off two agents for French Resistance groups; of three others picked up for the return flight to England, one carried 'a detailed report of the top secret V-weapon rocket development at Peenemünde'.[4] It is not known whether this message came from Frenchmen at Peenemünde or from Luxembourg via France. It is in any case sheer coincidence that it reached England just before the RAF raid.

The people of London and southern England and other places eventually attacked by the V-2 have much cause to thank the brave people who sought out fragments of information about Peenemünde, and those who ensured that it reached Britain. The French agent who brought the report by Lysander was Commandant Léon Faye. One month later Faye landed in France again, but was soon captured. Although he escaped from Gestapo Headquarters in Paris during an air-raid alert, he was soon taken again, and he eventually died in captivity. There were probably others who helped to send intelligence to Britain and who later gave their lives. For those who received and processed the Peenemünde information, it was work of the most interesting and stimulating nature; but for the men and women engaged in obtaining it, it was a cold, dangerous, deadly game.

In the end, it was the R.A.F. and that versatile aircraft, the De Havilland Mosquito, which gave Mr Sandys conclusive evidence of what was happening at Peenemünde. The Germans may have chosen one of the most remote parts of their country for their secret work and they may have kept security as tight as a drum. Foreign workers may only have been able to catch glimpses of half-understood devices; agents could only report random and often misleading conversations. Prisoners of war may have had a little fun deliberately misleading their questioners. But the Luftwaffe was unable to prevent R.A.F reconnaissance aircraft from flying over and taking photographs. These photographs eventually sealed Peenemünde's fate.

The task of photographic reconnaissance was allocated to A Flight of 540 Squadron; their airfield, at Leuchars on the east coast of Scotland, looked across a bay to the famous golf course at St Andrews. Peenemünde was 700 miles away. This small unit had been at Leuchars for several months. Its regular patrol area was Norway, Denmark, the Baltic and the north German coast beyond Rostock; areas further south were covered by 540 Squadron's main base at Benson in Oxfordshire.

Flying Officer Mike Hodsman, the officer responsible for intelligence and 'first phase' interpretation at Leuchars, remembers the special requests received at that time. (Because the large islands of Rügen and Bornholm were also suspected, these places also had to be photographed as well as the much smaller Peenemünde area.)

By late April and into May, a considerable interest was appreciated from the rapid increase in job requests in the peninsula adjacent to Peenemünde. We pondered over the large factory area, the numerous rail spurs and a strange mini-amphitheatre-like earthwork. But it was the jobs coming in ordering cover of 'the whole of Rügen island' and, later, 'the whole of Bornholm' which stunned both the interpreters and the aircrews for, regardless of the advantages that height, speed and lightness conferred on distant daylight photographic recce sorties, a cardinal consideration in ensuring success was to avoid hanging about over one target. Here they were, being asked to do jobs requiring several parallel runs so as to positively invite interception and the fire of predicted Flak.

It shook us rigid; the flight commander was stunned and it naturally upset the crews.

When the flight commander, Flight Lieutenant Gordon Hughes, flew down to Benson to ask for some explanation of these unusual orders, he was allowed to return and explain in the strictest confidence to his pilots and navigators, in the words of Flying Officer Hodsman, 'something of the almost incredible anxieties about the Peenemünde area.'

The flights were made. There were five sorties – on 20 May, 12, 21, 23 and 26 June – during the period of the Sandys investigation. Happily for the R.A.F. crews involved, their Mosquitoes were never fired upon by Peenemünde's Flak or caught by German fighters. There were no casualties, and many other areas were also usefully photographed. The frequent flights of the R.A.F. over Peenemünde caused much anxiety to the Germans on the ground, and the absence of Flak was, and still is, a cause of much annoyance to many people who were present but who did not realize that the Flak were under orders not to fire. One man at Peenemünde was talking about the R.A.F. flights to the captain of the Flak ship moored off Peenemünde; the captain said, 'I am afraid that one day they will come and bomb you.'

The story of how the Mosquito photographs were examined and the results interpreted has been told many times. The 12 June sortie – flown by Flight Lieutenant R. A. Lenton, MC (the Military Cross had been won in Crete) and Sergeant R. S. Haney – brought back a picture of a V-2 rocket lying horizontally on a trailer at Test Stand VII, but the interpretation officer on duty failed to recognize it for what it was. When Dr R. V. Jones, who had been disappointed when the main investigation had been taken out of his hands, was allowed to study the photograph a few days later, however, he did identify the object, thus achieving a major breakthrough. Further rockets were found after the next sortie to Peenemünde. (It is sad to have to record that none of the members of three of the four Mosquito crews which carried out the flights to Peenemünde survived the next six months. Flight-Sergeants E. P. H. Peek and J. Williams were killed over Holland on 24 September; Flight-Lieutenant Lenton and Sergeant Haney, who had brought back the first photographs of a rocket, died when their Mosquito was shot down by a German fighter near Trondheim on 26 October; and Flying Officers P. J. Hugo and M. L. H. Rose crashed at Benson airfield in January 1944.)

The R.A.F. photographs enabled Mr Sandys to conclude his investigation. Other benefits from the Mosquito flights included the production of an accurate map, showing every building at Peenemünde, which was made available to Bomber Command, and a scale model which helped in the planning of the subsequent raid. Valuable information was also gained about the German rocket-propelled fighter, the Messerschmitt 163, being test flown from Peenemünde airfield, although the V-1 flying bomb connection was not definitely established until much later in the year. It is interesting to note that at this time (and later) considerable photographic research was going on near the German-occupied Channel coast, where strange structures were being built in obvious connection with the secret weapons programme. An American official history states that no less than 40 per cent of all Allied photographic reconnaissance sorties between 1 May 1943 and 31 March 1944 was directed to German secret weapons, and that the staggering figure of more than 1,250,000 photographs was taken.[5]

As far as Peenemünde was concerned, those midsummer sorties of 1943 were all-important; but it should be noted again that the direction of interest there had come dangerously late. The R.A.F. had been making photographic reconnaissance flights over the Baltic since late in 1941. Peenemünde had been photographed in May 1942. Test Stand VII, from which V-2s had been fired since October 1942, had been interpreted as a testing area for the new kinds of explosive believed to be being manufactured in the two large halls (also photographed) in which V-2s were in fact being made. If the intelligence agencies in England had alerted themselves to Peenemünde earlier, the R.A.F. would almost certainly have brought back a photograph of a rocket earlier – but that is another judgement made with the luxury of hindsight.

Mr Sandys completed his investigation on 27 June, and it took only two further days to convene a meeting of the War Cabinet – actually of the Defence Committee (Operations) – at which he was invited to present his findings. It commenced at 10 p.m. in an underground conference room in Whitehall. Fortunately a full report of that late evening gathering – momentous for Peenemünde – is now available at the Public Record Office.[6] All eight regular members of the Committee were present: Winston Churchill in the chair, Attlee (Deputy Prime Minister), Eden (Foreign Secretary), the three service chiefs of staff – Pound (Navy), Brooke (Army) and Portal (R.A.F.) – and Sir Hastings Ismay, Churchill's chief of staff. Among nine other people specially invited were Duncan Sandys, Lord Cherwell and Dr R. V. Jones.

Mr Sandys opened the discussion. He reported that his investigations led him to believe that the Germans had developed at Peenemünde a rocket – almost ready for use – with a range of up to 130 miles (the V-2's actual range was nearly 200 miles). Peenemünde was also the location of the facilities for its mass production. He did not share the opinion, held by some, that the whole thing was a hoax.

After answering a few minor points, Sandys had to listen to the views of Lord Cherwell, who had been sceptical from the start and who now thought that 'it would assist the committee if he put the arguments on the other side.' Basically, his case was that the Germans were not then capable of solving the technical problems of producing an operational rocket, and that the whole affair was a clever German bluff and a cover for a more realistic weapon, possibly a pilotless, jet-propelled aircraft-bomb. When he had finished, Dr Jones was invited to give his opinion. Despite the views of Cherwell, a senior man in the scientific world and once Jones's tutor, the younger man stated bluntly that he thought the rocket threat was a genuine one but that large-scale attack was not yet imminent.

The committee was, therefore, faced with a two-to-one opinion. Those others present whose comments were recorded all accepted that the rocket was either a certainty or, at the very least, a strong probability. The committee quickly made four main decisions and a number of minor ones. The first decision was that Peenemünde was to be attacked by the R.A.F. as soon as possible. The remainder of the business does not concern this book.

It is obvious that Air Chief Marshal Portal, Chief of the Air Staff, had already had preliminary talks with Duncan Sandys on the subject of such a raid. The idea of an attack by a small force of fast Mosquito bombers – presumably in daylight but not stated in the minutes – was rejected by the committee, not on account of the danger of heavy losses but because the bomb tonnage capable of being delivered was deemed insufficient. Everyone present realized that the first attack on the establishment had to succeed; the facilities could be swiftly dispersed by the Germans following an inconclusive raid. Peenemünde needed to be given the full strength of the R.A.F.'s mighty Bomber Command – nearly 800 heavy aircraft capable of carrying nearly two thousand tons of bombs. But there was a major difficulty: Bomber Command normally operated under cover of darkness, and the summer nights would not be long enough for concealment until early or mid-August. The committee decided that this delay – possibly up to six weeks – had to be accepted.

One possibility seems not to have been suggested by anyone. The United States Eighth Air Force stationed in Britain had 300 B-17 Flying Fortresses capable of reaching and bombing Peenemünde, supposedly able to fly in formation and to defend themselves with their heavy armament against fighter attack. There were not yet long-range daylight fighter escorts available. An American raid could take place at once, and their daylight bombing in clear weather was more likely to be accurate than the R.A.F.'s night methods. An unescorted daylight operation as far as Peenemünde would have been a hazardous one, though it must be said that the Americans would soon be reaching out to targets on the Baltic Coast. On 25 July – three weeks before the R.A.F. could act – B-17s would attack an aircraft factory at Warnemünde, near Rostock, only seventy miles this side of Peenemünde. Also, during the day before the R.A.F. raid, the entire American B-17 force in England would make a much more dangerous flight to targets in southern Germany which lay much deeper in defended air space than did Peenemünde, which was only on the flank of the defences. It is quite possible that the Americans would have been willing to attack Peenemünde, and that they would – six weeks earlier – have achieved as much success as the R.A.F. were to do.

But there was one overriding reason why the Americans were not asked. All intelligence work so far had been in British hands, and the danger from the rocket was mainly to the civilian population of Britain. Peenemünde had been a British interest throughout. It is inconceivable that Britain's war leaders could have admitted that their own Air Force was not capable of bombing this target and that the Americans should be asked to take the risk of doing so instead. It is probable that the use of American bombers was never even considered.

That decision by the War Cabinet committee marked the end of the long intelligence search into Peenemünde and its rockets. The Sandys organization, though belatedly set up, had come to all the correct solutions in just two months, and its recommendations had been accepted. Peenemünde was now to be handed over to R.A.F. Bomber Command. It is worth recording that the proposed attack would have little relevance to the experimental work on the V-2, which was almost complete; if it were successful, however, a serious blow would be dealt to the rocket's production prospects.

NOTES

1. Jozef Garlinski, *Hitler's Last Weapons*, p. 31; this author acknowledges as his source Julius Mader, *Geheimnis von Huntsville*, Deutscher Militärverlag, Berlin, 1967, p. 126.

2. *Most Secret War*, p. 335.
3. A summary of all the material is now in the Public Record Office (PREM 3/110).
4. Hugh Verity, *We Landed by Moonlight*, p. 118.
5. *The Army Air Forces in World War II*, vol. III, p. 89n.
6. CAB 69/5.

CHAPTER 4

Bomber Command Planning

The order to attack Peenemünde came as no surprise to Sir Arthur Harris, the Commander-in-Chief of Bomber Command; he had undoubtedly been consulted by Portal before the recent War Cabinet meeting. But together with the confirmation of the raid by the Air Ministry came the precise areas chosen for attack. Such details were normally left to Bomber Command; on this occasion, however, Harris was only left the task of working out the tactics to be used. This chapter will describe the sometimes unusual but always interesting methods developed during the weeks between the decision to attack Peenemünde and the date of the raid itself.

The orders received by Bomber Command were that three separate areas of Peenemünde were to be attacked:

(i) The experimental establishment, destruction of which would interfere with research work and the development of the rocket apparatus.
(ii) The two large factory workshops, where it is believed the rockets nd/or projecting apparatus were being finally assembled.
(iii) The living and sleeping quarters, with the object of killing or incapacitating as many of the scientific and technical personnel as possible.[1]

The first two targets were obvious choices, but the third was not, for it was most unusual for the Air Ministry to ask so specifically for an attack on an area of housing. But this would be a night raid, and it was reasonable to expect the scientists and engineers to be at their homes. The target maps eventually issued to the R.A.F. bomb aimers showed that the Wehrmacht barracks in the old *Kraft durch Freude* holiday camp were in this third bombing area as well, and also – unfortunately – the smaller foreign labour camp at Karlshagen. Omitted were Peenemünde West airfield, from which V-1 flying bomb test flights took place, the power station and liquid oxygen plants, all the rocket test stands, and, of course, the large Trassenheide camp for foreign workers, more than a mile away from the nearest planned bombing area. The clear intention of the raid was the destruction of the laboratories and workshops used to design and produce the V-2 and the deaths of the senior personnel working on

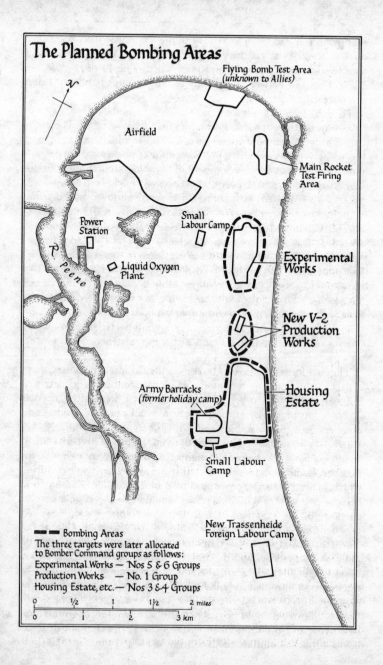

The Planned Bombing Areas

Flying Bomb Test Area
(*unknown to Allies*)

Airfield

Main Rocket
Test Firing
Area

Power
Station

Small
Labour Camp

Experimental
Works

R. Peene

Liquid Oxygen
Plant

New V-2
Production
Works

Army Barracks
(*former holiday camp*)

Housing
Estate

Small Labour
Camp

New Trassenheide
Foreign Labour Camp

▬ ▬ Bombing Areas
The three targets were later allocated
to Bomber Command groups as follows:
Experimental Works — Nos 5 & 6 Groups
Production Works — No. 1 Group
Housing Estate, etc.— Nos 3 & 4 Groups

0	½	1	1½	2 miles

| 0 | 1 | 2 | 3 km |

that project: it had nothing to do with the V-1 unless stray bombs fell on the airfield, or any of the very small numbers of Luftwaffe scientists who lived in the housing estate were killed. The British would not know of any link between Peenemünde and the flying bomb until after this operation.

Thus the scene was set for a most interesting undertaking. As mentioned in the Introduction, Peenemünde is believed to have been the only Bomber Command operation of the war in which the entire force was employed, by night, in a precision attack upon a small target. For those interested in the development of bombing tactics, the solutions suggested and the plan eventually adopted reflect some important principles connected with the techniques of finding, marking and bombing targets – principles later to affect the wider conduct of Bomber Command operations. Peenemünde also represents a good example of the flexibility of air power. Here was a location, exactly 500 miles from Britain, which posed a great threat both to the British civilian population and to the Allied prospects of invading Europe. No naval or military operation could possibly hope to reach this target. Yet, as has also been mentioned before, the ordinary squadrons of Bomber Command, mostly without any special training, would eventually take off to attack Peenemünde less than twelve hours after any member of those squadrons first heard of the existence of that place.

The first formal move by Harris was the calling of a conference of his six group commanders at the High Wycombe headquarters of Bomber Command on 7 July 1943, little over a week after the War Cabinet meeting. The gathering was a small one; the group commanders brought no staff officers with them, and it is unlikely that Harris was accompanied by more than one or two of his own staff. It would be five weeks before the nights would be long enough to allow Bomber Command to carry out this operation, five weeks during which many bomber crews would be shot down over Germany and become prisoners of war. Everything would be held 'very close to the chest' until the raid took place. The time lapse would, however, produce an advantage rarely enjoyed by Bomber Command. Normally, a raid was decided upon, the planning completed – though much of it was standardized – and the raid carried out, all in a period of no longer than eighteen hours. The Peenemünde plan could be drawn up in more leisurely fashion. Peenemünde also presented the planners with several important advantages as a target. If approached from the north, it could be reached without flying through the most heavily defended German night-fighter areas; the German defences could almost be outflanked. Neither was Flak at the target likely to be heavy. Finally, Peenemünde's position on the coast, with the distinctively shaped island of Rügen just to the north, was a valuable navigational benefit. The planning of the approach and withdrawal flights should pose no problems.

There would, however, be plenty of problems over the target. Bomber Command's standard tactics were devoted to the raiding of large industrial cities. An 'Aiming Point' was selected, and the Pathfinders attempted to mark this with coloured 'Target Indicators', or 'markers', at which the 'Main Force' aimed. But such were the difficulties which the Pathfinders often encountered in establishing their exact position at night that really accurate bombing was seldom achieved. If the Pathfinder marking was not too far astray, most of the bombs would fall on some part of the target, however, and serious damage would be caused. That was 'Area Bombing', the standard method of attack since early 1942. The only exception was when targets within the range of a device code-named Oboe were attacked. Oboe allowed a limited number of Pathfinder aircraft to place markers with great accuracy, but the range from the ground stations in England at which it could be used was governed by the curvature of the earth. As Peenemünde was well beyond this range, that valuable device would not be available. There was only one other unit specifically trained in precision bombing – 617 Squadron, of recent 'dambusting' fame; but Peenemünde was far too large a target for them, however accurately their bombs might be placed.

A further technical device was on the other hand to be of some use: the airborne radar sets, code-named H2S, now fitted in all of the Pathfinder bombers. These early sets were crude and not always effective, however, although coastlines produced clearer images on their screens than did inland areas.

The main difficulty was that of finding a way of identifying and marking the three small areas selected for attack and of keeping them marked accurately throughout the raid. A further complication was that the Germans were expected to be able to produce a dense smokescreen to cover the target areas, possibly before the first bombers even arrived. In addition, grave danger would be incurred if the initial attack was not successful: Bomber Command's experience was that the defences of targets not hit properly at the first attempt were rapidly reinforced and took increasing toll of the bombers in subsequent attacks.

The story of how Bomber Command evolved its plan to overcome the difficulties posed by Peenemünde has required a considerable but rewarding research effort. Part of the result can be based firmly on documentary evidence, but part can only be a reconstruction of events of which no record was ever made.

Attention must turn first to Bomber Command's No. 5 Group and its commander, Air Vice-Marshal the Hon. Ralph Cochrane. 5 Group was, seemingly, an ordinary group which flew as part of the Main Force to targets marked for it by 8 Group – the Pathfinders. But Cochrane's group – which Harris himself had commanded briefly earlier in the war – had occasionally been allowed to carry out special operations alone. A small force sent to Augsburg, deep in Germany, and a larger one to Le Creusot, deep in France, in April and October 1942 respectively had made daylight precision attacks against individual factories. The Augsburg force lost seven of its twelve Lancasters, but Le Creusot cost only one of the ninety-four dispatched. 5 Group had then raised and trained 617 Squadron for the famous attack on the Ruhr dams in May 1943, when two of the three dams were breached with a loss of eight of the nineteen aircraft involved. 5 Group thus had some experience of tackling precision targets, though also a reputation of occasionally sustaining severe losses.

A 5 Group operation which had more influence on Peenemünde was a raid to Friedrichshafen by sixty Lancasters, including four Pathfinder aircraft provided by 8 Group, carried out during the night of 20/21 June 1943, only eight days before the War Cabinet decision on Peenemünde and sixteen days before the Bomber Command group commanders' conference on the same subject. The target had been the Zeppelin works where *Würzburg* radar sets, an important part of the German air defence system, were being made. To achieve accuracy, the attack had been made on a moonlit night, and, because it was midsummer, the force had flown on to land in North Africa to avoid returning over Germany and France in daylight. It was the first so-called 'shuttle' raid to North Africa.

Two important aspects of the Friedrichshafen raid were the use of a 'Master Bomber', whose function was to remain in the target area throughout the raid, to observe the accuracy of the marking, and to radio advice both to his Pathfinders and to the main force of bombers; and the employment of a combination of 'offset marking' and 'time-and-distance bombing runs'. The Master Bomber technique had, of course, been pioneered by Wing Commander Guy Gibson, V.C., on the dams raid, but Friedrichshafen was the first time it had been used with a larger force. (At that time it was known as 'Master of Cere-monies' or 'Raid Commentator', but the later term 'Master Bomber' will be used here.)

Offset marking and time-and-distance runs will be important to the Peenemünde story, so they must be explained further. An acknowledged difficulty of the established Pathfinder technique of placing Target Indicator markers accurately on an Aiming Point throughout an attack was that they were often obscured by the smoke and dust of the subsequent bombing. 5 Group's offset technique was to place the markers at an easily visible point just outside the target area. The ordinary bombers then added a suitable 'overshoot' to their bomb-sights so that bombs aimed at the markers actually hit the Aiming Point. This technique had been only partially successful at Friedrichs-hafen: an unexpected wind change – always the Pathfinders' worst enemy – had resulted in the Target Indicators of the four marker aircraft being slightly misplaced, allowing only a moderate bombing performance.

It was here that the time-and-distance method used as an alterna-tive by other crews retrieved success from potential failure. The technique will be described in more detail later; it is sufficient here to say that the bombing photographs of those crews which used it at Friedrichshafen showed that their aim had been more accurate than that of the crews who used the offset markers.

The tactics employed at Friedrichshafen have an all-important relevance to the proposed operation against Peenemünde. It was an uncanny coincidence that the Zeppelin factory at Friedrichshafen was one of two outside Peenemünde which the Germans had chosen to mass-produce the V-2 rocket, so that this 5 Group raid, in setting back the commencement of the V-2 work there, had unwittingly struck the first British blow at the German rocket programme.

The reader must be warned that the next stage of the story has been reconstructed from conversations with people involved, and that no documentary record exists. I am satisfied, however, that my account is broadly accurate.

Sir Arthur Harris almost certainly consulted Air Vice-Marshal Cochrane *before* the other group commanders; even Air Vice-Marshal Donald Bennett of the Pathfinders was at first left out. Harris wanted to draw upon 5 Group's experience with precision targets, and it is possible that he was not just in search of suggestions but even asked Cochrane to do the preliminary planning. N. W. D. Marwood-Elton, Group Captain (Operations) at Bomber Command Headquarters at that time, writes: 'I have the impression that Harris delegated the detailed planning to be carried out, in the first instance, by Cochrane and his 5 Group staff ... I feel almost certain that Cochrane was asked to study the implications and draw up the plans.' Air Commodore H.V. Satterley, Cochrane's Senior Air Staff Officer, agrees with this.

It is probable that Cochrane's preliminary proposal was that 5

Group should bomb alone, using the techniques which had been successful at Friedrichshafen, with the main emphasis on time-and-distance runs, but keeping in reserve offset marking – carried out by borrowed Pathfinder crews – in case cloud or mist obscured the reference points needed on the ground. A Master Bomber would control the raid. For such an operation, 5 Group could deploy approximately 140 Lancasters, plus another twenty if 617 Squadron was used. The advantage of Cochrane's plan was that the crews would not be frustrated by the German smoke-screen or decoy markers, or by the dust and smoke of early bombing over the three Aiming Points. He could probably have allocated each of his aircraft a specific area to attack – a method feasible under the time-and-distance technique – and they would have followed one another into the target almost in a 'line-astern' fashion. This would avoid the 'jostling' likely if the whole of Bomber Command attempted to pass over this narrow target area, which would be a threat to both marking and bombing accuracy.

There is no doubt that Cochrane passionately believed that his was the correct solution to the Peenemünde problem. There were doubts at this stage of the war about the ability of the Pathfinders to mark targets properly when operating beyond the range of Oboe, and the rivalry between Cochrane and Bennett on this and other aspects of bombing policy was deep, long established, and well known. A useful informant here was Squadron Leader T. J. Beach, then Group Bombing Leader at 5 Group Headquarters. He told me: 'If there was a special job to do such as Peenemünde, then 5 Group had no intention of leaving the skill and glory to the Pathfinders – Cochrane would see that *his* men did the job and prove they could do the job well.'

So, at some date between 29 June and 7 July, Cochrane is presumed to have presented his plan to Harris. His suggestion – a precision raid by 5 Group using sophisticated techniques, rather than a mass attack by the largest possible force – represented an alternative philosophy not only of how Peenemünde might be dealt with but also of the whole future conduct of the bombing war. Unfortunately there is not space here to develop this interesting long-term argument. Harris rejected Cochrane's proposal; he was obviously not prepared to accept the risk of losing the advantage of surprise if the attack by a small force should fail. He insisted on the all-out effort. He did, however, extract several interesting points from Cochrane's scheme which he employed later in the Peenemünde planning process.

It is not known exactly what was said at the conference of group commanders on 7 July, but the decisions made by Harris immediately afterwards were contained in an operation order sent out two days later[2] which will be examined in detail in following chapters. The

Pathfinders were to mark the target using their standard technique, with some modifications to allow for the presence of three Aiming Points instead of the normal one. No firm decision was made about the use of a Master Bomber, and none about time-and-distance bombing by any part of the force. In fact the operation order was only provisional, and Harris was to make important changes during the ensuing weeks.

Harris's decision was a clear rebuff to Cochrane's policy and a confirmation of confidence in the ability of Bennett's Pathfinders to find and mark the three bombing areas at Peenemünde.

The order issued on 9 July began almost immediately to undergo important amendments. That original order read:

Date of attack. This attack [on Peenemünde] is to take place on the first suitable occasion when either there is sufficient cloud cover over Denmark to enable a dusk attack to be made or on the first suitable night which offers sufficient hours of darkness to enable the flight over enemy territory to be completed between evening and morning nautical twilights.

The interesting 'cloud cover over Denmark' possibility is an echo of yet another earlier 5 Group operation, in which, on a day when heavy cloud was forecast for Denmark and the western Baltic, forty-four Lancasters had been sent to carry out a precision attack on a U-boat construction yard in the Baltic port of Danzig (now Gdańsk), 200 miles further from England than Peenemünde. The Lancasters had indeed flown safely there but the bombing had not been successful, for the cloud en route caused navigational problems and most of the aircraft arrived just too late to bomb visually. Although only two were lost, the operation was a failure. This type of raid had obviously been considered for Peenemünde, in which case the complicated marking and bombing plan for a night attack just described would not be needed. But there was the obvious double risk that the forecast cloud cover would not materialize at just the right place and time, leaving the bombers easy meat for German day fighters, and that the ensuing attack might be so scattered and disorganized as to risk again the advantage of surprise. Peenemünde just had to be hit hard at the first attempt.

It is not known how seriously Harris looked for the 'cloud cover over Denmark' conditions in the ensuing weeks, but it is known that this type of operation never reached the serious planning stage. It is also known that some time after the order of 9 July was issued, Harris came to the conclusion that his raid would have to take place in clear weather and under a full moon to secure the best chance of success, even though Bomber Command rarely operated by moonlight, when the German fighters were a much greater danger. So, with the nights being too short until early August and the full moon not due until the middle of that month, nearly six weeks must elapse before the raid could take place – a time of further reprieve for Peenemünde, in which Bomber Command had to continue its normal operations, but also an opportunity for Harris and his staff to develop the plan at leisure.

Bomber Command carried out sixteen major raids on Germany, Italy and France during these weeks. Of outstanding interest, and of some significance to Peenemünde, was the series now known as the Battle of Hamburg when, between 24 July and 3 August, there were six heavy attacks, four on Hamburg and two on cities in the Ruhr. Three of the four Hamburg raids were particularly crushing, one, on the night of 27/28 July, producing the catastrophic firestorm which killed 40,000 people in the city.[3] The concentrated bombing – beyond the range of Oboe – had been carried out on moonless nights using standard Pathfinder marking techniques. Hamburg's position, near the coast and on the wide river Elbe, made it a distinctive target for the H2S radar sets of Bennett's crews, and their success must have given Harris confidence in the decision he had taken to attack Peenemünde with his full strength, relying predominantly on the Pathfinder technique rather than on Cochrane's methods.

Also important in the Battle of Hamburg was the first operational use of the British anti-radar device, Window. This consisted of thousands of metallized strips of paper, released by the bombers for as long as they were within range of the German ground radar sets. To the delight of the R.A.F., it was found that the slowly descending, fluttering clouds of paper strips jammed both the ground radar sets and the close interception radar sets used in the German night fighters. Window thus seriously impaired the effectiveness of the defence, and bomber losses fell dramatically. Although the Germans would obviously proceed to alter their tactics, the new device would still be effective by the time Peenemünde was attacked, only two weeks after the end of the Battle of Hamburg. Its success was a major factor in Harris's decision to risk sending Bomber Command to Peenemünde by moonlight.

Meanwhile, the last few preparations and refinements were in train. At the War Cabinet meeting on 29 June, it had been decided to discontinue photographic reconnaissance over Peenemünde so as not to betray an undue interest. One more flight was, however, made on 26 July in order to discover if there had been any last-minute developments. The Mosquito crew found clear conditions; they were still not fired upon by the Flak defences, and returned safely. 540 Squadron's entire Peenemünde effort had thus passed without the loss of any aircraft or crew. Their contribution to the intelligence investigation had been of the utmost value, providing yet another example of the versatility of air power. The photographs brought back revealed no startling developments at Peenemünde itself, but showed what appeared to be a decoy fire site in the remote countryside across the river Peene, about three miles to the west, where thirteen large and seventeen small timber frameworks had been erected, ready, it was believed, to be set alight in order to draw any bombing away from the real target. It was a familiar German device, and Bomber Command was duly warned. The photographs also showed, more ominously, an increase in the number of smoke generators around the target area and what appeared to be new Flak positions although, from information now available, it is probable that there had only been a movement of existing anti-aircraft guns.

It was also during this period that Sir Arthur Harris made three important further amendments to his plan, in addition to his recent decision to bomb Peenemünde by moonlight. The first of these – that a Master Bomber should be used – was probably in fact made relatively early, although it was not in the 9 July operation order. The Peenemünde Master Bomber was to be provided not by 5 Group but by 8 Group, the Pathfinders, who had never before used the technique; but this was a proper decision for a full-scale Bomber Command attack and one with which Cochrane would not have quarrelled. The choice of who should carry out the task was made by Air Vice-Marshal Bennett in consultation with Group Captain C.D.C. Boyce, his Senior Air Staff Officer. After consideration of the commanders of all six heavy squadrons in 8 Group, Group Captain J.H. Searby, commanding officer of 83 Squadron, was selected. Boyce says, 'Bennett probably mentioned Searby first. He was chosen because he was very experienced, very calm, sound and steady.' John Searby was a thirty-year-old Lincolnshire man whose soldier-father had been killed in 1916 in the Battle of the Somme. A former Halton apprentice, he had been a sergeant-pilot in 1939 and had since flown approximately fifty bombing operations. Before coming to the Pathfinders, he had served under Guy Gibson in 106 Squadron, which he later himself commanded. It was probably only a coincidence that Searby was an ex-5-Group man. He was told nothing of future plans.

It was probably to confirm this choice that Group Captain Boyce flew as a passenger in Searby's Lancaster in a raid to Turin on the night of 12/13 July and observed Searby in action. It was then decided to hold a Master Bomber rehearsal. Without being told its purpose, Searby was ordered to act in this capacity during a small-scale attack on Turin on the night of 6/7 August. Owing to weather conditions, the operation did not in fact take place until the following night. Searby says:

> I thought the rehearsal was something to do with a special future operation, possibly an Augsburg type operation or an attack on one of those curious buildings seen near the French coast recently or to 'take out' the Fiat works in Turin. The rehearsal was a very messy business; it was a very indeterminate operation. Afterwards, I was told absolutely nothing about any future operations and, as I heard nothing for some time, I thought that whatever it was had fallen through.
>
> I was astonished when the order came, on the day before the Peenemünde raid, to report to Pathfinder Headquarters with my navigator and bomb aimer and was shown a model of a target near a coast. We weren't told the name of it even then.

Although the decision to use a Master Bomber was in line with the ideas of Air Vice-Marshal Cochrane, the Pathfinders did not oppose it; it is in fact quite likely that a Master Bomber would have been used whether Cochrane had suggested it or not. But the next move by Sir Arthur Harris represented a much greater concession to Cochrane's philosophy. At some stage between 9 July and 22 July, Harris decided that he would allow 5 Group to carry out their time-and-distance bombing *during* the main attack but independently of the Pathfinder marking which would be taking place at the same time. It was a typical Harris decision, giving way to innovation but not staking all on it. Cochrane was, of course, delighted and hoped that, if his group was successful, it would lead to more of his ideas being accepted. He called a conference of his station and squadron commanders, ostensibly to ask for their opinions; from the following account provided by a junior officer who found himself at this conference, however, this may have been only a formality. Pilot Officer John Whiting was an Australian pilot with 467 Squadron:

> Some bright spark had thought up the important-sounding position of 'Flight Bombing Officer'. As I was the newest and most junior commissioned officer in the flight, I was given the job – a job, presumably, that no one else wanted. The duties were somewhat vague to say the least. My opposite number on the other flight was Gerry Godwin who was also freshly commissioned and a fellow Australian but he was some years older than I.

One morning, the C.O., Wing Commander Gomm, announced that Godwin and I were to attend with him at Group H.Q. that afternoon for a special meeting. We duly arrived there but turned up a little late and, as is the way so often with meetings, the back seats filled up first. By the time we arrived, the only seats remaining were those in the front row. Here we sat down. Cochrane was in the chair. I remember looking around the room and seeing a mass of senior officers – wing commanders and upwards; the gold braid was thick. Godwin and I were well and truly outranked.

The meeting got under way. Cochrane said that an important raid was being planned. He couldn't tell us where it was but the target had to be knocked out, if possible, with one blow; if not, Bomber Command would have to go back the next night and, of course, the Germans would be waiting for us! I think we were told that the target was a relatively small one.

Next came a discussion on how best to attack this target. It was well known that the time-and-distance run was Cochrane's 'baby' and I was a little disgusted to hear senior officer after senior officer speak and advocate it. I believe that these men were crawling to Cochrane. I may, however, have been unfair to them. It may have been that they genuinely believed what they were saying but I doubt it.

After all of the senior officers who had been invited to speak had expressed 'their opinions', Cochrane then turned to Godwin and myself and said that he would very much like to hear what the men who were actually going to do the job had to say. I certainly wasn't the public speaker and it was even more obvious that Godwin had no intention whatsoever of getting on his feet. Using his greater years of experience, he out-fumbled me. So, by default, I found myself the spokesman.

I said that the only speaker whom I could even faintly agree with was the bloke at the back of the room. I recall hearing many suppressed titters because this humble pilot officer was referring to a group captain as 'the bloke'. Having overcome my youthful faux pas, I then went on to say that I would much prefer to see not a time-and-distance run but a low-level attack in moonlight with delayed action bombs. A deadly hush overcame the hall. I was thanked by Cochrane and that was that. Needless to say, Whiting's idea was not accepted.

At that time, I was young and probably not as articulate as I might have been and my statements were almost certainly prompted by a gut feeling rather than by a reasoned appraisal of the situation. I think that low-level flying fascinated many young pilots. It certainly fascinated me. It was the ultimate in exhilaration. In my opinion, the time-and-distance run was subject to far too many variable factors to impress me as a satisfactory method of bombing. I am certain that it must have looked good on paper but, unfortunately, the war wasn't fought that way.

(Pilot Officer Whiting in fact flew on the Peenemünde operation and returned safely from it. His squadron commander, Wing Commander C. L. Gomm, died two nights before Peenemünde when his Lancaster was shot down in Normandy, on the way to a raid on Milan. Pilot Officer G. P. Godwin, Whiting's companion at that conference, should have flown to Peenemünde, but his aircraft developed a fault before take-off. Godwin and all his crew were killed on a raid to Kassel on the night of 22/23 October 1943; they had needed only one more operation to complete their tour.)

Cochrane insisted that every 5 Group crew taking part in the coming operation must practise time-and-distance bombing. Each squadron commander prepared a list of his more experienced crews, and training started on 9 August. The men were not allowed to go on leave until the Peenemünde operation was over, and they were not, of course, told for what type of target they were training.

The essence of time-and-distance bombing was that a series of easily identifiable reference points had to be visible on the ground during the run up to the target and in a direct line with it. Close co-operation between the bomb aimer – observing the ground with his bomb-sight set vertically – the navigator and the pilot was also essential. The bomb aimer guided the pilot over the first reference point, calling out the exact moment that the aircraft passed over it. He then gave further directions so that the pilot could keep the aircraft heading exactly towards the second reference point; the same compass heading would thus compensate for any cross-wind and point the bomber directly at the target. Another time-check was made when the aircraft passed over the second reference point, and the time taken to fly between the two was used by the navigator to calculate the exact time required for the actual bomb-run from a third point to the target. No marking was required, and the target could be attacked through cloud, mist or a smoke-screen – *as long as the early reference points were visible*.

5 Group's Bombing Leader, Squadron Leader John Beach, was let into the Peenemünde secret.

I was summoned to Cochrane's office where he was in conference with Satterley. They had, apparently, had a considerable discussion as to whether they should merely brief me as to the bombing requirement in general or take me into their complete confidence.

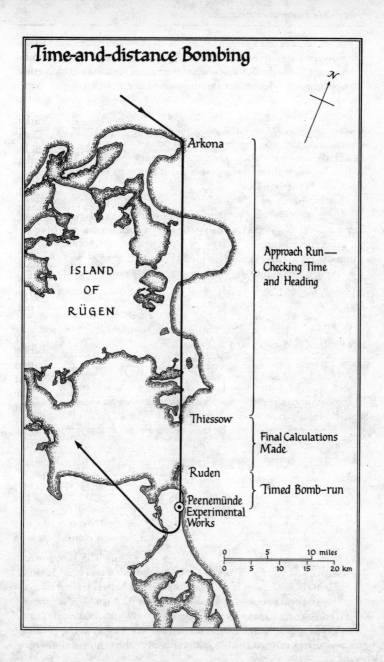

Time-and-distance Bombing

N

ISLAND OF RÜGEN

Arkona

Approach Run—
Checking Time
and Heading

Thiessow

Final Calculations
Made

Ruden

Timed Bomb-run

Peenemünde
Experimental
Works

| 0 | | 5 | | 10 miles |
| 0 | 5 | 10 | 15 | 20 km |

I have always felt greatly honoured in their decision to take the second line and they made it clear that we alone knew target details, though I don't think I knew what the actual importance of Peenemünde was until after the raid had taken place.

Beach was shown a map of the area with the easily recognizable island of Rügen to the north, and told of the approach over the many distinctively shaped bays between Arkona in the north of the island and Thiessow in the south, and then over the tiny island of Ruden. A line between these three points led directly to the Experimental Works at Peenemünde.

The Wainfleet bombing range, on the Lincolnshire coast near Skegness, was to be used for the time-and-distance practice. Squadron Leader Beach found that, by using the railway line from Louth Station to a junction near the village of Willoughby, a Lancaster could simulate the approach flight from Arkona to Thiessow and then fly a suitably timed run to the bombing range. He remembers the results of the first series of practice runs:

> Cochrane was appalled. In fact, he appeared shattered that crews had done so badly and that his whole plan might fail. We couldn't tell what had happened to cause this – my own feeling was that operational crews with tremendous experience felt insulted at being asked to carry out practice bombing – almost unknown on squadrons at that time – and, having been given no inkling of the importance of the exercise, felt that brass hats had nothing better to do than produce unreasonable and stupid ways of keeping them under the official finger. Be that as it may, pilots flew erratically – both in speed and direction – bomb aimers were casual in reporting the exact time over pinpoints, and navigators didn't think that a few seconds mattered in bomb release on such a silly exercise. Result – practice bombs over a very wide area of the Wash with a few actually on land! I fancy Cochrane had something to say to his squadron commanders and they to their crews. A second practice was ordered.

The results of the second practice showed much improvement, although they were still not as good as hoped for. There is little documentation of these events, but Sir Arthur Harris later recorded that the first practice produced bombing errors of 1,000 yards or more, the second reducing the average error to 300 yards.[4] One pilot says that Cochrane took up a Lancaster and surprised everyone by placing his practice bomb just thirty-eight yards from the centre of the target when the next best crew could do no better than sixty yards. There was no time for a third set of runs, but at least Cochrane had grounds for thinking that further improvement would take place on the night of the operation.

It should be mentioned that the crews came from standard Main Force squadrons: 5 Group's specialist squadron, 617, was not involved. Cochrane was determined to show that ordinary crews in Bomber Command could improve their accuracy dramatically if given the chance. Peenemünde could be an excellent test of his theories.

As the days of early August passed and the moon period approached, a final element was incorporated into the Peenemünde planning, designed to reduce the risk of heavy loss in the coming operation.

After the recent successful series of raids on the Ruhr and Hamburg, speeches had been made in Britain warning the Germans that 'Berlin was next'. This part of the propaganda war was useful to Sir Arthur Harris because he intended to dispatch a small force of Mosquito bombers to create a diversion at Berlin on the night of the Peenemünde raid. The Mosquito operation began nearly a week in advance. They bombed the German capital three times, always flying out over Denmark and then turning south, passing within sixty miles of Peenemünde. The bluff was actually twofold. The first intention was to rouse the people at Peenemünde with the air-raid sirens which, it was assumed, would be sounded when the R.A.F. flew so near. The second was to persuade the Luftwaffe that these raids were a preliminary to the much-heralded British offensive against Berlin, which would be the destination the next time a force of heavy bombers was detected flying over Denmark. On the night of the Peenemünde raid, the Mosquitoes were to pass near the area about an hour before the main attack commenced.

The preliminary raids took place on the nights of 12/13, 14/15 and 15/16 August. The Mosquitoes were provided by 139 (Jamaica) Squadron which, only a month earlier, had been given the task of assisting Bomber Command's heavy force in a variety of diversionary functions. The credit for organizing these three small successful missions belongs to 8 Group Headquarters, of which 139 Squadron was a member. Nineteen sorties were flown to Berlin in the three nights. The people of Peenemünde became used to their sirens sounding, and when no attacks followed many decided that the next time they would stay in bed. Berlin suffered minor damage and its people also lost some sleep. The Luftwaffe started thinking of how they could defend their capital city when the R.A.F. heavy bombers came.

One Mosquito was lost on return from the first of these three preliminary raids. It may have run out of fuel after sending a signal saying that it was in difficulties; – Berlin was at extreme range for these Mosquitoes when they had to fly the roundabout northern route. The pilot, Flight Sergeant H. M. Valentine, an Englishman, and his navigator, Flying Officer K. W. Rawlins from Trinidad, were really the first R.A.F. casualties of the Peenemünde operation. Their names are now on the Runnymede Memorial to the Missing.

These three raids ended the waiting period for the August moon, and concluded Bomber Command's planning. To assist them in finding and attacking their small target, the bomber crews would have the advantage of the anti-radar device Window, which was still believed to be effective; the Pathfinders would have the advantage of operating by moonlight, with a Master Bomber for the first time directing a major Bomber Command raid. For added interest, 5 Group would be using their time-and-distance technique. Success was not guaranteed, of course; cloud or mist in the area or too much smoke over the target itself or sudden changes of wind or the early loss of the Master Bomber and his deputies or poor marking – any of these factors could bring about failure. And then there was that great danger of sending the bombers out in the moonlight. If the Mosquito diversion to Berlin failed to deceive the Germans, there could be a veritable slaughter.

NOTES

1. Draft Target Instruction Sheet loaned privately by a former Peenemünde scientist.
2. Reproduced in full here as Appendix 1. It is believed that this paper is not in the Public Record Office; it was contained in a folder of documents later used by the R.A.F. Staff College and a copy was loaned to me privately.
3. For a full description see my book *The Battle of Hamburg*, Allen Lane, 1980.
4. *Bomber Offensive*, p. 183.

CHAPTER 5

'Peenemünde? Never heard of it!'

The twelve-night-long moon period, during which Bomber Command did not normally fly over Germany but which Sir Arthur Harris had decided on for the Peenemünde attack, commenced on the night of 11 August. The operation had to wait several days, however, for suitable weather conditions. Bomber Command did not rest completely, for it was still being sent to the lightly defended cities of northern Italy in the campaign to knock the Italians out of the war. The full strength of the four-engined bomber force – 656 aircraft – went to Milan and Turin on 12 August, three smaller forces on the 14th, 15th and 16th. These last three raids are interesting in that Harris never sent more than 200 aircraft – he was clearly conserving Bomber Command for Peenemünde. The week's operations had cost but eighteen aircraft of the 1,149 dispatched – a loss rate of only 1.6 per cent. This was, however, the end of Bomber Command's easy times. Peenemünde was to come, and there would be no more lightly defended targets in Italy and France for the next six months.

Sir Arthur Harris had been watching the weather carefully. The operation had three requirements: a full or nearly full moon; no cloud over Peenemünde or the important islands north of it needed for checkpoints on the final approach to the target; and clear weather at the airfields in England for landing after the raid. A low-pressure area with cloud had affected Germany's Baltic coast during the first few nights of the moon period, but at Harris's regular morning conference of Tuesday 17 August there was better news. The unfavourable weather was believed to have moved well away, and although a warm front with further cloud was forecast for southern Germany, the whole of the centre and north of the country were believed to be relatively clear. A little high fine-weather cloud – strato-cumulus – was forecast for Peenemünde, but Harris had already decided to attack at medium level. There would be almost a full moon, and no difficulties were forecast for the English airfields.

Harris did not hesitate; he ordered the raid for the coming night. A weather reconnaissance Mosquito was to go out and check conditions during the day.

Two quite separate factors made the choice of this night even more propitious. One of the main objectives was to kill as many technical men as possible, and a raid on a Tuesday night, near the middle of the week, could expect to find them present in greatest numbers. The second factor was of more importance to the safety of the aircrews than to the effectiveness of the bombing. Before his morning conference, Harris already knew that the American 8th Air Force had planned two extensive operations into southern Germany for that day. Every Flying Fortress unit in England was to be used to attack the Messerschmitt aircraft factory at Regensburg and the ball-bearing factories at Schweinfurt. The Regensburg force would fly on to North Africa, but the Schweinfurt force would return to England. There would be no fighter escort for these 376 bombers once they had flown past a point just inside the German border. Both targets involved much deeper penetration into Germany than anything attempted before by the Americans.

These audacious operations were bound to provoke a fierce reaction from the Germans; some of the night-fighter units were likely to be drawn into the day battle, and some day-fighter units occasionally used in night operations were also likely to be involved. As a result, the German fighter units which Bomber Command could expect to meet during its Peenemünde operation would probably have suffered attrition during the day, and the evening might find some of them drawn away to the south. The Americans could not have prepared an operation more suited to Bomber Command's purpose, though in fact they had been waiting their opportunity for many days; it was no more than coincidence that the same twenty-four-hour period should witness three such interesting and historic operations.

There is one ironic aspect of the R.A.F. and U.S.A.A.F. missions. Schweinfurt, the home of the German ball-bearing industry, was believed by those responsible for the overall planning of Allied bombing to be the most important 'bottleneck target' in Germany. Knock out the ball-bearing factories by American daylight raids and the town of Schweinfurt by R.A.F. night bombing, it was thought, and a crippling blow would be struck at Germany's war effort. The Americans had accepted the directive gladly; it suited well their concept of how the strategic bomber should be used. But Sir Arthur Harris believed, with deep conviction, that the ball-bearing bottleneck argument had been overstated. Tactically, he did not think Bomber Command could be effectively used against distant small towns like Schweinfurt when it normally operated only over the mainland of Germany in non-moon periods. He had no intention of bombing Schweinfurt if he could avoid it. Here, hard on the heels of

Air Vice-Marshal Cochrane's wish to pioneer more advanced techniques, was another example of the different philosophies concerning the use of the R.A.F.'s heavy bombers. Many of the American crews who were to fly that day to Schweinfurt had been led to believe that it would be a joint U.S.A.A.F.–R.A.F. target, and that the British would be following them to Schweinfurt that night. It was truly ironical that Bomber Command would, instead, be carrying out a precision attack, in moonlight, on a target much smaller than the town of Schweinfurt – but 320 miles to the north.

Back at his headquarters at High Wycombe Harris ended his conference, and soon after 9 a.m. a preliminary order was sent to all group commanders, warning them that the long-awaited Peenemünde raid was to take place that night. It had been given the special code-name *Operation Hydra*. The diversionary attack to Berlin by Mosquitoes was also to take place. The routine code-name for Berlin was *Whitebait*.

A team of staff officers prepared the detailed operation orders to be sent out to the groups later that day. As has been described, much preliminary work had been carried out in recent weeks; the task of these officers was to mould Bomber Command's routine tactics to the special requirements of Peenemünde. It is worth repeating that not one man on any Bomber Command airfield had ever heard of Peenemünde, nor would he do so until these operation orders were transmitted; only fuel and bomb-loading details were sent on ahead. All that Group Captain Searby, the Master Bomber, and his navigator and bomb aimer had seen was a model of a target, and only the crews of 5 Group had carried out any special bombing practice. The orders now to be prepared would tell the Pathfinders and the squadrons of the five Main Force groups exactly how to reach Peenemünde, how to mark and bomb three separate targets there, and how to return home. (Only a broad outline of the final Peenemünde plan is given here; it will be more convenient to deal with the finer points later. Unfortunately, those officers or civil servants who selected material for retention and eventual release to the Public Record Office failed to keep a single copy of the Bomber Command Operation Order issued on 17 August 1943, but there are sufficient supplementary documents available for its contents to be reconstructed.)

The fortunate location of Peenemünde on the Baltic coast and on the flank of the main German night-fighter defences meant that a simple route over Denmark could be taken. The bomber crews preferred flying over the sea or over German-occupied countries like Denmark rather than over Germany itself, and the presence of

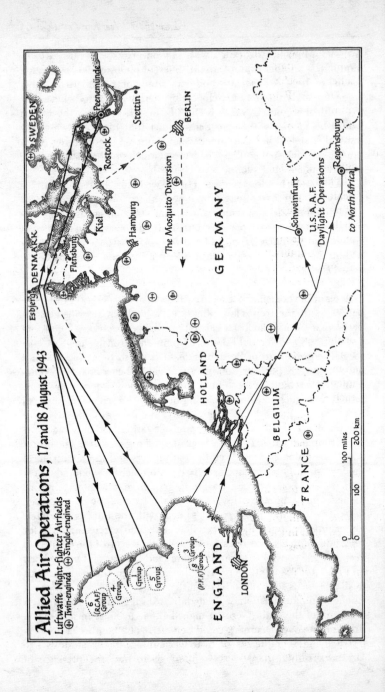

Allied Air Operations, 17 and 18 August 1943

Luftwaffe Night-fighter Airfields
⊕ Twin-engined ⊕ Single-engined

SWEDEN

Peenemünde
Stettin
Rostock
BERLIN
Kiel
Hamburg
Flensburg
Esbjerg DENMARK

The Mosquito Diversion

GERMANY

Schweinfurt
U.S.A.A.F. Daylight Operations
Regensburg
to North Africa

HOLLAND

BELGIUM

FRANCE

6 (R.C.A.F) Group
4 Group
1 Group
5 Group
3 Group
8 (P.F.F) Group

ENGLAND

LONDON

100 miles
100   200 km
0

Sweden, only forty miles from the outward route at one point, was a comforting thought in case of aircraft being seriously damaged or suffering mechanical trouble.

The first Pathfinder markers were due to be released at eleven minutes past midnight, R.A.F. time; German time was one hour ahead. The Main Force would start bombing four minutes later, and their attack was to last for forty minutes. As has been said, the targets were three separate areas of Peenemünde, known as 'Aiming Points' in tactical parlance; the three attacks on them were called 'waves'.

The manner and order in which the three Aiming Points were to be dealt with posed several problems and had obviously been the subject of much thought. Bomber Command normally attacked downwind, so that the wind would blow smoke away both from the Aiming Point and from its approaches. At Peenemünde, however, the presence of not one but three Aiming Points in a line down the narrow peninsula and the position of the navigational checkpoints on the island of Rügen to the north dictated an approach from the north-north-west. Should these Aiming Points be attacked in turn from north to south or in the reverse order? The original operation order, issued on 9 July, had clearly envisaged that the wind would be blowing from the south or the south-west and that the three targets would be attacked from north to south so that, at each stage, the wind would keep smoke away from the next Aiming Point. The following table shows the order intended in the original plan and the forces of bombers allocated to each target.

Aiming Point	Target	Bombers
1st	Experimental Works	Nos. 3 and 5 Groups
2nd	Production Works	No. 1 Group
3rd	Housing Estate	Nos. 4 and 6 Groups

Now, however, the wind was forecast as blowing from the west-north-west (the actual forecast was from 290 degrees), and the order of attack had to be reversed. But 5 Group had practised its time-and-distance bombing with the intention of attacking the Experimental Works, so its position in the timing of the original plan was also changed. The new plan was:

Aiming Point	Target	Bombers
1st	Housing Estate	Nos. 3 and 4 Groups
2nd	Production Works	No. 1 Group
3rd	Experimental Works	Nos. 5 and 6 Groups

The allocation of entire groups to waves in this way was contrary to Bomber Command routine. A normal attack on a city consisted of six waves, with the aircraft of each group spread over two, or sometimes three, waves. It would be a particularly unusual privilege for the Stirling squadrons of 3 Group, with their lower ceilings and lighter bomb-loads, to be present in the first wave. 5 Group and the mostly Canadian 6 Group were in the most potentially dangerous wave, arriving over the target at the end of the attack when German fighters might be more numerous.

The unusual means by which the Pathfinders would transfer the marking from one Aiming Point to another twice amidst all the confusion of the attack will be described later. Two deputy Master Bombers were selected in case Group Captain Searby was shot down or otherwise put out of action: Wing Commander John Fauquier, the tough Canadian commander of 405 Squadron, was the first deputy, Wing Commander John White, a flight commander in 156 Squadron, the second. Call signs were given to various parts of the bombing force; 'Sparrow', 'Crow', 'Raven' and 'Blackbird' were all used, but no record appears to exist of how these were allocated.

A major change was in the proportion of incendiary to high-explosive bombs to be carried. The normal city-target raid required at least fifty per cent incendiary bombs; city targets were burnt down rather than blown to bits. But Peenemünde was not densely built up, and, moreover, smoke from fires was the last thing that the Pathfinders wanted to hinder their already complicated task. So it was to be a mostly high-explosive raid; only one-third of each wave of bombers would bring in a few incendiaries at the end. Peenemünde was to be blown to bits.

The return flight would again be over the Baltic, Denmark and the North Sea. The total mileage would be around 1,250, depending upon the location of home airfields, and the flight time would be seven to eight hours, depending upon aircraft type. It was a long-range operation, but by no means approaching the extreme of which Bomber Command was capable.

The diversionary raid by eight Mosquitoes to Berlin has already been mentioned; there would be no larger-scale diversion, although the eighty-strong force of Wellingtons and Bomber Command's training groups were available, and no radio-countermeasures aircraft were to be used. A full-scale Intruder effort was called for, however, and six long-range Fighter Command squadrons would provide Mosquitoes and Beaufighters to patrol German airfields or routes likely to be taken by German fighters. A few Halifaxes would take advantage of the full moon to drop supplies and, perhaps, agents to Resistance groups in Europe. Some of these flights would be to dangerous dropping zones in Denmark, the aircraft going under cover of the passage of the Peenemünde-bound bombers.

The final orders for the Peenemünde operation were duly completed and issued in the early afternoon.

Out on their airfields, the bomber squadrons had been told that a *Goodwood* operation was being prepared. *Goodwood* was the so-often used code-name for 'maximum effort'. The bomb- and fuel-loads were the only clues available to the identity of the target, and there is evidence that even some of this information was abnormally late in arriving because of the unusual nature of the mission. The Operations Record Book of 83 Squadron notes that, although the warning order for the raid arrived at 10 a.m., the armourers had to wait until after lunch before details of the marker and bomb-loads arrived. 'Suspense grew apace,' wrote the recording officer.[1] The fuel loading was the vital clue needed by the bomber men to make a guess at the location of a target, and this information flashed around airfields as soon as it was received. There was not enough petrol for Italy, and most settled for Berlin, with Nuremberg as a possibility. The aircrews knew that there had been public speeches warning the Germans that 'Berlin was next', but Berlin by moonlight was an alarming prospect.

A total of 1,924 tons of bombs was loaded on to the aircraft – 1,650 tons of high explosives, a mere 274 tons of incendiaries. One bomb aimer, who recorded the bomb-loads of each of his thirty bomber raids tour in his diary, found that Peenemünde was the only one in which his crew carried an exclusively high-explosive load. A mass of other material had to be provided: machine-gun ammunition, high-octane petrol – 1,760 gallons for the Lancasters and up to 300 gallons more for the Stirlings and Halifaxes – 214 Pathfinder Target Indicators and 216 flares, 200 or more bundles of Window for every bomber, and leaflets to be dropped over Denmark and in the Peenemünde and Stralsund areas of Germany.

Morale on the bomber squadrons was particularly high at this time, boosted by the obvious successes of the spring and summer over the Ruhr and Hamburg, the benefits of the recent introduction of Window, and the low loss rate of recent weeks, with some experienced crews reaching the end of their tours safely and many new ones safely negotiating their first few operations. Nor were the men tired, for Harris's policy of conserving his resources for Peenemünde meant that only small forces, working by rotation, had been out in recent nights. The squadrons of 4 and 6 Groups, based in Yorkshire and thus more distant from the Italian targets, had not flown operationally for nearly a week. The most tired were the men of 3 Group and of the two Halifax Pathfinder squadrons, 35 and 405, who the night before had been on the long haul to Turin – a successful raid, with only four aircraft lost from the 154 dispatched. The 3 Group squadrons, however, had found their airfields closed by morning fog and had been diverted all over southern England.

This diversion was to be the cause of a serious depletion in the force which could be sent to Peenemünde. Orders were sent to the diversion airfields to get the ninety or more Stirlings involved back to their bases as quickly as possible, but the fog persisted in many places well into the morning. The Stirlings came home late, often with mechanical defects, always with tired crews. At least sixty-one would disappear from 3 Group's battle order for Peenemünde.

That fog was only one of a number of unusual factors which helped to cut down the proposed size of the force. The moon period was the traditional part of the month for sending as many crews as possible away on leave, and the need for secrecy had prevented any change in this practice. In theory, sufficient crews were always retained to deal with any major operation; but a comparison between the aircraft sent by squadrons to Peenemünde and those sent on recent raids during the non-moon period indicates that possibly forty to sixty more aircraft could have gone if crews had not been absent on leave.

Next came the complete deletion from the night's effort of five fully operational Wellington squadrons capable of providing nearly eighty aircraft. The conversion of all Wellington squadrons to four-engined bombers was proceeding only slowly. The Wellingtons had operated normally until the end of the Battle of Hamburg, just two weeks earlier, but had not flown with the Main Force since then. Sir Arthur Harris had not mentioned them in his early Peenemünde operation order of 9 July for reasons which are not clear: possibly he thought that the conversion process would proceed faster than it did; possibly he felt there was a danger that the twin-engined aircraft operating by moonlight would be mistaken for night fighters by the gunners of the four-engined bombers – but this was a risk the Wellingtons had often had to take. There may have been another reason: two of the squadrons were manned by Polish airmen, and it may have seemed unwise to send them to bomb a target where there were known to be many Polish forced workers, although the main labour camp, at Trassenheide, was a good way away. This, however, is only speculation and cannot be said to explain why the Wellington squadrons were relieved from major operations for more than three weeks. Harris did recall them at the end of August, and they continued in action until mid October, sometimes flying to Berlin – at least as distant and much more dangerous than Peenemünde.

The next depletion was in 5 Group. Air Vice-Marshal Cochrane, presumably with Harris's approval, decreed that only those of his crews who had practised time-and-distance bombing should take part in the raid; thirty Lancasters which were available with crews were thus left behind.

At the airfield at Linton-on-Ouse, there was an unusual cause for a further loss of numbers: the new sleeping accommodation into which the Canadian aircrews of 408 Squadron had just moved was found to be infested with insects. As a result, the entire squadron was declared non-operational and sent on leave for a week, and their sixteen Halifaxes stood idle. Two more squadrons – 196 at Witchford and 431 at Tholthorpe – were out of action because they were converting to Stirlings and Halifaxes respectively, but a proportion of Bomber Command was always non-operational for this reason. In partial compensation, another Canadian unit, 426 Squadron, had just become available again; since mid June it had been converting to the Mark II version of the Lancaster. Half the unit was now ready for operations, and Peenemünde would be their first flight with their new aircraft. So, for reasons ranging from the absence on leave of aircrew, through the untimely fog in East Anglia and Air Vice-Marshal Cochrane's quest for perfection to bugs in Nissen huts in Yorkshire, Bomber Command would send 596 bombers to Peenemünde, some 240 aircraft less than its true maximum strength.

Forty-four of Bomber Command's fifty-eight squadrons went into action. The largest effort was by 12 Squadron, at Wickenby, which sent twenty-five Lancasters; the smallest contribution was the solitary Stirling which was all the 622 Squadron at Mildenhall could muster after most of its aircraft had been diverted because of the morning's fog. The best group effort was by Air Vice-Marshal C. R. Carr's 4 Group, at a peak of strength at this time; their 145 Halifaxes exceeded by twenty-eight aircraft the contribution of the next strongest group.

Appendix 2 will give details both of Bomber Command's Order of Battle on 17 August 1943 and of the operational effort and losses of the squadrons taking part in the Peenemünde raid. The following table gives the entire R.A.F. effort for the coming night.

Duty	Lancasters	Halifaxes	Stirlings	Mosquitoes	Beaufighters	Total
Bombing Peenemünde	324	218	54	—	—	596
Berlin Diversion	—	—	—	8	—	8
Intruders	—	—	—	28	10	38
Resistance Supplies	—	8	—	—	—	8
Total	324	226	54	36	10	650

It should be added that nine short-range fighters – five Typhoons, two Hurricanes, a Mustang and a Whirlwind – were to carry out Intruder operations to areas just across the English Channel, but these flights could have no effect upon the outcome of the Peenemünde operation.

While their aircraft were being prepared for the raid, squadron and flight commanders were busy compiling 'battle orders', the lists of crews who were to fly. The selection was made simpler on most units by the fact that they had not been flying the previous night. The exception to this happy position were the aircraft of 3 Group which had been diverted to distant airfields on their return from the Turin raid. The following are typical of the difficulties experienced when their crews did get back.

It was the first operation for my crew. The wing commander informed us that we were only going on the raid because the squadron was committed to sending a certain number of aircraft. I gained the impression that, because we lacked experience, he thought we wouldn't return. (Flight Sergeant H. Triplow, 214 Squadron)

Flight Sergeant Triplow and his crew not only returned safely from Peenemünde but completed their full tour of operations.

On the previous night, we had been to Turin, which was to have been the last operation before going on leave. I was to rush to Bury St Edmunds, collect an engagement ring and then go to Buckinghamshire, where my fiancée was staying with friends. We were planning to hold an engagement party on the night of the 17th of August. After debriefing from Turin, we changed and went to collect our leave papers at the Guardroom only to be told by the Service Police that our leave had been cancelled and that we were to report to our Squadron Office immediately.

As we were told at briefing that, if the raid was unsuccessful, we would have to return to Peenemünde until the job was done, I remember thinking that Freda may think that I was 'backing out' because I could not tell her a good story when I telephoned her to say that the engagement party would be postponed. (Flight Sergeant J. L. Elliott, 620 Squadron)

Flight Sergeant Elliott also returned safely from Peenemünde and was immediately sent on leave, but he fell asleep fifteen minutes after his party started 'and so missed all the fun.'

We had been diverted to another airfield coming back from Turin. Orders were sent to get all aircraft back to base as soon as possible but it was still midday before we reached our airfield at West

Wickham. The C.O. told us that the target for the coming night was an important one but that he realized some of the crews were very short of sleep. If any crew was too tired, he said, they could be stood down. It was a 'come and see me in my office' routine, making it very difficult for us to do anything about it and, in fact, no one went to see him. I think most of the chaps took their 'wakey-wakey' pills and just got on with it. (Sergeant A. R. Clarke, 90 Squadron)

Sergeant Clarke's squadron managed to get fifteen crews and aircraft ready for Peenemünde – the largest effort in 3 Group.

There were the usual difficulties over finding replacements for individual crew members who were not available for various reasons; the following example may be typical of many.

I had been posted with my crew to the squadron and, full of youthful anticipation, we commenced ops. The first was aborted due to engine failure just before crossing the Dutch coast; the second was even more hectic, having to ditch in the English Channel returning from a raid on the Ruhr. As a result of the last episode, my crew was split up and I was floating around the squadron as a spare bod, trying to be as inconspicuous as possible having discovered rather quickly that this business was not just a 'bed of roses'. I expected to be posted back to the training unit to pick up another crew but this didn't happen, and to my horror one morning on reporting to the Flight Engineers' Office, I found I was to fly that night with a crew whose flight engineer had been granted compassionate leave. I didn't know anyone in this crew at all and I remember that the usual pre-flight nerves and stomach rumbling took place. (Sergeant E. A. Gosling, 78 Squadron)

A Canadian crew of 427 Squadron at Leeming was short of a man because their regular wireless operator had been made drunk by his friends in the Sergeants' Mess the previous evening and was now too sick to fly. His temporary replacement would be killed by a German cannon shell that night.

A substitution for an even more unusual reason took place in a 15 Squadron crew. This account, by Sergeant L. C. Wood, the bomb aimer, also describes activities and attitudes typical of young, wartime aircrew.

After lunch, we went to check that all was well with our aircraft and did our Night Flying Test. It was a glorious, sunny day and we were in shirt-sleeve order. After we landed and while we were chatting with the ground crew, Bob Grundy, our pilot, mentioned that I had become twenty-one the previous Thursday and, to celebrate, the ground crew took my shirt off and painted my body with yellow paint. When I promised that we would have a joint aircrew/groundcrew 'thrash' at the earliest opportunity and that I would share a cake my mother was sending me, they cleaned me up with petrol and let me dress in a more airmanly fashion. This was just as well because, when we returned to the Flights, there was a message for the crew to report immediately to the adjutant's office.

When we arrived, the adjutant told us that our former rear gunner, who had gone absent to avoid flying on a recent operation, was up before a court martial the following day and he took statements from each of us. Principally, he seemed concerned that the rear gunner was aware that he was on operations the night he disappeared. He concluded by telling us that, as we were flying that night, he would have our statements typed and we could sign them the following morning. He warned us to report to his office at 14.00 hours the following day in our 'best blue' as we would be witnesses at the court martial.

15 Squadron did not have a man to replace the air gunner being held for the court martial, and had to borrow one from 622, the other squadron at Mildenhall. This was Sergeant Ron Scandrett, who had not yet flown on operations. When this crew was shot down near Peenemünde, Scandrett was a prisoner of war for several weeks before realizing that he had flown his one and only operation with a crew from another squadron. It is believed that, because the main witnesses for the court martial were not available the next day, the original tail gunner had to be charged with a lesser offence. The outcome is not known.

The Australian 460 Squadron at Binbrook had for some time been planning a great party to celebrate its thousandth Lancaster sortie. In the belief that the full moon would result in a stand-down from operations, the party had been fixed for that night at Cleethorpes Pier Dance Hall. Some aircrew had left Binbrook early to get 'warmed up', and the civil and service police were kept busy retrieving them. Only one crew failed to return on time, and the Australians sent twenty-four Lancasters to Peenemünde.

So, in their various ways, the squadrons completed their selection. Pilots – and sometimes others – from recently arrived crews were put down to fly as additional members with more experienced crews – a routine measure which was not popular but was considered useful preliminary training. A study of squadron lists shows that no less than seventy such new men were chosen to fly to Peenemünde, an unusually high figure which might indicate that the coming operation was not considered particularly dangerous by some squadron commanders. There were wide variations in attitude, however; for example, 1 Group sent only one second pilot while 4 Group sent twenty-seven. In contrast, none of the station commanders or group staff officers who occasionally flew on operations asked to go along, although one staff officer (to be named later) decided to do so at the last minute. However, seventeen squadron commanders put themselves down to fly, ten of them in 5 and 6 Groups, which were to form the potentially dangerous last wave of the attack.

A total of 4,241 men – from the United Kingdom, Canada, Australia, New Zealand and a scattering of other countries – were eventually to take off in the bombers for Peenemünde.

While all this activity was in progress on the bomber airfields, a reconnaissance Mosquito had been checking that the weather over the Baltic was still clear. Flight Sergeant F. Clayton and his navigator, Pilot Officer W. F. John, took off at 10.55 a.m. from the Pathfinder airfield at Oakington and flew in their unarmed aircraft out over the North Sea and across Denmark as far as the large island of Sjaelland, 150 miles north-west of Peenemünde. To go any closer might give a hint to the Germans of Bomber Command's intentions. Pilot Officer John made his observation: '4-10ths cumulus and fracto-cumulus at 7,000 feet, 8-10th cirrus between 22,000 and 23,000 feet.' [2] The Mosquito returned safely after a flight of nearly four hours and its report soon reached Bomber Command Headquarters. The high cloud would be no problem, and it was hoped that the scattered lower cloud would not become so dense as to cover Peenemünde and the approach route over the island of Rügen. There was no need even to consider postponing the operation. (Flight Sergeant Clayton – on his fifty-fourth operation – and Pilot Officer John were both killed when their Mosquito was shot down near Lille while flying a similar sortie to the Stuttgart area on 14 November 1943.)

The Americans flew their planned missions to Regensburg and Schweinfurt, although they had suffered a setback when the morning fog in East Anglia delayed the take-off of the Schweinfurt force. As a result, the two formations had to fly into Germany three hours apart. The Luftwaffe had a field day; sixty Flying Fortresses were shot down. But this gallant American endeavour certainly drew in some of the German night-fighter units, and at least six aircraft which would otherwise have flown to Peenemünde were destroyed; others were damaged, and many German night-fighter aircrews passed a less than restful day.

*

While the R.A.F. groundcrews toiled on, the aircrews had no work for most of the day except for the short flight test of the aircraft that would carry them that night. At Bottesford, a visiting E.N.S.A. theatre company put on an extra performance that afternoon for the men of 467 Squadron who would miss the evening show because they would be flying. The play was Noel Coward's stirring drama, *This Happy Breed*. No charge was made to the Australian and English airmen who made up the squadron. Then, in the late afternoon or early evening, the aircrews on the thirty-eight airfields involved started to congregate for the 'main briefing'.

The first unusual aspect of the Peenemünde briefing was the extra security precautions. Sergeant George Whitehead was at Holme-on-Spalding-Moor, due to fly as a second pilot.

> I went to the briefing with the pilot I had been allocated to. I remember him as being very efficient; that gave me a lot of confidence. The regular bods, who knew the drill, expressed amazement that there were so many service policemen hanging around. Once inside the briefing hut, there was an ostentatious locking of the door – an obvious turning of the key with a clunk.

Many other men remember the unusually elaborate security that evening. 'The whole atmosphere suggested that the operation was going to be something pretty big.' 'There was naturally an atmosphere of special excitement and mystery about the whole thing, with much speculation.'

This atmosphere of expectancy was heightened at many airfields by the presence of visiting senior officers. Air Vice-Marshal Bennett took Mr Duncan Sandys to Wyton to watch Group Captain Searby brief his squadron. Searby obviously responded to the importance of the occasion and gave what he later considered to be one of the best briefings of his career. The Senior Air Staff Officer of 8 Group, Group Captain C. D. C. Boyce, had gone to another Pathfinder airfield, Bourn, to attend 97 Squadron's briefing.

> On the spur of the moment I decided to go on the raid myself; I suppose because it was something special. I told the squadron commander that I would like to go along and could he find me a nice reliable pilot to fly with. I had my flying suit in my car and I drew the rest of the equipment there. I didn't tell the A.O.C., Bennett, but he probably wouldn't have minded.

Group Captain Boyce, known as 'Bruin' Boyce from his teddy-bear-like figure, thus made his second flight in connection with Peenemünde; his first had been to Turin when Group Captain Searby was being considered as the Master Bomber. Boyce flew on this night as second pilot in Squadron Leader E. E. Rodley's Backer-Up crew. Credit is due to him – a personality little known outside the Pathfinders – for quietly taking these risks.

Then the briefing officers revealed their maps of the target and the routes.

> We saw the red tapes across Denmark and the Baltic. I thought, 'Oh Jeezus – Berlin! The northern route to Berlin!' But then we saw that the tape came to an end on the coast and doubled back again. They told us it was a place called Peenemünde. We felt great – anything but the Big City. (Flight Sergeant W. H. Layne, 97 Squadron)

> I think that, like most of the other aircrew, I remarked, 'Peenemünde? What's there? Never heard of it!' (Sergeant P. L. T. Lewis, 83 Squadron)

The aircrew were not to be told what there was at Peenemünde; not even the briefing officers knew that. The original Bomber Command operational order, issued more than five weeks earlier, had stated that Peenemünde was a place where the Germans were producing new countermeasures against R.A.F. bomber attack, particularly a new form of radar. This was repeated – with some minor variations and local embellishments – at every briefing. The subterfuge served several purposes: the bomber crews would be encouraged to press home their attacks; R.A.F. men who were taken prisoner could not reveal the extent of British knowledge about the true purpose of Peenemünde; English civilians would get no hint that rockets might one day fall on their country. When further details were given, there was much apprehension among the aircrew over the fact that the raid was to take place in broad moonlight and at comparatively low levels; but the lightness of the local Flak at this 'virgin target' was stressed, and the plan explained that Mosquitoes would keep the German fighters over Berlin. 5 Group squadrons, due to fly in the last wave when the effects of the diversion over Berlin might have worn off, were told that 'being a better group than the rest in Bomber Command' had led to their being selected 'for the most important part of the raid'.

The briefing and intelligence officers had even more scope to develop their imagination and individual styles when it came to giving details about each squadron's particular target. It must be remembered that the purpose of a briefing was not only to inform crews of the basic details of a raid but also to inspire them to the best possible effort. That second purpose was not easy to achieve night after night.

There were no qualms among the squadrons detailed to bomb the Peenemünde Production Works or the Experimental Works, but there was some surprise among the men who were told that the housing estate was to be their target; it was obvious that women and children would be hit. Such crews were told that this was unfortunate, but that it was essential that the top scientists were killed: it was no good destroying the laboratories and workshops if the scientists survived and were left free to start all over again. It was claimed that this was the first occasion that Bomber Command had been sent out on a 'deliberate killing raid'. Several squadrons were, falsely, told that agents had discovered that there would be a particularly large gathering of scientists at Peenemünde on that night and the raid would catch many of them in their beds. The general reaction of the crews was, 'We weren't too proud about bombing this part of Peenemünde but we didn't dwell on it.' There was some humour. One wag asked if it was known whether the scientists slept with their beards inside or on top of their blankets, and 115 Squadron, recently moved to a new airfield at Little Snoring, were told, 'There will be little snoring at Peenemünde tonight.' At Holme-on-Spalding-Moor, a prize was promised for any crew who came back with a pair of scientist's steel-rimmed spectacles hanging from his undercarriage.

Then came the real bombshell of the evening. Every squadron was warned, in the gravest possible terms, that the work being done at Peenemünde was so important that, if this first raid was not a success, it would be repeated as often as necessary until the desired results were obtained, regardless of loss. This message came directly from Sir Arthur Harris, and there is little doubt that he meant what he said. Very few of the airmen had heard anything like that before, and they were certainly impressed.

> This was the type of admonition which, in Johnson's memorable quote, tended to 'concentrate the mind wonderfully'. (Flying Officer R. G. McCadden, 76 Squadron)

> That dire warning at briefing remains with me, as I imagine it does with all survivors. (Sergeant A. Cordon, 207 Squadron)

> We were told that our lives were not to be considered in the destruction of this target. (Sergeant J. G. McLaughlan, 405 Squadron)

At Tholthorpe, the following device was used to increase the effect.

> We were literally getting up and leaving the room when we were called back in and resumed our seats. The station commander said

that he had just received a signal – a personal one from Harris – of the utmost importance and that, if Peenemünde was not wiped out that night, we would go out again the following night and so on. That sobered everyone up and confirmed that this was a serious and grave operation. Not one of us had ever heard a message such as that to conclude a briefing.

There wasn't the usual babble and horseplay and I remember coming out on to the airfield, right into the rural surroundings and sunshine and I thought 'this can't be happening to us on such a lovely day'. (Sergeant K. W. Rowe, 434 Squadron)

The briefings ended, usually with a final exhortation on the importance of the raid, with talk of the outcome 'affecting the whole course of the war,' and 'the lives of future bomber crews depending on you.' The crews mused on what they had heard.

I think a lot of us came out of briefing a bit mystified and not a little intrigued. I recall my own reaction very clearly. It was one of great excitement at the prospect of taking part in a raid that was obviously different and also vitally important – rather more, in fact, than just another run-of-the-mill attack on a German industrial centre. At the same time, I took it for granted that the chances were that the operation would most likely prove to be a trifle sticky. But I genuinely believe that, at the time, even this did little to dampen my enthusiasm. Maybe I should explain that I am, by nature, a sucker for the big occasion and the Peenemünde briefing held all the promise of just such an occasion. (Sergeant O. E. Burger, 77 Squadron)

Briefing had been a dismal affair. The officer concerned spoke as though he was convinced he was going to his death (he didn't) but morale slumped alarmingly. (Flying Officer J. W. Ward, 102 Squadron)

The usual feeling was that we were taking a heavy load of bombs and dumping them on some city and that, if we kept on long enough, it might make some difference to the outcome of the war. But, on the Peenemünde raid, my impression was that the chaps realized we were on something very special. (Sergeant G. G. A. Whitehead, 76 Squadron)

We had no doubts, from the moment briefing began, that losses would be heavy. Bombing on a time-and-distance run under a full moon anywhere in Europe was not our idea of fun. Assurances at briefing of dummy raids etc. strangely enough only served to heighten the expectation of heavy losses instead of reducing them, illogical though that may seem.

When the target was known, we just gave a philosophical shrug and envied those aircrew who were on leave. (Sergeant J. E. Hudson, 49 Squadron)

NOTES

1. Public Record Office AIR 27/687.
2. Operations Record Book, 1409 (Meteorological) Flight, Public Record Office AIR 29/867.

CHAPTER 6

The North Sea

> We reached our dispersal area long before they had finished loading the bombs. It was a superb, sunny evening and, as we squatted on the ground passing the time, we were visited by the Padre. I'm sure that it was a well intentioned comforter from the C.O. but, at the receiving end, it appeared more like the last rites. (Flight Sergeant W. C. B. Smith, 50 Squadron)

The first bomber to take off for Peenemünde was a Stirling of 90 Squadron at West Wickham airfield in Cambridgeshire. The Stirlings of 3 Group were to share the first wave of the attack with the Halifaxes of 4 Group but, because the Stirlings were slower-climbing aircraft, they needed to be on their way first. The even faster Lancasters of the Pathfinders who would need to be over Peenemünde before the attack started would also take off later. The first Stirling to be airborne – at 8.28 p.m. – was piloted by Flight Lieutenant George Crew; for him and his crew this would be the last flight of their first operational tour. They were destined to bomb Peenemünde and return safely, but Crew was to die on 25 May 1944 while flying with a Pathfinder squadron to Aachen. Further take-offs were soon in full swing throughout eastern England. On several airfields, the ground personnel had worked out that this was an unusual and perhaps particularly dangerous operation, and the bomber crews found that they were being waved off by larger gatherings of Waafs and airmen at the start of the runway than normal.

Many a crew of Bomber Command were killed when their planes, so heavily burdened with bombs and fuel, developed faults on take-off, crashed and exploded. There was no such calamity on this evening, but the following account does typify the effect of the 'maximum effort' and the 'press on regardless' spirit expected of and usually shown by Bomber Command aircrews. Pilot Officer Don Moodie was an Australian with 460 Squadron at Binbrook. He had been allocated an old Lancaster, recently under repair, which he had not had time to test fly in the normal way during the day.

> One of the engines would not start and, by the time we got it going, the others were starting to overheat. In due course, we lined up on

the runway which took off towards the village and, full power applied, the aircraft was slow to get moving and was nose heavy. As a result, we were out of runway and still on the ground. Binbrook airfield is well above the surrounding terrain and the ground dropped away sharply to the village. This allowed us to bounce out into space and push up speed without further contact with the ground and the take-off and initial turn and climb proceeded.

During the take-off, the navigator advised the crew that smoke was pouring out of the Gee set and this was switched off before any fire broke out. It was later determined that the electrical power to the unit was not properly regulated and the set had burnt out. In the ensuing fuss, the sextant was knocked from the table and later proved to be unserviceable. Fortunately for us, the weather was good and dead reckoning navigation commenced and other aircraft were plainly in sight on most of the trip.

The usual crop of last-minute withdrawals of bombers which developed difficulties comprised at least twelve aircraft, two of them Pathfinder Backers-Up; there was almost a third when a 35 Squadron Halifax, at Graveley, developed a major engine fault just before take-off. It had been to Turin the previous night, and, again, there had been no time to fly the usual air test during the day. Flight Lieutenant Tim Green was the crew's bomb aimer.

There was a long delay while the bombs and markers were reloaded on to a reserve aircraft and we were eventually ready to take off but only after the last possible time of reaching the target for our marking time with the first wave of the attack. The Station Commander came round, then the Squadron Commander came round and there was a long discussion on what could be done. We were desperately anxious to go. It was the last operation of our tour and we were all keyed up to do our job on the raid which we knew was an important one. We wanted to go if we could. We came up with the idea that we could cut approximately twelve minutes off by taking a more direct route, just off the Frisians, and by increasing our cruising speed by five knots. The Squadron Commander was quite reluctant to let us do it. No one pushed us. In the end the decision was made to do it – very much a crew decision.

Flight Lieutenant Davidson and his crew did take off, thirty-one minutes later than planned, and, by taking the measures suggested, reached Peenemünde just in time to mark the target during their allocated wave of the attack.

The last take-offs were mainly in 5 and 6 Groups. Pilot Officer W. J. Lowe, a bomb aimer in 49 Squadron, remembers his departure.

The main runway was in direct line with the cathedral at Lincoln, five miles away, and, as we lifted off, I always looked out to port and could see Holt Farm, the home of Les and Nancy Blackbourn our very special friends. The peaceful view of the farm, of Fiskerton village itself and of the cathedral in front, was a sight that had never failed to impress me on the many times we had taken off. Little did I think, as we took off on the evening of August 17th, that it would be two long years before I would see it again.

On his return from a German prison camp, Pilot Officer Lowe immediately married and spent his honeymoon at Holt Farm.

The last two aircraft to leave were both Lancasters from 1 Group squadrons; due to take off much earlier, they had developed last-minute engine trouble. However, Flight Sergeant C. R. Smith, an Australian of 460 Squadron, and Flight Lieutenant D. G. R. Weeks, of 12 Squadron, were able to leave Binbrook and Wickenby at 10.04 and 10.07 p.m. respectively and still managed to arrive in time to bomb with their allotted wave.

A total of 596 four-engined bombers had successfully taken off and were bound for the German rocket establishment.

The heavy aircraft climbed steadily away to the east, as they had done on so many evenings since 1939. For the early crews, it was still light.

I remember, vividly, on this warm summer evening, the sight of the 3 Group aircraft at the first rendezvous point – the town of Cromer – this huge gathering of Stirlings in daylight and setting out across the North Sea like an armada. Grinning crews were 'V-signing' each other from the cockpits and turrets. (Sergeant K. G. Forester, 90 Squadron)

The long climb to gain altitude soon led to the discovery by some crews that their aircraft were developing technical troubles; a few of them had to take the decision to turn back. These 'early returns' or 'boomerang' sorties were a regular feature of every Bomber Command raid, and much official effort was devoted to keeping their numbers to a minimum. Twenty bombers were to turn back before the crossing of the North Sea was completed, dumping their bombs in areas known to be clear of Allied shipping and then returning to their home airfields. The causes of the early returns were mostly routine: eight aircraft had engine failures, a further nine had other technical difficulties, and three had crew members ill – two pilots and a navigator.

The following description of one of the Peenemünde early returns is typical.

> When we reached 10,000 feet and tried to turn on our oxygen supply, we found that the oxygen tanks were empty. We didn't believe the readings on the gauges at first and I remember the futile attempts to find the cause of the failure. I also remember our frustration at having everything electric, electronic and mechanical in 'apple pie' working order and a stupidly simple thing like the oxygen supply out of order.
>
> You know the significance of this particular mission so you will be able to imagine how keyed up we were and how much everyone wanted it to be a successful raid. We anguished over the failure of the oxygen supply and our skipper even went so far as to open up a mini debate among all seven members of the crew, but we realized that we could not find our way to the target and back at roof-top level (below radar) and that it would be suicide to try it alone at any other altitude open to us.
>
> We returned to base. This was one of the rare occasions when we were angry and ready to blame the ground crew for neglect. We were also ready to see that they were made to suffer for it if they were at fault. However, the maintenance crew were cleared of any blame because it was found that a major leak had drained the system after inspection. (Sergeant J. Sheriff, 57 Squadron)

Some of the early-returning aircraft found their landings difficult because a few German bombers were operating over East Anglia and airfield lighting could only be shown for the briefest periods; but again there were no crashes, and the accident-free record of the Peenemünde operation remained intact.

The number of aircraft which turned back represented 3.4 per cent of the force which had taken off. This is a significantly lower figure than was normal for this period of the war, and it is clear that some crews – possibly between ten and fifteen – who would probably have turned back on any other night took the decision that, because this raid was so obviously important, they would press on instead. The Operations Record Book of 51 Squadron[1] relates that when Pilot Officer G. Richards suffered an engine failure in his Halifax and could not maintain height, the crew threw all their spare equipment overboard, reached Peenemünde, bombed, and then returned safely. Pilot Officer Richards was recommended for an immediate D.F.C. It was a double cause of celebration because it was the last flight of this crew's operational tour.

*

The aircraft took their different paths out across the North Sea to that point marked on the navigators' charts as 'Position A'. This was where the routes of the Main Force groups would meet and the bomber-stream be formed at 55.10 North, 07.00 East, 300 miles from the English coast and sixty miles from Denmark. With a light wind on their tails, the bombers took approximately ninety minutes for the flight from the English coast to this assembly point. A device called Gee, which transmitted signals from different points in England and was used to obtain a succession of fixes, showed that the wind had veered slightly to the north. Some of the less experienced navigators failed to detect this, and their aircraft slid gradually south of the ordered track. The bombers had climbed steadily all the way across the North Sea; the Lancasters would cross Denmark at 18,000 feet, the Halifaxes and Stirlings at slightly lower altitudes. Later, they would all lose height to attack Peenemünde.

Night fell while the bombers were still over the sea. The moon became more prominent; there was no cloud at the heights at which the bombers were flying. That moon was a cause of some anxiety; very, very few of the men in the bombers had ever set out on operations to Germany on such a bright night.

We stood out like a toilet in the desert. (Flight Sergeant B. Treacy, 460 Squadron)

I had the impression that the experienced crew I was flying with were not happy about the moon, though there was no more than the odd comment about it. Otherwise, it was deceptively peaceful. (Sergeant G. G. A. Whitehead, 76 Squadron)

The flight out was uneventful but scary nevertheless. (Pilot Officer W. K. Hynam, 100 Squadron)

Even today, when I see a cloudless sky with a full moon, I think about that night we went to Peenemünde. (Sergeant F. Wadsworth, 12 Squadron)

Two bombers – both Stirlings – reported meeting German fighters over the sea. The first quickly lost its attacker by corkscrewing away. The second recorded two combats, but neither side was hurt much. In view of what was to come later in the night, these encounters can be left without further description.

NOTE
1. Public Record Office AIR 27/492.

CHAPTER 7

The Luftwaffe

Much earlier in the war, Air Marshal Hermann Goering had claimed that the R.A.F. would never bomb Germany – a boast that was proved foolish, although his Luftwaffe often caused serious loss to Bomber Command. By no more than chance, the tactical circumstances at the time of Peenemünde were particularly interesting, and the handling and performance of the German fighters would have made this a significant night in the ever-unfolding story of the air war even if the target for the bombers had been less important than Peenemünde.

For two years since 1941, the night-fighter defence of Germany had been entrusted to a sophisticated tactical system called *Raumnachtjagd*, of which a literal translation is 'room night fighting'; here we shall use the phrase, 'the box system'. According to this arrangement the coast of Germany and of those Occupied Countries through which Bomber Command usually flew to Germany was divided into a series of overlapping 'boxes' approximately thirty-five miles across. The whole of the coastal area from Denmark to France had been protected by a double belt of such boxes, and there were more inland, particularly on the approaches to major German cities. Each possessed a group of ground radar sets which enabled a 'fighter control officer' on the ground to pick out one of any number of bombers flying through his box and direct a night fighter on to it. The fighter made the final contact and engaged the bomber with its own airborne radar. Bomber Command had partially reduced the effectiveness of the system by the introduction of the bomber-stream which passed through as few boxes as possible, but the ground-controlled night fighters had still taken a steady toll whenever the R.A.F. visited Germany. The aircraft which manned the box system were the long-endurance, twin-engined types – Junkers 88s, Messerschmitt 110s and Dornier 217s.

A further night-fighting force had been recently established in an endeavour to counter the growing R.A.F. strength. A certain Major Hajo Herrmann had been allowed to form a much smaller group of single-engined fighters for use only over a German city under attack. The local Flak was ordered to restrict its fire to a certain altitude, above which Herrmann's fighters were free to hunt. They carried no radar but sought out the bombers in the beams of searchlights or against the general glow of fires and British Pathfinder markers. These needed no sophisticated ground organization, but they did require that the probable target could be identified early so that they could reach the city while the raid was still in progress. The new tactic, known as *Wilde Sau* (Wild Boar), had achieved some success and official recognition. Herrmann's organization was still small, but it was expanding, and there were high hopes that this cheap, simple system could double the effectiveness of the German night defences. (Appendix 3 will give the Order of Battle of the German night-fighter units at the time of the Peenemünde raid. It is suggested that those readers who are unfamiliar with the system of abbreviations used for German fighter units might read the note on this subject in Appendix 3.)

This promising state of affairs – the combination of the well-tried box system covering the approaches and the new Wild Boar tactic over the target – was almost immediately shattered when Bomber Command started using Window during the Battle of Hamburg, only three weeks before Peenemünde. It has been described earlier how the clouds of fluttering metallized paper strips rendered most of the German radar sets ineffective. At the stroke, the box system, as the main line of defence for the Germans, was finished.

But the Germans are a resourceful people, and a vigorous fight back against Window had begun even before the Battle of Hamburg was over. A proportion of fighters had been released from their boxes and allowed to fly freelance, as it were. Some went into action over Hamburg and sought their victims visually, Wild Boar style. Others listened to a broadcast 'running commentary' – a primitive one by later standards – which gave as much detail as possible about the position and the probable future movements of the bomber-stream. These fighters used their initiative to get among the bombers and find their own quarry without further help from the ground. Many of the newer breed of German crew were not too sorry to see the end of the box system; they believed that these new, loosely controlled, free-lancing tactics would allow more aircraft to play an effective part in night operations. The box system had always favoured the limited number of *Experten* – aces – who had usually been given the most promising boxes whenever the bombers appeared.

They told us that the old system was more or less finished and we were to be sent to fight over the cities. We were pleased to receive such orders. Don't forget that I had been training for three years to shoot at bombers – that's all. I had no ambition to sleep with girls

or get drunk, just to shoot at R.A.F. bombers. That was all I
thought about, and these new tactics suited us young pilots very
much. Until then we had only had second or third turn in the boxes.
(Leutnant Peter Spoden, II/NJG5)

But it was still very early days for these new tactics. Only two R.A.F.
raids had been flown against German targets since the Battle of
Hamburg, to Mannheim and to Nuremberg, in southern Germany,
and few of the German night-fighter units had gained much experience in the new methods.

The Wild Boar tactic pioneered by Major Herrmann had been
unaffected by the Window setback, and those who believed that this
was the way forward now pressed their case. But General Josef
Kammhuber, who had built up the box system and was now com-
mander of Germany's entire night-fighter force, was reluctant to
abandon his creation completely; he hoped that new types of radar
could be produced which would avoid the worst effects of Window.
But it is known that, at some stage between the end of the Battle of
Hamburg and the date of the Peenemünde raid, Goering sent Major
Herrmann to Kammhuber's headquarters in Holland to explain the
Wild Boar technique more fully, and then formally ordered
Kammhuber to instruct all his night-fighter units to adopt it without delay. A conference of front-line commanders was held and
this radical change explained to them. In future, the main strength
of the twin-engined night-fighter units was to be directed, by
means of radioed instructions from the ground, to whatever target the
Germans believed to be the destination of the British bombers.
There is no evidence that General Kammhuber made any serious
objection to Goering's decision. It must have made sense to use the
fighters in this way until a technical answer to Window could be
produced.

The boxes were not to be entirely abandoned, however; a proportion of the twin-engined fighters – possibly 10 to 15 per cent – was to
be held back to man them, in order to guard against the sudden
appearance of small R.A.F. forces not well protected by Window, or
of individual bombers which had strayed off course or had been
damaged and forced to take a lonely route home. But the priorities
had definitely changed now; only a small proportion of the heavy
fighters had been released from the boxes in the early freelance
operations against Window.

The importance of these developments for the Peenemünde operation was that this night would be the first of the new emphasis on Wild
Boar fighting. The War Diary of one German night-fighter *Gruppe*,

II/NJG 1, based at St Trond airfield in Belgium, contains this entry:

17.8.43. Tag der Revolution der deutschen Nachtjagd. Völlige Umstellung auf 'Reportage und Wilde Sau'. (Revolution day for the German night-fighter force. Full conversion to commentary and Wild Boar.)[1]

The Messerschmitt 110s based at St Trond normally manned boxes within fifty miles of their home airfield; Peenemünde was 440 miles away, even if the Messerschmitts flew there directly.

Peenemünde was destined to be a 'first' for another German development.

Parchim airfield, 100 miles south-west of Peenemünde, was the home of the 5th *Staffel* of NJG 5. The *Staffel* 'weapons man' was Oberfeldwebel Paul Mahle, an imaginative fellow. On a recent visit to the Luftwaffe's development centre at nearby Tarnewitz, Mahle had been intrigued by the sight of a Dornier 217 torpedo bomber with an upward-firing cannon for use against fighters when operating low over the sea. He believed that such a weapon, fitted to a night fighter, would enable the pilot to attack in relative safety from underneath instead of being exposed to the fire of the bomber's rear turret when attacking from the conventional *von unten hinten* position from the rear and slightly below. Major Rudolf Schoenert, also an enterprising man, agreed to fly the Dornier 217 to Parchim, and he helped to achieve the fitting of not one but two 20-millimetre cannons in a Messerschmitt 110.

It did not take long for the guns to be installed, set at an angle so as to fire slightly forward. The biggest problem was the sight, which had to be fitted in the narrow space between the pilot's head and the cockpit roof. Practice attacks were made on a drogue towed by another aircraft. Wind resistance, which gave rise to some anxiety, was found to be negligible at the close range at which it was intended to use the new weapon. The main tactical advantage, apart from the safety of the attacker, was that no allowance need be made for deflection.

Two fighters at Parchim had been fitted with the upward-firing guns by the time of the Peenemünde raid; they had not yet been used in action. The new weapon was later christened *schräge Musik* – 'slanting', 'offbeat' or 'jazz music'. Everyone at Parchim had great hopes of it.

But the principles of *schräge Musik* were not new.

It is possible, by flying one's own machine at the same speed and in the same direction as his, to obtain conditions under which accurate fire can be delivered ... because the allowance for one's own speed and for the enemy's speed then cancel out and it is only necessary to consider the comparatively

The 'schräge Musik' Attack

Radar approach ending in a visual sighting

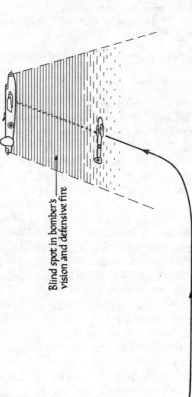

Blind spot in bomber's
vision and defensive fire

The fighter, from the safety of the blind spot
under the bomber, fires into the petrol tanks
of one wing.

(The drawing is not intended to be to scale. The angle of the
fighter's approach path in particular is exaggerated.)

small allowances required for air resistance and for gravity drop of the bullet. If, further, the direction of the fire is *upwards* and *forwards*, at certain angles these two remaining errors approximately cancel each other out with the result that very small allowances on the sight are necessary.

This conveys perfectly what Oberfeldwebel Mahle and the pilots at Parchim were trying to achieve; but it is actually an R.A.F. note written at the end of the First World War.[2] It is unlikely that the Luftwaffe men knew of the earlier R.A.F. work on the subject. It is certain that Bomber Command intelligence officers had no knowledge of the new German development.

It is always interesting to attempt the reconstruction of an air battle from the scattered and usually incomplete evidence available. The Peenemünde operation has not failed to provide an intriguing challenge.

The Germans had probably known during the day that a major R.A.F. operation was likely to take place that night. Luftwaffe radio listening posts in France and the Low Countries could measure the approximate number of test radio transmissions made by British bombers during their pre-operational flight tests, and it can be assumed that this information had provided an estimate of the new strength of aircraft likely to be operating. David Irving's book revealed that the Germans, having earlier broken a low-level R.A.F. code, were able to say that the seaside town of Cromer would be one of the bombers' departure points: it was from Cromer that the aircraft of 3 and 8 Groups, based on East Anglian airfields, usually flew when taking a northern route to Germany, and it was indeed used again that night. The Germans must have been surprised; they would not have been expecting a major raid by moonlight, and certainly not one involving any deep penetration of German defended air space. Nevertheless, all German night-fighter units had been warned that they might be needed.

When Window caused such havoc to the German radar system, on its first use, there was one type of radar set which was not affected. This was the *Freya*, employed by the Germans, among other things, for long-range work out to sea from their coasts. Because of its geographical position, the *Freya* station on the Dutch island of Texel was usually the first to report that British bombers were flying out across the North Sea, and it can be assumed that Texel sent in the first report on this night. The first contact had been with the eight Mosquitoes setting out for their diversionary raid on Berlin; they had been detected flying seventy miles away at approximately 9.30 p.m. (Unless otherwise stated, all times quoted are those used by the R.A.F.; German time was one hour ahead.) Texel had then reported the larger force of bombers bound for Peenemünde, and after that it had been no more than a matter of routine for the bombers to be tracked by further *Freya* stations on the Frisian Islands, in the German Bight and on the Danish coast.

It was one thing for German commanders to know the position of a raiding force; their estimate of the future course and intentions of the bombers was quite another. Two conflicting factors must have been deep in the German thoughts on this night. The first – the reasonable belief that the R.A.F. must be mad to send their heavy bombers on a distant raid on this moonlight night – was counteracted by the German obsession about the possibility of an attack on Berlin; the British had been preaching 'Berlin next' for some time, and they had sent those unexplained small nuisance raids three times during the past week. From the orders which the Germans eventually issued, it is obvious that the initial plan had a dual intention. The first was to cover any shallow penetration raid on such important targets as Flensburg, Kiel, Bremen, or even Hamburg should the R.A.F. decide to turn over the rubble of this unfortunate city again; the second (and here could be seen one of the advantages of using heavy night fighters in the more flexible Wild Boar role) was to switch the fighters to Berlin if the bombers flew on over Denmark.

It is unlikely that many officers in the Luftwaffe control organization knew of the importance of Peenemünde. It is probable that not one of them thought that the main force of R.A.F. bombers approaching Denmark could be heading for that place.

The British had also kept their secrets well.

The impression is sometimes given that, at this period of the war, one senior Luftwaffe officer was able to direct the operations of all the German night-fighter units over the entire spread of Western Europe. Something approaching that desirable state of affairs would be reached a few months later, but, as has been mentioned, the Peenemünde operation took place on the very first night of a new era of German night fighting. There was no direct overall control; there was no such thing as a single commentary broadcast to the night-fighter crews throughout the operation. What did exist was a predetermined plan that, except for a handful of fighters left behind to patrol local 'boxes', every German fighter should attempt to reach the R.A.F.'s target for the night and carry out Wild Boar tactics there. Numerous 'operations officers', often of quite junior rank and in many, widely separated control rooms, were assessing incoming information and broadcasting their best advice to the fighters on many frequencies. There were certainly senior officers in the background, consulting each other by telephone, often over long distances, about the likely identity of the target for the R.A.F. bombers and trying to establish a common plan; but the interpretation of that plan was in the hands of those scattered subordinates.

The two relevant senior officers on this night were General Josef Kammhuber, who as commander of X I I Fliegerkorps was nominally chief of the night-fighter forces – though not of the single-engined units – and his superior Generaloberst Hubert Weise, commander of the *Befehlshaber Mitte*, who was in charge not only of fighters but also of Flak and the whole range of other aids available to the air defence of Germany. Kammhuber had his headquarters at Zeist, in Holland, very close to the operations room of the 1st Jagddivision at Deelen airfield near Arnhem. (The massive and sophisticated underground operations bunker here, code-named Diogenes, would not be ready for use until September.) General Weise was in the Luftwaffe's central operations room at the former Olympic Sportfield at Wannsee, just outside Berlin. It is believed that Goering was either at Wannsee with Weise, or at least in close touch with him. So, while it is true to say that Weise had overall control of the situation and that Kammhuber had direct control of the fighters, in reality much would be left to the initiative of subordinate officers and, ultimately, of individual night-fighter pilots, many of whom were carrying out their first Wild Boar operation.

David Irving tells the intriguing story of how communications through the operations room at Deelen failed during the most important part of the Peenemünde operation, of how General Kammhuber could issue no orders to his units, and of how, after a delay, the operations room of '4th Fighter Division' at Metz, in northern France, took over control of the night battle. (Metz at that time was actually the headquarters of the 3rd Fighter Division, soon to be redesignated the 4th.) 'After the war,' Irving writes, 'Kammhuber was informed by British officers that two Germans employed at the Arnhem–Deelen operations room were, in fact, British agents, and they may well have been briefed to sabotage the defence effort on that one night, if on no other. This, however, must remain pure speculation.' [3]

For anyone making a special study of this one night's operations, that tantalizing statement written in 1964 cried out for further investigation. Questions to Sir Arthur Harris and Bomber Command staff officers revealed no knowledge of a secret operation designed to help the R.A.F. bombers on their dangerous way to Peenemünde.

This is not surprising; there was no advantage in telling Bomber Command that such an operation might be in progress.

An attempt to get positive information from Holland also failed. A letter to Arnhem, asking if Dutch resistance men might have been involved, brought this reply from P.R.A. Van Iddekinge, the town archivist:

> I have been trying to find former Resistance members who might be able to help you. Much to my regret I have not been very successful. The only result so far is that I was informed that one of the main telephone cables – from the Operations Centre near Deelen to St Trond in Belgium – was sabotaged more than once and that, consequently, it would be impossible by now to establish whether 17/18 August 1943 was one of the dates. None of the Resistance men I know, moreover, would ever claim this remarkable and important feat of arms.

General Kammhuber was still alive in Munich when this research was carried out and he politely answered my letters. He stated that he was informed of the 'Deelen sabotage' story by an R.A.F. officer who interrogated him several times between September and December 1945 at Latimer House, a country home in Buckinghamshire where senior German officers were extensively questioned about their war-time activities. (Latimer House is still in use as the Joint Services Staff College.) The officer who conducted the main questioning of Kammhuber at this time is known to have been Squadron Leader Spencerley (who died in 1970), but Kammhuber was insistent that the officer who told him about Deelen was named King and that King talked to him several times. The Ministry of Defence forwarded letters to the last known addresses of all 'Kings' who had served as officers in either the Signals or the Intelligence branches of the R.A.F. at that time. There was only one, enigmatic reply from one of the former Intelligence officers who regretted that he was 'not able to answer questions about the war.'

There is no way of being certain that 'King's' claim to General Kammhuber that communications at Deelen were deliberately broken was based on fact; it may have been a ploy designed to make Kammhuber talk more freely. On the other hand the British may have indeed sent a request to agents or underground men in the Deelen area to do what they could to sever communications for those few vital hours. I would like to have been able to state with certainty that some brave Dutchmen or Germans had saved the lives of many R.A.F. aircrew in this way, but unfortunately that is not possible. What can be said is that, when at least eleven former night-fighter men were asked about any serious communications failure on this night, not one of them remembered any difficulty. The truth is that, if Deelen did cease to broadcast, there had been sufficient other means of sending out information to fill the gap.

We can now return to the actual operations of the Luftwaffe. The main strength of the long-range night fighters was ordered up at about 10.30 p.m., while the bombers were still more than 100 miles from the Danish coast. The units in Belgium were away first. II/NJG 1, a crack *Gruppe* based at St Trond, dispatched thirteen Messerschmitt 110s between 10.38 and 10.48. Other units soon followed, the ones in Holland next, then those in north-west Germany and Denmark, and finally the *Gruppen* of NJG 5, a relatively new and inexperienced *Geschwader* stationed around Berlin and on the Baltic coast – the nearest *Geschwader* to Peenemünde. Many were directed at first to radio beacons well to the west of Peenemünde or Berlin, in case the R.A.F. attack should develop on Kiel, Hamburg or another city in that area. Radio beacon *Hahn*, near Hagenow airfield forty miles east of Hamburg and 100 miles west of Berlin, was certainly used as an initial holding position for many of the German fighters.

The last unit of twin-engined fighters to take off was the 3rd *Staffel* of NJG 3, recently sent to Kastrup airfield just outside Copenhagen. Local thunderstorms delayed things here, and Oberleutnant Paul Zorner, the Staffelkapitän, eventually left with only four or five of the eight Messerschmitt 110s available; he judged that the remaining crews were too inexperienced to cope with the thundery conditions which still lingered. 'They didn't say anything but I think that the newer crews were happy to be left behind. Conditions were difficult but the old hands with me weren't worried.'

Decisions about take-off time were particularly critical for the single-engined fighters of Hajo Herrmann's three Wild Boar *Gruppen* with their limited endurance. Herrmann's units were at Hangelar (near Bonn), Rheine (north of Münster), and Oldenburg. His command was virtually an independent one. He preferred to receive his information from Generaloberst Weise's general control room at Berlin, rather than from General Kammhuber's purely fighter room at Deelen. It was essential for Herrmann's unit to have close liaison with Flak commanders about the altitudes above which his fighters could operate without fear of being hit by Flak, and this liaison was better achieved through Weise's organization. Herrmann delayed his take-offs.

I first talked with Weise, or a member of his staff, or possibly even with Goering himself, when the R.A.F. were still over the North

Sea. Initially, there was a large range of possible targets – Hamburg, Lübeck etc. I didn't think of Berlin at first because of the shortness of the night and I never thought of Peenemünde, which I knew about as a test centre for strange aircraft but I only knew a little about the rocket work there.

I had another chat with Berlin when the first R.A.F. aircraft reached Denmark. They told me that they were now forecasting Berlin as the target; they had become hypnotized by Berlin. They advised me to make for Berlin but to be prepared to divert to another target if required.

Herrmann accepted this advice and ordered all his units to leave directly for Berlin. Herrmann was to take part himself, and he took off from Hangelar.

The last of Herrmann's pilots to take off was Oberleutnant Friedrich-Karl Müller, a pre-war Lufthansa pilot.

I was out hunting in the woods about eight kilometres from Hangelar airfield. Herrmann had told me to go and shoot a wild boar; he wanted its head for the Officers' Mess. It was a nice summer night out in those woods. I was sitting on a heap of potatoes but had no luck. I was a little too early; they mostly came out of the woods about midnight.

Then I heard sirens and saw the top of the cone of three search-lights over our airfield. I couldn't hear the fighters taking off but I knew that they were. They only lit that cone for our take-offs – and there was I sitting on a heap of potatoes watching for wild pigs! I set off at once with my motor cycle and sidecar to the castle which was our H.Q., got my flying suit, took off in our Fieseler Storch and reached the airfield in four or five minutes. I had taken about thirty-five minutes from that heap of potatoes to sitting in my Fw 190 ready to take-off.

Herr Müller is still a keen hunter; I had to travel to a hunting lodge deep in the Hunsrück for my interview with him.

It is generally accepted that 213 German fighters took off for action on this night, 158 twin-engined aircraft and fifty-five of Major Herrmann's Messerschmitt 109s and Focke-Wulf 190s. It is not known whether these figures include a few fighters from NJG4, based in northern France, believed to have been sent to the Ruhr area to fill the gap left by the wholesale dispatch to the north of the local units. One Messerschmitt 109 suffered an engine fire and crashed a few minutes after taking off from Hangelar, and a Messerschmitt 110 from St Trond was badly damaged when it crash-landed after an engine failed on take-off, but there were no fatal casualties. A handful of the German fighters were being kept back for duty in the box system, but the remainder were now committed to the Luftwaffe's first great Wild Boar operation. Those not dispatched directly to Berlin would soon go there when the danger to cities further west had passed. Peenemünde was 110 miles from Berlin.

If one transposes this operation into British terms, it is as though night fighters from as far apart as Plymouth and Aberdeen were sent to Newcastle, some via a holding point near Liverpool, when the target for the enemy bombers was in fact Edinburgh.

The R.A.F. did not intend to allow the Germans to deploy their night fighters without interference. For several months, long-range squadrons of Fighter Command had been operating in that support-ing role aptly called 'Intruding'. They had the ability to send fighters as far as most of the German night-fighter airfields to try to catch and shoot down aircraft at the vulnerable times of take-off and landing. Even if German fighters were not caught, the general disruptive effect was always a cause of annoyance. Fighter Command, asked for a maximum Intruder effort, had been able to provide ten Beaufighters and twenty Mosquito crews for the night's main work. Half had been allocated to the first phase, timed to catch German fighters taking off. Eight more Mosquitoes would be flying operational training sorties to Holland and France, but these proved uneventful, and they play no real part in the Peenemünde story.

The first Intruders to take off were from an unusual squadron and carrying out an unusual operation. 141 Squadron at Wittering was the R.A.F.'s first Serrate unit. Serrate was a device which enabled a British fighter to detect the presence of a German night fighter by picking up its radar emissions. 141 had been operating it since mid June 1943 with steady success; the war of fighter versus fighter in night operations was not one of dramatic results but of steady attrition. Led by the brilliant exponent of the combined night-fighter and Intruder role, Wing Commander J. R. D. (Bob) Braham, the squadron could boast an unusual strength of skill and experience amongst its pilots and radar operators. They were still flying the ageing Beaufighter, but, together with other squadrons, would soon be equipped with new Serrate Mosquitoes and would play a major part in bomber support operations during later stages of the war.

Wing Commander Braham's plan was that his crews would not operate directly over German airfields but would hunt 'freelance', inter-posing themselves between the outward bound bomber-stream cross-ing the North Sea and the German airfields in Holland and north-western Germany. He hoped that the radar echoes of the five Beau-fighters in his first wave would attract German fighters which his air-craft could engage. Five other crews would repeat the process when the bombers returned later in the night. Braham would fly in the first wave.

Four of the Beaufighters in the first wave made no contact of any kind, but Braham attracted two German fighters. The very ex-perienced Luftwaffe unit IV/NJG 1 at Leeuwarden was one of the few which the Germans had allocated to local defence, and five of its Messerschmitt 110s under an up-and-coming ace, Leutnant Heinz-Wolfgang Schnaufer, were sent out over the North Sea towards the Beaufighters' radar echoes. Using his Serrate, Braham attacked the first German plane, which was shot down in flames into the sea. The second had probably been trying to close on the Beaufighter, but Braham outmanoeuvred it, got behind, and shot it down also. One German was seen to jump by parachute, and Braham later recorded how he thought of finishing him off but was persuaded not to by his radar operator – who was Jewish.

Braham's successes in this neatly planned operation were against two experienced German crews. The pilot of the first Messerschmitt 110 – Feldwebel Georg Kraft, who had shot down fourteen R.A.F. bombers – was killed, but his radar operator survived. The pilot of the second German fighter, Feldwebel Heinz Vinke, with more than twenty R.A.F. bombers to his credit, crash-landed in the sea and was later picked up safely, but the other two in his crew – Feldwebel Schödel and Unteroffizier Gaa – both died; one of them had been the man on the parachute. He must have drowned. The deaths of Georg Kraft, Karl Schödel and Johann Gaa were the first of the Peenemünde operation. (Feldwebel Vinke later crewed up with Unteroffizier Rudolf Dunger, the radar operator who survived from Braham's first success, pushed his score up to fifty-four night victims and won the Knight's Cross with Oak Leaves but, ironically, was shot down by a Spitfire and lost with Dunger in the North Sea when making an air-sea rescue flight. Leutnant Schnaufer was shot at by his own Flak when he landed at Wittmundhafen; he finished the war as the leading German night ace with 121 successes. Wing Commander Braham's two successes brought his score to seventeen night victories – the R.A.F. were not presented with the more numerous opportunities available to the German aces – and gave him a lead of one over his rival at the top of the R.A.F. night list, Wing Commander John Cunningham.)

The ten Mosquitoes of the first phase flew further afield and carried out conventional Intruder patrols over five airfields astride the bomber route to Peenemünde. R.A.F. intelligence was good; the airfields – Ardorf, Stade, Jagel and Westerland in Germany and Grove in Denmark – were all the homes of front-line night-fighter units. But this timing of the Intruder patrols – always a difficult matter – was slightly wrong on this night; the German fighters had all taken off on their new Wild Boar operations before the Mosquitoes arrived. Nine of the ten Intruders found their airfields correctly; most of them dropped two 500-pounder bombs on the airfield or on some useful nearby target and then remained in the vicinity for as long as possible. Flying Officer Vivian Bridges, a pilot of 25 Squadron, describes what was probably a typical operation for those crews who had not yet gained much experience in this work.

We crossed the coast at 5,000 feet, coming in just south of Sylt. We could see the coastline and islands. There was a hell of a lot of defence activity here – anti-aircraft fire and searchlights. I remember clearly seeing an aircraft hit about five miles away; there was a flash and then something caught fire. I only watched it for a little while.

We had been told to bomb anything useful that we could find. We went to the airfield first but there was no activity and I decided to bomb the railway which we could see. I flew along it from south to north until we found this junction. We hadn't any bomb sights; we just pointed the aeroplane downhill and let go. Then we flew home – with a big sigh of relief when we got out to sea. It was my first Intruder operation and I was terrified. We had no special training but we were sent out because we were fairly experienced in home defence work. I suppose it just seemed a good idea at the time to use crews in this way. They just said, 'Go over there and see what you can do.' Compared to the work I did later with 100 Group, this was a pretty amateurish effort.

Squadron Leader Frank Brinsden, another 25 Squadron pilot, and his navigator, Flying Officer Fane-Sewell, need not have been flying at all. Having completed their tour of operations, they had been posted to a Beaufighter squadron in North Africa and were packed ready to leave. But, that afternoon, they had been asked to fly one more operation because of the 'maximum effort' requested in support of the Peenemünde operation. Having agreed, they spent a frustrating hour near Westerland airfield, on the island of Sylt, dodging searchlights and Flak. Brinsden describes what happened next.

With our patrol coming to an end but with bombs and ammunition intact, we decided upon a bombing run across the airfield. We climbed away westwards but then let down quickly and flew a wide orbit back towards Westerland at sea level.

All was dandy until, over the airfield when banking in a turn towards some large buildings, a searchlight shone right into the cockpit and Flak came from everywhere. Night vision and the ability to read instruments was lost and I obviously became disorientated in the violent weaving because, in the next few seconds, we hit the water – fortunately on an even keel. One bounce, with no control, and, by the engine noises, no propellers and we were back in the sea.

The Mossie dinghy had ejected itself, as the handbook said it should, and, after taking the sails from our seat packs, which we later erected in the dinghy, and scratching around for our maps and charts, it was a simple matter to haul in the painter and step aboard. Still a glorious moonlit night, calm and warm and only the sound of friendly Merlin engines of another Mosquito heading westwards and home.

Altogether an unexciting tale of a last sortie although exciting enough to Pete and myself. Whether we achieved anything, we will never know. From time to time one reminisces about the last few minutes of the attack and thinks, 'I should have done so and so,' but this is futile really. One does one's best at the time. We became a little foolhardy at the end of the patrol – and came unstuck.

The two airmen were met by German soldiers when they drifted ashore at Sylt next morning.

There was to be one more incident in this interesting first phase of the Intruder operations. Flight Lieutenant D. H. Blomeley, of 605 Squadron, had been patrolling Jagel airfield for fifteen minutes when he was himself attacked by a German fighter. In the ensuing combat in bright moonlight, the enemy was identified as a Messerschmitt 109. The German made several passes and then made the mistake of overshooting the Mosquito, giving Blomeley the chance to fire one quick burst. The German was seen to crash into a lake, and Blomeley actually tried to photograph the tail of the fighter sticking out of the water with his camera gun. The identity of the German is not known; he may have been from a local day-fighter unit which had decided to try to get rid of this troublesome Intruder.

The Intruder operations had produced a clear advantage for the British – three German fighters destroyed for the loss of one Mosquito. These successes were, however, of significance rather to long-term attrition than to the outcome of the Peenemünde operation. The take-off of the main German night-fighter force had not been disrupted in any way.

NOTES
1. Bundesarchiv R L/540.
2. The quotation is from *Long Range Upward Shooting*, kindly provided by Group Captain A. E. Dark, C.B.E., whose father was a First World War air armament officer.
3. *The Mare's Nest*, pp. 102 and 113–14.

CHAPTER 8

Denmark

When the R.A.F. bomber-stream formed at Position A, sixty miles from the Danish coast, the aircraft had reached their normal operational height – twice the altitude at which they would bomb Peenemünde. It was an essential part of the plan that they should make their approach as though they were attacking a normal city target. Twenty miles out from the Danish coast, the bombers started to release Window. Each aircraft would release two bundles per minute while flying through the night-fighter boxes in Denmark, but then the rate would fall to one per minute for the remainder of the flight to Peenemünde. The landfall on the Danish coast was on the southern tip of the island of Fanø. This distinctively shaped feature was clearly visible in the moonlight to those crews who had made good crossings. Some who approached the coast too far to the south realized their error when they saw the dangerous Flak and searchlight defences of the German island of Sylt, and sheered away quickly. The Danish town of Esbjerg, to the north, was also showing a heavy concentration of searchlights, but few bombers had strayed in that direction.

Two more aircraft had to turn back with mechanical trouble. One was piloted by Flight Lieutenant John Rowland of 12 Squadron.

We had a bit of a confab about what to do. The rear gunner was very fed up about not being able to get his turret going as he had had the same trouble before and it was very hard work rotating it by hand. I decided to ask everybody, in turn, if they thought we should turn back as, with the bright moonlight and the low level attack, it seemed a bit dicey to go on.

Everybody in turn said, 'I don't know, leave it to you,' until last of all I asked Charlie, the flight engineer, a warrant officer on his second tour. He replied, firmly, 'Let's push off home.' Everyone immediately agreed; everyone had wanted to go back but didn't want to be the first one to say so!

I asked the nav if there was any target nearby where we could drop our bombs and he said that Sylt was only a few miles to the south of us and perhaps we could bomb the aerodrome there. This we decided to do and we lost height to 15,000 feet and very shortly afterwards the bomb aimer said he could see Sylt. We opened the bomb doors and dropped our load and then turned for home. Because we had bombed Sylt, we were allowed to count the trip towards our tour and nobody questioned our early return with a u/s rear turret.

I have always had a slightly guilty feeling about it, coupled with regret at having missed a very unusual target that was 'in the news' quite a bit subsequently.

The other aircraft which had to turn back at this point, another 1 Group Lancaster, also released its bomb-load 'on the airfield at Sylt'. There is no record to show what damage was caused at Sylt, but Danish records show that one bomb-load fell on friendly Fanø, thirty miles further north!

It was navigational error which led to the destruction of the first bombers to be lost from the Peenemünde force. The German town of Flensburg, right on the Danish border and a port where U-boats were built, was well known for Flak. Although it was thirty miles south of the route across Denmark, conditions were so clear that many crews could see a bomber caught in the searchlights at Flensburg and 'disposed of by the Flak in a frighteningly efficient way'. One observer of this incident was Pilot Officer Gerry South, on only his second operational flight, his first to Germany. He was second pilot in a Halifax of 405 Squadron.

I was keeping out of the way of the working members of the crew and assimilating as much 'gen' as I could for future use. The first sign of major enemy activity was when some unfortunate bomber was coned in searchlights. 'Flensburg,' said the bomb aimer, 'always a spot to avoid, that.' The warning stuck and, though no doubt I subsequently saw much heavier Flak, Flensburg remains a baleful memory.

The bomber destroyed over Flensburg was from the same squadron as Pilot Officer South. The pilot – Flying Officer H. S. McIntyre, a Canadian – three more Canadians and three Englishmen all died: the first British deaths of the night. They had been on their sixth operation with this Pathfinder squadron but had not yet 'qualified' as a marker crew.

Approximately twenty minutes later, another crew paid the penalty for navigational error. Sergeant Peter Crees of 434 Squadron was nearby and saw what happened.

We were about ten miles away to the north. I was in the astrodome and saw this 'master' searchlight switched on and it had the bomber straightaway. I had never seen a searchlight catch an aircraft like that without weaving around first. No more than half a minute later, we saw the Flak – seen as just little flashes at that distance – and there were just two or three shots before the plane was hit, burst into flames and went down. There were the usual remarks – 'Someone's caught it over there.'

By coincidence, the bomber destroyed was also from the same squadron as the witness of its destruction. The Halifax hit over Sylt was piloted by Flight Sergeant F. J. Walker. This time there were two survivors; one of them was Sergeant George Irving, the flight engineer.

All hell broke loose when we were in the vicinity of Sylt! Suddenly, everything was as bright as day because we were trapped in the beam of a master searchlight. Before we could take evasive action, we were hit amidships by the anti-aircraft fire. We were carrying an overload fuel tank and it seemed that there was a direct hit on it and probably other places because the aircraft appeared to be out of control.

I was unable to go aft because of the fire and couldn't communicate with the mid-upper gunner and rear gunner. So I went forward but found that the pilot and bomb aimer appeared to be dead; I think they died instantly. I had Flak wounds in the right leg. At that time, the aircraft seemed to be spinning. I went to the navigator's position, towards the nose of the aircraft, and gestured to him that we should bale out as the aircraft was, by this time, completely enveloped by flames.

The bale-out for me was not exactly smooth. Although I left the aircraft all right, I must have got into the wrong position because I remember a severe wallop in the face and was sure that I had lost my nose. Shortly after leaving the aircraft, I saw an explosion on the ground which I presumed was our aircraft. I was followed most of the way down by searchlights and was greeted by a group of German military because I landed on the runway of the German airfield of Westerland.

Many of the R.A.F. men express surprise that they saw so little evidence of activity while crossing Denmark in the bright conditions which usually favoured German night fighters so much. This was territory normally defended with vigour by NJG3 with its chain of airfields stretching from Vechta, south of Bremen, to Aalborg in the north of Denmark. Moreover, this *Geschwader* had the advantage of having had more experience – during the Battle of Hamburg – of coping with the difficulties caused by Window than any other German night-fighter unit. But probably three quarters or more of the fighters here had been sent off on the new Wild Boar operations and, when the bomber-stream crossed Denmark, were on their way to Berlin. Only a handful, supplied by the German detachments at Westerland and Aalborg, were manning the local boxes. The twelve to fifteen thus left to engage the bombers made a poor showing: the entire stream appears to have crossed Denmark without losing a single aircraft. There were four combats, in which bomber crews claimed two German fighters damaged, but not one German cannon shell or bullet struck a bomber. (One German report says that the R.A.F. bomber lost at Sylt was shot down by a night fighter, but all British witnesses agree that its destruction was caused by Flak.)

It is possible that the earlier flight over Denmark of the small Mosquito force – which was also releasing Window – had disrupted the defence, but a more likely reason for the German failure was that the best crews, who normally manned the boxes when bombers approached, had gone off on the Wild Boar operation, and the inexperienced men left behind just could not cope with the Window released by the Main Force and the other protective devices carried by the bombers. Unteroffizier Benno Gramlich was pilot of such a crew.

> We flew from Aalborg and, normally, we had the task of trying to intercept the fast courier and transport planes flying from England to Sweden. We had tried every tactic for months on end without success; we particularly wanted the confirmed success of a victory. Our morale was miserable. We were young, ambitious, aggressive, and wanted to prove ourselves with that first success.
>
> My chance came in the night of 17/18 August 1943. Incoming flights over the North Sea, target possibly Berlin. Operations in a box near Esbjerg. It was full moon, the northern sky was pink. We saw the bomber about one kilometre away. As we closed in to 400 metres, the bomber suddenly dived away in a steep spiral. It probably had a warning device – he couldn't have seen us. We followed – steeper – into the darkness. In those seconds, I swore to myself no longer to behave according to the book but to open fire at whatever range and from whatever position I was in when I first saw the next bomber.

It remained to be seen whether the German abandonment of their old defensive system would be compensated for by success elsewhere later in the night.

The bombers had turned onto an east-north-easterly course on reaching the Danish coast and also commenced a steady loss of height and an increase of speed which would bring them to Peenemünde –

240 miles away – in just fifty-eight minutes. The roar of the bomber-stream was heard by thousands of Danish people. Lights were seen on the ground when curtains were deliberately drawn and doors opened to show the R.A.F. men that there were friends below, and the V-for-victory sign was flashed in morse code. The bombers carrying leaflets for the Danes released them; the latest war news and encouragement for these beleaguered allies were thus delivered in economic fashion.

The Danish press was obviously subject to German censorship, but one enterprising local editor was able to publish this subtle little piece for his readers on the day after the bombers flew overhead to Peene-münde.

FLYING NIGHT ANIMALS IN INCREASING NUMBERS

The advantage about bats is that they multiply so incredibly fast. They hide in places where their enemies cannot get hold of them and there they breed in peace and quietness. Though the animals have suffered heavily for some years, it is not of great importance. They will be able to hold their own.[1]

An R.A.F. Halifax of 138 Squadron took advantage of the diversion caused by the flight of the bomber-stream over Denmark to drop a load of arms by parachute to a Resistance group. The dropping zone was near Lake Madum, in Denmark's largest forest, twenty miles south of the town of Aalborg and 100 miles north of the route being taken by the Peenemünde bombers. Unfortunately for the Danish men involved, a German night-fighter pilot saw the parachutes descending and warned the local authorities. Also, the containers dropped more than a mile from the place where the Danes were waiting. After they had recovered the containers and while they were driving away from the area, they met a lorry-load of German soldiers sent out to look for them. In the chase which followed, the gas-driven Danish lorry was no match for the petrol-driven German one. The Resistance leader, Lieutenant J. P. Jensen, ordered his lorry to stop and his men to escape into the forest. One man was shot by the Germans in the ensuing scrap; another was captured and formally executed at Aalborg later – the first Dane to die in this way. This incident may have helped to precipitate the breakdown of relations between the Danish and German authorities. The Germans took over the government of Denmark at the end of the month.

Each bomber crossed the narrow neck of mainland Denmark in only eleven minutes, and the stream then flew on over the many Danish islands in the Baltic. There was little cloud, no haze, and, in the moonlight, every ground feature was clearly visible. For many of the men who flew to Peenemünde, this view of alternating land and sea, of bright strips of sandy beaches and even of breaking waves on those beaches, is one of their strongest recollections of that night.

> The outward flight lives in my memory as the best operation we flew so far as I, as the bomb aimer and hence the map reader, was concerned. In that brilliant moonlight, keeping to our correct track over the mainland and islands of Denmark was a cinch! (Sergeant A. M. Glendenning, 158 Squadron)

> The majority of raids in which I participated have been forgotten in detail but Peenemünde has always remained clear. There was so much to see and it was a thrilling experience to fly low at night, in full moonlight, and to see so much ground detail both over Denmark and in the target area. I think this overshadowed the object of the raid – to destroy a target. It seemed a pity that had to be the reason for such an experience. (Sergeant V. A. Thomson, 76 Squadron)

At one point on the route across the Baltic, the bombers' course passed within forty miles of neutral Sweden and within sixty of the brightly lit city of Malmö. Some of the crews who found they were ahead of their flight plan lost time by flying still nearer to this unusual sight. The aircraft of Sergeant J. Sheriff, of 57 Squadron, had been forced to return to England because of mechanical difficulty, but Sheriff has recorded what other members of his squadron told him later about seeing Sweden.

> I remember quite a number of the other crews mentioning the thrill of seeing towns and villages that were not blacked out. They were thrilled, not only at the sight of lighted towns but also at the sudden realization that, 'Good Lord; there are some people down there actually living like human beings!' After four years of living in total black-out, it was difficult to believe that those people were living completely peaceful, carefree lives.

One Halifax gunner, on his seventh operation and with the prospect of twenty-three more to go, reports wistfully that he thinks his crew 'were hoping we could get lost and land in Sweden.'

The final factor which made this part of the Peenemünde operation so pleasantly memorable for the R.A.F. men was the almost complete lack of German activity, even though the bombers passed only fifty miles from the important German port of Rostock and were now rapidly approaching Peenemünde. There are only two reports of combats along this section of the route and, as both reports refer exactly to the same time and location, they probably belong to the same incident. In a confused action involving a Stirling, a Halifax, and perhaps a German fighter, the Stirling claimed the destruction of a Dornier 217 and the Halifax was hit in the nose by a burst of machine-gun bullets from 'a Junkers 88' which was, in reality, probably the Stirling. The Halifax's flight engineer was wounded in the foot. The only German fighter which may have been missing in this area was actually a Messerschmitt 110 piloted by Leutnant Karl Gerber, the adjutant of III/NJG5. He and his radar operator disappeared somewhere over the sea and their bodies were never found; but their loss may have been the result of action later in the night and at another place.

Only one bomber – a Halifax – was forced to turn back from the Baltic. It had been slightly damaged by Flak over Denmark and two of its engines developed trouble. The bomb-load was immediately released and the Halifax returned to England. A total of 569 bombers passed safely through these quiet parts of the Baltic and prepared to enter the target area.

Midnight ushered in the twenty-second birthday of Sergeant George Aitken, a tail gunner in 156 Squadron. When the remainder of his crew sang 'Happy Birthday to you' over the intercom it was, for Aitken, 'something very special which I will never forget'.

NOTE

1. From *Lolland-Falsters Stiftstidende*, provided by the Nykøbing Central-biblioteket.

CHAPTER 9

Berlin

While the heavy bombers were flying in comparative safety over Denmark and the Baltic, there was much excitement over Berlin. The R.A.F had carried out its diversionary raid on the capital.

The eight Mosquitoes of 139 Squadron, led by their commander, Group Captain L. C. Slee, had earlier flown from their base at Wyton to Swanton Morley, a forward airfield near the Norfolk coast, and had topped up their fuel tanks before taking off again for the long trip to Berlin. After an uneventful flight out over the North Sea, Denmark and the Baltic, the Mosquitoes crossed the German coast at a point west of Rostock, eighty miles from Peenemünde but near enough to cause the sirens to sound there. A twelve-mile-long lake, the Müritsee, clearly visible in the moonlight, provided a good navigational reference point fifty-five miles out from their target.

The eight Mosquitoes all reached Berlin, the first of them just before 11 p.m. (midnight German time). The plan was that they should fly at different heights and on different headings over the city. Each Mosquito had the modest load of three 500-lb. bombs and one Target Indicator, and they would also release Window. The eight Target Indicators were the most important part of this little operation. Such weapons were normally the forerunners of a heavy raid.

The Germans reacted as expected. The strong Flak and searchlight defences of Berlin opened up, and I am again obliged to David Irving for the information that eighty-nine Flak batteries fired a total of 11,774 rounds and that the ceiling of the fire was twice reduced – at 11.07 p.m. and 11.31 p.m. – to allow the Wild Boar operation to take place. It must have been an exciting time for the Luftwaffe. For the first time, it seemed, they had been able to assemble a large force of fighters – possibly 150 – at the target city before the main strength of the R.A.F. arrived, and they had secured that vital co-operation with the ground defences. Flak, thick and heavy up to 18,000 feet, would tend to force the R.A.F. bombers above that height, and there the night fighters would catch them. The searchlights could assist both arms of the defence on this clear night.

Six of the eight Mosquito crews performed their task safely, though it was an understandably tense time. Warrant Officer V. J. C. Miles was the pilot of one of the Mosquitoes.

> My memories of the raid were that, on my first visit to the 'big city', it lived up to its reputation. The searchlights seemed to be in their hundreds, the Flak was thick, hot and heavy, and my luck was good. After we had dropped our bomb-load, my navigator spent the next few minutes – they seemed like hours – kneeling on his seat, watching for signs of fighter aircraft and the approach of searchlights.
>
> Once we cleared the Berlin defence area, the rest of the trip was uneventful.

The Mosquito of Flight Lieutenant R.A.V. Crampton was coned by searchlights and fiercely engaged by Flak. Crampton managed to remain unscathed for some time but, when over Brandenburg and almost out of the Berlin defensive area, his starboard engine was hit by shell fragments. He closed it down and flew the 430 miles back to Swanton Morley on his remaining engine. Lack of fuel caused this faithful Rolls-Royce Merlin to cut out on landing, and the Mosquito was written off in the resulting crash. Flight Lieutenant Crampton spent six weeks in hospital with head injuries, but his navigator was unhurt.

The remaining Mosquito was not so fortunate. It was spotted by one of Major Herrmann's Wild Boar pilots, and the resulting combat was witnessed by Oberleutnant Friedrich-Karl Müller, who had taken off late from Bonn and had just arrived in Berlin.

> There were a lot of searchlights waving about nervously. I couldn't see any bombs or markers but I did see just one aircraft going down on fire – a small aircraft – and I heard a voice on the R/T: '*Horrido. Horrido. Horrido. Schütze 31.*' I switched on and replied, '*Wilde Sau 3. Ich gratuliere zum Abschuss.*' '*Wilde Sau 3*' was my own call sign, and I was telling him that I had witnessed the success he had claimed.

Schütze 31 was Feldwebel Werner Hakenjos. His victim was the Mosquito of Flying Officer A. S. Cooke and Sergeant D. A. H. Dixon, flying their third operation with 139 Squadron. Both were killed. Cooke was an American from Wichita Falls, Texas, who had joined the R.A.F., and Dixon was a Scot from Glasgow. The Mosquito crashed near the town of Nauen, sixteen miles west of Berlin. (Feldwebel Hakenjos was killed in action on 17 March 1944.)

The effects of the raid on Berlin really mattered little to the R.A.F., but they will be briefly described. The city records[1] state that only six bombs exploded but that thirteen heavy Flak shells which had failed to burst in the air also exploded on the ground. Four men – one a foreign worker – were killed and five people injured. All four deaths are listed as being caused by the falling Flak shells and not by bombs. Eight dwelling houses and five commercial premises were damaged, only one seriously. By coincidence, two of these buildings, in the Zimmerstrasse, housed publishing firms of particular interest: the V. B. Verlag, which produced Goebbels's *Völkischer Beobachter*; and the main publishers of the Nazi Party who had once brought out *Mein Kampf*. Another bomb made a crater outside Zimmerstrasse No. 10, a branch office of the Gestapo.

The R.A.F. action over Berlin was soon finished: the last Mosquito had probably gone by 11.40 p.m. But the Berlin Flak fired long after, and the night fighters continued to circle round, both expecting the R.A.F. Main Force to arrive soon. Whoever was controlling the night-fighter defence at this stage had, at 11.35 p.m., issued the order that all those night fighters not already at Berlin were to make for the city. This was thirty-six minutes before the R.A.F. were due to open the attack at Peenemünde.

The British diversion at Berlin had been well planned, well executed, and could hardly have achieved its purpose more success-fully. A major advantage for the Peenemünde force had been gained for the expenditure of two Mosquitoes lost and two men killed.

NOTE

1. *Der Polizeipräsident als örtlicher Luftschutzleiter, S. I. Ll. 5425.*

CHAPTER 10

Over the Target

The head of the bomber-stream reached the final turning point on the route to Peenemünde. The headland of Arkona, on the northern end of the island of Rügen, was only forty miles from the target and a distinctive feature easily picked out in the clear conditions with the moon now at its brightest. The bombers turned and headed for Peenemünde, the many bays on the east coast of Rügen providing perfect landmarks to keep them on course. A Canadian pilot remembers the beautiful full moon to the south and the sight of more and more bombers converging on the final approach. 'It made me feel proud of our navigational ability that we could all be coming together at the same place, at the same time, so far from home.' Many aircraft had arrived early and were orbiting or 'dog-legging' just north of Peenemünde. The leading bomb aimers, at first disappointed to find a thin sheet of stratus cloud ahead of them, soon found with relief that it was just above their operational height.

Group Captain John Searby, the Master Bomber, arrived without difficulty and made his first flight across the peninsula on which Peenemünde stood. Squadron Leader Norman Scrivener was his navigator:

> My job was done when we reached Peenemünde. I had worked out a course for the return flight and I had nothing to do until we finished over the target. It was as clear as a bell. Everything stood out just as shown on the map and on the model I had been shown at Huntingdon. We could see everything – blocks of buildings and open spaces, railway lines when the moon shone on them, little patches of water. The shore line stood out very well. But that soon changed – like a lot of these things. The plan had been made and the briefings done and this should have been as simple as pie; but no sooner did we do our first run down the peninsula before the attack opened than I remember seeing those little streams of smoke blowing across the whole area.

The Germans had activated their smoke-screen – a routine precaution – but their Flak and searchlights remained quiet for the time being so as not to draw attention to the target they were protecting.

Much has been written in earlier chapters about the importance of the Pathfinder marking to the outcome of the attack on this small target. There would be four phases, but the success of the last three and of the bombing of the Main Force would all depend on the success of the initial marking now about to take place. The following table lists the three elements of the plan. ('Blind Markers' were Pathfinders who released their Target Indicators after establishing their position by H2S radar. 'Visual markers' did not carry out their job until the bomb aimer could pick out the Aiming Point visually. 'Red Spot Fires' were a new type of longer-burning markers which were ignited barometrically at 3,000 feet and which burned for up to ten minutes after reaching the ground. 'Zero' or 'Zero Hour' was the time at which the Main Force commenced bombing.)

INITIAL MARKING PLAN

Part 1. Sixteen Blind Markers to release one Red Spot Fire each on the northern edge of Ruden island, seven miles out on the approach flight to the first Aiming Point. These 'Red Spots' were to be re-marked throughout the attack by thirteen later Pathfinder crews and would provide a final reference point just off the target for all approaching crews, Pathfinders and Main Force.

Part 2. The Blind Markers fly on to drop three red Target Indicators and sixteen illuminating flares each, as near as possible to the first Aiming Point between Zero minus 4 minutes and Zero. These radar-aimed red Target Indicators were to guide the Visual Markers to the approximate position of the Aiming Point. The flares were to provide illumination for the Visual Markers.

Part 3. Between Zero minus 2 minutes and Zero plus 2 minutes, six Visual Markers were to mark the exact Aiming Point with four yellow Target Indicators each.

Only one aircraft from the initial force – a Blind Marker – had not arrived; it had turned back earlier with mechanical trouble. The twenty-one other crews set about their task. They were all flying Lancasters from 7, 83, 97 and 156 Squadrons; the Halifaxes of 35 and 405 Squadrons would operate in later stages of the Pathfinder plan. The initial markers flew at heights well above those of the Main Force; the Blind Markers flew at 13–16,000 feet, which allowed their radar sets to take in a large enough area to establish their position, and the Visual Markers all recorded heights between 10,400 and 14,000 feet.

The very first part of the Peenemünde marking plan went badly wrong. The Pathfinders had been advised by their radar experts that the small island of Ruden would show up well on the H2S sets; but, for more than one reason, the decision to use Ruden as a marking point turned out to be a tragedy for the Allied side of the operation. The majority of the Blind Markers did not detect it on their radar sets and did not release their Red Spot Fires until they reached the northern coast of the Peenemünde peninsula, mistaking that coast for Ruden. In some confusion, these Blind Markers then flew on and released their red Target Indicators where they believed the first Aiming Point – the housing estate – to be. This one incident proved to be of vital importance to the opening phase of the raid.

The first markers were released at 12.10 a.m. – one minute early – by the crew of Flight Lieutenant Brian Slade, a senior Pathfinder captain at the age of only twenty-one! A most useful official document shows the estimated positions at the time of marking or bombing of many of the crews at various stages of the raid.[1] They were plotted from the flashlit photographs of ground detail taken at the time of marking or bombing. One map shows the approximate position of eight of the Blind Markers and reveals that six of the eight placed their markers two miles south of the correct position. The initial error made in missing Ruden – two miles – had been maintained in the ensuing release of the Target Indicators. Only one Blind Marker was in the correct place, right over the housing estate. The remaining seven could not be plotted because of the increasing smoke-screen or for other reasons. The result was, therefore, that a large group of early markers had been placed two miles south of the target and only a much smaller group over the correct position. The credit for placing that one accurate load is believed to belong to Pilot Officer D. B. Clements, the H2S set operator in the crew of Pilot Officer L. W. Overton of 156 Squadron.

Next came the Visual Markers – all six present and on time – and they were able to do something to save the situation. One of the crews did not release their markers because they could not be sure of their exact position and the photograph of another could not be plotted because of smoke. Although a third crew put their yellow markers down even further south than the misplaced red ones, the remaining three – two from 83 Squadron and one from 7 Squadron – all found the correct Aiming Point and marked it despite the increasing German smoke-screen. Flight Lieutenant Peter Cutchey was one of the successful bomb aimers. His pilot was Squadron Leader S. Baker of 7 Squadron.

We had arrived early and banked out to sea, to the east of Peenemünde, to waste the unwanted time with the maximum safety. From there, I had a wonderful view of the whole area and could pick out the general area of our Aiming Point, though not the individual buildings. I watched the smoke-screen start up but that didn't do them any good as far as I was concerned.

We came back in on a very hairy, weaving bombing run. Why were we weaving? Tubby Baker always moved the aircraft around quite a lot but he always steadied down for the last bit. He used to say that I was the finest bomb aimer for hitting the target after a curved approach. That's how I survived seventy-three trips with chaps like Tubby Baker. People who went in straight and level, with long bombing runs, just didn't survive. But Tubby always levelled out for those last fifteen seconds.

As we came in, Tubby headed towards the already positioned red Target Indicators but I directed him further north. As we came in to where I judged our Aiming Point should be, I could see groups of buildings by now and then I picked up the sports field which was on my target map and I knew I was on the right target. I aimed my markers to the left of that sports field.

It wasn't so much the moon that helped me see the Aiming Point but the flares dropped by the earlier Pathfinders. A flare spreads its light over a large area. There wasn't a large group of them but there were enough for me to see the ground.

The Visual Markers had performed their task well, and when the first Backer-Up Pathfinder crews appeared they were able to ignore the earlier, wrongly placed markers; most dropped their Target Indicators – green ones – over the housing estate. But the process described above had taken several minutes, and Zero Hour for the Main Force had passed before the situation had clarified. The Master Bomber had quickly realized that a mistake had been made and started broadcasting to the Main Force crews that the early markers should be ignored. Wing Commander John White, the Deputy Master Bomber, had also helped by placing his reserve markers in the correct position, but, for possibly three minutes, the Main Force had been bombing the early markers, and a large area of burning buildings could now be seen amidst them.

That error of two miles would, in almost every direction from the housing estate, have resulted in these bomb-loads falling harmlessly into a forest area, into farmland or into the sea. But just two miles south of the housing estate lay the Trassenheide labour camp, full of foreign workers.

So, at fifteen minutes past midnight (1.15 a.m. local German time), the main attack on Peenemünde had commenced. This was the timetable for that attack.

MAIN FORCE BOMBING PLAN

Wave	Target	Force
1st 00.15 to 00.30	Housing Estate	54 Stirlings and 12 Lancasters of 3 Group 145 Halifaxes of 4 Group 14 Pathfinder Backers-Up, 19 Non-Marking Pathfinders
2nd 00.31 to 00.42	Production Works	113 Lancasters of 1 Group 6 Pathfinder Shifters, 12 Pathfinder Backers-Up
3rd 00.43 to 00.55	Experimental Works	117 Lancasters of 5 Group 52 Halifaxes and 9 Lancasters of 6 Group 6 Pathfinder Shifters, 12 Pathfinder Backers-Up

Because navigation to the target had been so easy and because there had been no undue delay in the initial marking, the Main Force bombing began promptly. Many crews had been in the Peenemünde area for some time and were only too anxious to drop their load and get started on the journey home. Orders about bombing height had varied a little between squadrons, but the general rule was that it should be as low as the crew thought possible between 6,000 and 10,000 feet, with an absolute minimum of 4,000 feet for safety. Bombing at such heights was a novel experience for the crews and there were mixed feelings; there was certainly a concern for the effects of the German defences: 'Time and again, one had seen aircraft forced down below 15,000 feet and shot down by the German light Flak and we knew how deadly accurate it could be. To bomb from such a low height at Peenemünde was not psychologically easy.' But a Stirling crew member says, 'But, oh, it was nice to be bombing at the same height as the Lancs for a change.' Two thirds of the squadron records contain details of bombing heights and, for this first wave of the attack, most crews chose 7–8,000 feet; only three came in above 10,000 feet. Returning crewmen told the usual stories of bombs 'hanging up', resulting in aircraft having to make a second run over the target or dumping surplus bombs on the return journey, of near collisions, and of men looking up and seeing an aircraft, bomb doors open, just above their own. There was only one slight collision, between a Halifax and a Stirling, resulting in no more than light damage, and there were no serious casualties due to aircraft being hit by 'friendly' bombs.

The crews had rarely been able to observe the effects of bombing at such close quarters. The following descriptions are all from men who went in on the first wave.

The first markers went down directly ahead, as if made to order; it was all straightforward – more like a practice flight. I could see the dark shapes of buildings quite plainly, our bombs straddled them and erupted in mushrooming red and I remember saying, 'Bang on, Skip! We hit 'em. Bang on!' The navigator gave our Skip a course out of the target and, with our nose down, we got out of there in a hurry. (Sergeant P. Foolkes, 90 Squadron)

I shall always remember looking out of the blister on the port side of the cabin and seeing the *sea* bouncing back off the shore due to the amount of explosives being dropped. The bombs just showered down and they seemed to be well on target. (Sergeant H. Coles, 83 Squadron)

The target area was an incandescent mass as we flew over on our bombing run, directed by the Master of Ceremonies. Not on any bombing attack have I experienced such a buffeting as we received over the target but I suspect this was caused mainly by blast from bomb explosions on the ground only 6,000 feet below rather than nearby Flak bursts. There was not the rattle of shell fragments against the fuselage such as usually comes from a close Flak burst. (Flight Sergeant W. L. Combs, 15 Squadron)

On the bombing run, a Halifax with bomb doors open was stuck fifty feet above us. I warned the pilot and we edged out from under it. Flak was banging on our starboard wing tip and, as we bombed, the excited words of the Skipper, Ted Sheppard, have always stayed with me: 'Christ almighty, boys! Just look at the fires – just look at the fires!' They were, indeed, spectacular with the colours of the markers all mixed in. (Sergeant K. G. Forester, 90 Squadron)

The bomber crews remember the early part of the attack on Peene-münde for another reason – the ineffectiveness of the defences. As far as is known, not one German fighter was in the Peenemünde area while the initial marking and the whole of the first-wave bombing took place. One searchlight was seen early in the attack, but the Flak had been slow to open fire. This quotation is typical of many memories.

Being in the first wave was an enormous advantage. The markers were dropped, we bombed, we turned for home, and we might as well have been on a joyride – no Flak, no fighters, nothing! It was a beautiful evening, moonlit, broken cloud, and a picture-book operation, a lot easier than many training operations we had previously completed. (Sergeant E. H. Burgess, 78 Squadron)

But the Flak soon started to become more intense, particularly the light Flak which, on normal raids, did not reach to the height at which the bombers flew.

It was at Peenemünde that the light Flak mesmerized me – the various colours – the spiralling effect – the hosepiping; we were normally much higher, among the heavy stuff. This time, it all seemed to be light Flak and this, and the light from the incendiaries below, was really memorable. (Sergeant A. H. L. Atkinson, 76 Squadron)

The spell of immunity could not last, and two bombers were caught by Flak towards the end of the first wave. Sergeant J. E. T. Pearson was the mid-upper gunner in the first of these aircraft – a Halifax of 158 Squadron.

We had been told that our absolute minimum bombing height was 4,000 feet and, just before the bombing run, I heard the pilot and bomb aimer deciding that we would take that minimum height. The station commander had got up and stressed, at the end of the briefing, how important this target was and how lightly it was defended. I remember him saying that Peenemünde was defended by four large catapults. That had got a laugh and we took him at his word and went in as low as we could.

I heard the call, 'Bombs gone,' and at the same time swung my turret round and saw that flames were licking round the starboard inner engine. There had been a lot of light Flak, a constant stream of it coming up from the ground. I called out that we'd been hit; I think that I was the first to realize it. Someone said, 'O.K.,' as though they'd seen it at the same time; it may have been the skipper, Bill Caldwell. I heard him ordering the fire extinguisher to be pressed and the engine to be feathered. The fire didn't gain very fast but it was very persistent and it eventually got a grip and the wing itself caught fire. I had thought that we may get away with it until I saw the wing burning.

Things happened rapidly after that. I heard Caldwell saying, 'Prepare to abandon aircraft.' He seemed quite calm and the aircraft was still flying, apparently under control. There was no panic in the aircraft when I left; I thought the others would all follow and out I went.

I still have this vision of seeing the wing well and truly alight but I saw no more after that because I was only a short time in the air. On the way down, I can remember seeing the target all lit up – a couple of miles away I suppose – and hearing a lot of aircraft noise. I was very surprised when I found that the navigator and myself were the only survivors. I never found out any firm details and I can only assume that the wing came off or the aircraft blew up.

The brave Flight Sergeant Caldwell, a New Zealander only nineteen years old, and two Englishmen, a Scotsman, and a Canadian of this typically mixed Bomber Command crew were the first British deaths over Peenemünde. Caldwell's commission came through a few days after his death.

Three minutes later, a second aircraft was hit by Flak and exploded in the air with its bomb-load still on board. This is believed to have been the 77 Squadron Halifax of Sergeant F. E. Shefford. No trace was ever found of him or his crew. (Appendix 2 contains details of all the R.A.F. aircraft lost on the Peenemünde operation.)

The first wave – fifteen minutes of heavy bombing – ran its course. The German smoke-screen continued, but it never succeeded in covering the first Aiming Point completely. The Pathfinder Backers-Up renewed the marking without any serious gaps. Flight Lieutenant Tim Green was the bomb aimer in the 35 Squadron Halifax which had been delayed on take-off but, by various methods, had reached Peenemünde in time to mark at the end of this first wave.

The visibility was marvellous and I had strong hopes of clear marker identification in spite of the lack of real landmarks near our Aiming Point but, a few miles out, it became clear that this was a vain hope because of the amount of smoke. Scattered bombs and the residual smoke from flares and markers meant that our Aiming Point was not going to be visible. Some markers were already down but it seemed possible that they might be burnt out by the moment of our arrival over the target. The crowding on the approach was giving us a poor run. Jimmy Davidson, the skipper, was obviously having a bad time following my directions and I needed to make some difficult decisions. It was possible that we might represent the only markers for the next stage of the raid and, in any case, any other marker aircraft would have the same smoke problems with the likelihood that they would get worse.

In spite of the poor run and the limitations I have described, we decided to mark. This decision was also influenced by the knowledge that the Master Bomber had things apparently well in hand. I was able to see our markers burst but, because they did so above the ground and because of the smoke and the movement of the aircraft to avoid the crush, I couldn't form a good judgement. I think we undershot – but not by much – although I wasn't really able to form more than an impression.

My general impression was that the effectiveness of the raid was very rapidly declining at this stage, with any concentration in the bombing overshooting the target.

It was the final operation of our tour but there was no great emotion; we still had a long way to go. The excitement would be when we got back.

The remark of Flight Lieutenant Green that 'the effectiveness of the raid was declining' and his reference to 'the bombing overshooting' are significant, although this would affect the second and third waves rather than the first. The marking of the first-wave Backers-Up had been accurate and well maintained. Some Target Indicators had cascaded too far east, over the sea, but the Master Bomber quickly detected them and warned the Main Force crews to ignore them. Most of the first-wave bombing had been good; one tail gunner later joked that he had 'distinctly seen a German scientist going past his turret.' The German decoy fire site, four miles to the west, had been set alight; not one R.A.F. bomber was misled by it. But the fiercely burning labour camp at Trassenheide continued to attract bombs. It was well known that some Main Force crews were willing to ignore markers and could not resist 'stoking up' a good fire; photographs would later show that some aircraft were still bombing Trassenheide up to twelve minutes after Zero Hour.

At least 250 bombers had dropped nearly 500 tons of high explosive and more than 100 tons of incendiaries during this phase of the attack. Only two had been shot down.

At 12.31 a.m., fifteen minutes past Zero Hour, the second phase of the Main Force attack commenced. This – the attempt by the whole of 1 Group to destroy the V-2 production works area – was undoubtedly the most optimistic part of the whole operation. The target comprised just two assembly buildings, each less than 300 yards long. But 106 of 1 Group's powerful Lancasters had arrived, each capable of carrying more than four and a half tons of bombs; sixteen Pathfinder aircraft would also add their loads to this wave. At least ninety of the great 4,000-lb. blast bombs and nearly seven hundred 1,000-lb. high explosive bombs were carried by the force allocated to the destruction of these two buildings.

Before the bombing could take place, however, the Pathfinders had to do something which had never been attempted before and which they had not even practised: they had to move the marking from the first bombing area to this new one. To this end, each of the six Pathfinder squadrons had provided one of its most experienced crews to act as a 'Shifter'. The Pathfinders planning team had calculated that, if an aircraft flying at 12,000 feet but with its bomb-sight set for only 5,000 feet aimed its markers at a given point on the ground, the incorrect setting would place the markers exactly one mile short of the position at which they had been aimed. Just before the end of the first phase of the bombing, the six Shifters were to come in and aim their loads of red Target Indicators at the centre of the green Target Indicators being dropped by the first wave Backers-Up. These red markers should then fall directly over the new Aiming Point, which was exactly one mile short of the first. It was a solution that seemed to have all the advantages of simplicity.

One of the six Shifters had turned back with electrical trouble, but the markers of the others all went down within a two-minute period. The results illustrate yet again the difficulty experienced by the Pathfinders in marking the small targets at Peenemünde with the means available to them at that time, even in the most favourable of circumstances. The earlier green markers, which the Shifters were using as their 'false' aiming mark, were being accurately dropped at that period but, for no obvious reason, one of the Shifter marker-loads fell three quarters of a mile short, and three more overshot by the same margin. The situation was retrieved by the skill of the remaining Shifter crew and by the action of the Master Bomber. The red markers of Squadron Leader C. J. Lofthouse, of 7 Squadron, were placed exactly over the two production buildings. Group Captain Searby realized that most of the others had overshot and was able to warn the Main Force to ignore them just before the powerful squadrons of 1 Group commenced their attack.

The following quotations are all from men who took part in the subsequent bombing. The reader should remember that the scenes on the ground are mostly the result of the earlier attack on the housing estate and the Trassenheide camp.

This is when the real tension builds up but, this time, slightly elated. As we approach, we were pointing straight at the centre of the fires which had started – and still no fighters! There was heavy calibre Flak, exploding far too high for our bombing height, but quite a lot of light stuff.

As flight engineer, I started calling off our height and speed to Jimmy English, my skipper, and, hands on the throttles and trimming tabs, kept warning him of the minimum height for bombing. If you have not lived and fought with Australians, then take it from me, I cannot repeat their language. He told me what he would do with the throttles and trimming gear if I tried to use them before he shouted 'go'.

Over the target, we were being kicked about in front and underneath, mostly by exploding 'cookies' (4,000-lb. bombs). My God,

I now knew what a fly feels like being dangled over a coal fire on which chestnuts are roasting. Below was just a jumble of fire and wreckage. We couldn't miss when Arthur, the bomb aimer in the nose, shouted 'Bombs gone.' (Sergeant W. L. Miller, 460 Squadron)

Peenemünde was growing very 'lively'. On the ground, everything was going up and burning as it isn't possible. This was a mixture of flashes from the ground defences, which seemed to increase their firing in the same measure as we were raining them with bombs, and of explosions which were all more spectacular one from the other. It looked like coal burning – an inferno! Flames were of every colour possible – red, orange, green, blue and what not! Explosions succeeded one another at a rate that surpasses imagination. (Sergeant J.-J. Minguy, 101 Squadron)

The target looked as though one wave of bombers had already hit it and that the whole country was erupting into something terrible. The explosions below were so tremendous that, as we made our pass over the area, it was like riding a car over a ploughed field. There was a great sigh of relief when we altered course for home and my poor old backside muscles relaxed a bit. They had been going 'threepenny bit and two and six' for at least half an hour and it felt good to be on the way home, knowing that this target had been completely destroyed. (Sergeant A. C. Farmer, 12 Squadron)

The raid certainly appeared to be going well. Many of the 1 Group squadron records convey satisfaction at the performance of the men involved in this second wave. Individual crew reports go on to show that much diligence was exercised in order to ensure success. Time-keeping was good and the ordered bombing heights were observed. The 'creepback', so often observed in raids on cities, failed to materialize. Several crews who were not satisfied with their first bombing runs circled back to try again.

But the raid was not proceeding as favourably as appearances suggested. It is not possible to say exactly what happened to every load of Pathfinder markers and Main Force bombs because many bombing photographs revealed only a smoke-covered area of land or, worse still, an expanse of sea. The photographs of only twenty-one aircraft of the second wave – two Pathfinder Backers-Up and nineteen Main Force – could be plotted. From these, however, and from German reports, it is possible to deduce what was really happening. There is no doubt that the burning camp at Trassenheide acted as a beacon throughout the raid and that many R.A.F. crews thought that it must be in the first of the three planned bombing areas. Both Pathfinders and Main Force crews would thus tend to overshoot for most of the raid.

Another factor had also come into play. Many of the people on the ground at the time remember the unusually brisk breeze which was blowing eastwards towards the sea. Unexpectedly strong cross-winds had ruined many Pathfinder attempts to mark targets in the past. The markers could be placed accurately – either visually or by radar – but, once they had burst and were cascading above the ground, the wind took them away. This happened at Peenemünde, and it is certain that large numbers of the 1 Group bomb-loads were aimed at markers which were drifting towards the sea. Unfortunately for the R.A.F. plan, there was absolutely nothing of importance to the leeward side of that small area covered by the two production buildings, and many bombs dropped by the second-wave aircraft fell into woods, on to the beach, or even into the sea. The Master Bomber had detected this about three minutes before the end of the first-wave bombing, and from then until the end of the attack most of his efforts would be devoted – with only limited success – to exhorting both Pathfinders and Main Force not to drift off to the east of the target.

The bomber crews of the second wave at least had the advantage of carrying out their task when the German defences were least effective. The light Flak – never very intense – had undoubtedly been subdued both by the general attack and by the efforts of some of the Pathfinder crews carrying loads of small anti-personnel bombs with orders to drop them on any position seen in action. The heavy Flak, mainly outside the bombing area, had been less affected by the general attack, but continued to fire at too great a height. However, towards the end of this phase German night fighters were beginning to arrive in the area, and there were a few inconclusive combats on the approaches to Peenemünde and more where the bombers were leaving the target. Then, right at the end of the second wave, a Lancaster of 100 Squadron was shot down by a night fighter and crashed into the sea near the target.

The second phase lasted only eleven minutes and ended at 12.42 a.m. Approximately 124 bombers – nearly all Lancasters – had dropped over 480 tons of high explosive and 40 tons of incendiaries on various parts of Peenemünde and on surrounding areas.

The third and final wave of the bombing followed immediately, with the squadrons of 5 and 6 Groups and their accompanying Pathfinders attempting to destroy the most important part of Peenemünde, the Experimental Works. The aircraft which reached the target area – 114 from 5 Group, fifty-seven from 6 Group and eleven Pathfinders – carried a greater bomb tonnage than any other wave. In addition, the 5 Group crews now had the opportunity to show whether the time-and-distance technique they had practised could provide a successful demonstration of the more sophisticated tactics which Air Vice-Marshal Cochrane was anxious to see employed by Bomber Command. It would be a good test, because the Canadian squadrons of 6 Group would, at the same time, be carrying out their bombing in the normal manner. Both were under difficult operational conditions. The ground was now very thick from the German smoke-screen, from fires, and from bomb explosions, and some patchy, low cloud was also coming into the target area. On top of all this, German fighters were arriving in increasing numbers. The crews of the third wave were going to have a tough time.

The six Pathfinder Shifters who were to mark the new Aiming Point by using false altitude settings on their bomb-sights had all arrived on time, but unfortunately this technique was no more successful than it had been at the start of the second wave. Five of the six photographs taken by the Shifters were later plotted. Two of them – Squadron Leader A. P. Cranswick of 35 Squadron and Pilot Officer R. King of 83 Squadron – overshot by 1,000 yards, but a third was a mile over, and two more were actually on the *first* Aiming Point, nearly two miles astray. The records of the Master Bomber's broadcasts to the Main Force reveal that he did not detect that these new markers and the subsequent backing-up markers were overshooting so badly: all his efforts at this stage were devoted to keeping both marking and bombing from drifting away from the target to the sea.

The main description of the air battle now developing at Peenemünde will be kept for a later chapter, but the following quotation, from the pilot of one of the Shifter crews, shows how dangerous the situation was for Pathfinders.

As we approached the target, we witnessed the attack by a twin-engined fighter on a four-engined bomber just off our port wing. I remember that the fighter and its prey were well lit and I assume that the light came partly from bright moonlight and partly from fires on the ground. The fighter made only one approach from astern and below and it set the bomber on fire immediately. I had to decide whether to allow my gunners to fire on the fighter, if within range, or to remain quiet and hope he would miss seeing us. My decision was that discretion was the better part of valour since we had not yet performed our mission. The fighter broke off the attack to starboard right under us and you can believe that all eyes were on the lookout for an attack from that moment on but, fortunately, none came. (Pilot Officer H. Gowan, 405 Squadron)

Canadian Main Force crews were not notoriously rigid followers of flight plans and timetables, and a study of the records of the 6 Group squadron reveals a characteristic spirit of independence. Their bombing was supposed to be spread evenly over three periods of four minutes each, but many crews arrived early and did not wait for their allotted time. One crew, from 427 Squadron, had actually bombed at the opening of the preceding wave – at least twelve minutes too early – and many others had done so before the second wave was over. When the third wave commenced, many of the remaining crews bombed immediately and, understandably perhaps, got away from Peenemünde as quickly as possible. The squadron records also show that many Canadian crews did not observe the ordered bombing heights: several were well above 15,000 feet. There were exceptions, however. The eleven crews who returned from 428 Squadron all recorded bombing times and heights according to plan. A Canadian pilot from 426, Squadron Leader W. H. Swetman, waited in the area for twenty minutes in order to bomb at his allocated time. He returned safely to find himself promoted and appointed to the command of his squadron, the previous commander having been killed at Peenemünde. It is pleasant to be able to record that Squadron Leader Swetman survived the war.

Despite their free-thinking attitude, every Canadian crew came in and faced the German defences and there was no unduly scattered bombing. Some survivors who were shot down will be met later, but this quotation can represent those Canadians who bombed and made it back to England safely.

Our first sight of the target was like coming around a corner to face the lights of a Christmas tree. There was no second pilot on this trip so Keary, my bomb aimer, was up on the flight level with myself and Mulholland. He was also a witty fellow but our total crew reaction was, 'Jesus Christ! Whose surprise party is this one?' The sky in front of us was full of activity.

There was not another word said, except by the bomb aimer after he had gone back to his position and by the navigator. We made our run in total fright, except for 'Right, right – Left, left – Steady – Bomb doors open – Steady – Bomb away – Steady – Bomb doors closed – Steady – Flash camera – Run Over – Off target.'

It took for ever to make that run, the whole crew were tense. Over the target it was like daylight. It was the only time I ever saw at least ten other bombers, almost like we were in formation. It was also the only time I ever saw German fighters in the air. They were dodging around with several good targets in the moonlight. I saw at least five bombers going down; one blew up in the air within a thousand yards of us.

The first word off the target was from White, the navigator. It took the tension away and broke us into a real lift-up mood. 'My god damn gum has hair in it but I am going to swallow it quick because it's my ass hole.' (Sergeant J. McIntosh, 419 Squadron)

For any student of the air war, the most interesting aspect of the Peenemünde operation must be the results achieved by 5 Group's time-and-distance bombing in this final phase. Unfortunately, the experiment did not receive the full test for which Air Vice-Marshal Cochrane had hoped because the orders given at the briefings had been that, although the 5 Group crews should carry out their time-and-distance runs, they were to aim their bombs at the Pathfinder markers in sight at the end of those runs unless the markers were obviously misplaced. If crews were in doubt about the accuracy of the markers, they were to be guided by the instructions of the Master Bomber. *Only if there were no markers in sight or if the Master Bomber advised that markers were badly misplaced, was the time-and-distance method alone to be used.* This was, of course, a major departure from the technique which Cochrane had pioneered, but these orders had been issued from Bomber Command Headquarters, and Cochrane had been forced to pass them on to his squadrons. (It is unfortunate that no original copy of them could be found, but Sir Arthur Harris records the position about the 5 Group orders quite clearly in his memoirs; he probably had a copy at his elbow when he wrote that passage.[2] Subsequent events fit in closely with Harris's version. One interesting aspect is that Group Captain Searby, the Master Bomber, was not told about the separate 5 Group bombing method at all.)

The 5 Group crews found that their first checkpoint, at Arkona on the northern tip of Rügen, was clearly visible, and they were able to keep on track across the distinctive bays on the east coast of that large island. (Look back to Map 3 on page 59.) There was also no difficulty in identifying the second checkpoint, at Thiessow. Then, during the five-mile flight down to the small island of Ruden, the navigators rapidly completed their calculations on the strength and direction of the wind encountered. Finally, from the island of Ruden which the Pathfinders were endeavouring to keep marked with their Red Spot

Fires the final timed run commenced – four miles in a few seconds more than one minute.

This account by a 5 Group pilot describes what was probably a typical time-and-distance run.

There did appear to be more haze and cloud about than had been forecast but 'Pop' Matheson, my bomb aimer, was able to make satisfactory landmarks and, by the time we approached Ruden Island, the visibility, except for the target itself, was pretty good. We were able to pick up the point for the run in without too much difficulty and 'Bunny' Perry, the navigator, gave me the course and airspeed according to his calculations. The target itself was completely hidden by smoke and markers seemed to be dropping all over the place, some, I suspect, dropped by the Germans as well as by our chaps. The sky above and around seemed smoke-laden and reflected the light from markers and fires.

We spotted the odd Lanc drifting across and caught a glimpse of another aircraft burning but, strangely, once having commenced our run, most of my attention was taken up checking air speed, height, direction and listening to the countdown, especially near the end, which helped me at least to ignore a lot of what was going on around. Most of the crew came forward and seemed intent, observing the run and listening to the countdown. Towards the end, we encountered quite a bit of turbulence and, as the count finished, I shouted to the bomb aimer to let everything go. Of course, he was ahead of me in anticipation and didn't waste one second. (Flight Sergeant B. W. Kirton, 49 Squadron)

It is obvious, from a study of squadron records, that the 5 Group crews were most diligent. Only two out of more than a hundred bombed before time, and only three recorded bombing heights of slightly more than the 8,000 feet maximum ordered. Many made two and some even made three attempts. And all this in the midst of fierce German fighter action!

A Lanc went down in flames on the starboard side. A few seconds later, looking up, I saw a twin-engined fighter with its nose down, coming from above and behind straight for us. The rear gunner had seen it too. We both shouted almost at the same time, 'Fighter, dive to port!' The pilot did so immediately and down we went. I kept my eye on the fighter. He didn't deviate but went past where we would have been and shot a Lancaster down that had been flying just below us. Whether we were the night fighter's intended victim or the one that was shot down will never be known. Our

time-and-distance run was in ruins. (Sergeant J. E. Hudson, 49
Squadron)

It is also clear from squadron records and from the later plotting
of bombing photographs that, although most of the 5 Group crews
carried out their time-and-distance runs properly, many of them then
obeyed their orders to bomb the nearest markers at the end of the
timed run or to follow the instructions of the Master Bomber. Unfortunately, this was during that period of the raid when the Master
Bomber had not detected that most of the Pathfinder marking was
overshooting. Most of the 5 Group bombs were aimed at those markers
and thus did not fall, as intended, on the Experimental Works. (There
will be further comment on this, and a map showing the results of the
various bombing methods used in the third wave, in Chapter 15.)

Group Captain Searby was approaching the end of his difficult task
as Master Bomber. It had been very much a crew effort. Searby,
piloting his own heavy Lancaster throughout, made a total of seven
runs over the Peenemünde peninsula, circling back each time over the
sea. While the gunners kept a careful lookout for fighters, three other
members of the crew – the navigator and the flight engineer standing
in the cockpit with Searby and the bomb aimer in the nose – kept
watch on developments on the ground and pointed them out to
Searby. I have been in touch with three surviving members of this
crew, including Group Captain Searby himself, and all agree that the
bomb aimer, Flying Officer W. G. Ross, a schoolteacher in civilian
life, 'a quiet, reserved and efficient chap', made the best contribution.
Group Captain Searby added his own observations of the raid's
progress, assessed all the reports, and broadcast his instructions, sometimes to the Pathfinders, sometimes to the Main Force.

The task had been difficult from the start because of the effective
German smoke-screen and smoke from the bombing, the poor performance of some of the Pathfinders, and the effect upon the markers
of the strong cross-wind. Surviving members of the crew all agree that
the really close and successful control of the raid which had been
hoped for had not been possible. The cumulative strain of flying over
a defended target for more than forty minutes was intense. A German
Flak ship[3] directly beneath their path gave Searby's crew a particularly hot time each time the Lancaster circled back for a new run;
moreover in the later stages of the attack they ran the same risk as the
Main Force crews from the obviously increasing number of German
fighters – except that the Main Force mostly had to make only one
run over Peenemünde before making for home. It is reported also that

the Master Bomber was subjected at one stage to the 'ribald replies' of dissatisfied Main Force pilots and that, during the second wave of the attack, 'a cheerful Australian voice' could be heard singing 'God bless you and keep you, Mother McCrea.'

The activities of the two reserve Master Bomber crews should also be mentioned. Wing Commander John White had intervened at a crucial moment and placed his markers near the correct point when other marking was going badly astray. He had then remained in the area in case the Master Bomber was shot down. The second deputy, the Canadian Wing Commander John Fauquier, was also present from beginning to end and eventually dropped his bombs in the very last minute of the planned raid period, but he took his Target Indicators home. Squadron Leader Peter Powell, another Canadian, was Fauquier's navigator.

> From our vantage point, circling the target throughout the raid, we witnessed some of the most accurate marking and bombing we had ever seen. Miraculously, in spite of our lengthy stay in the target area, the only time we were shot at was by a few stray bullets from one of our own aircraft.
>
> The Master Bomber did a fine job throughout. This was fortunate for us as we were able to sit back and watch, fascinated, as one would a theatre spectacular. And we didn't even have to pay to get in!

There is no doubt, however, that Group Captain Searby found it almost impossible to exercise effective control in the final stage of the attack. There was smoke everywhere and the Pathfinder marking was becoming more scattered. Searby, by his own admission, was becoming 'quite frustrated', and Flying Officer Ross, his bomb aimer, 'was getting very anxious; he kept urging me to make smaller circuits to keep the target in view.' At 12.48 a.m., Searby made his seventh and final run over Peenemünde and his last broadcast: 'Watch your bombing. Make a steady run and bomb the greens.'[4] At the end of this run, Searby told the Main Force that there would be no more messages and turned his Lancaster for the first time to the west, homeward bound. 'Despite all the difficulties, I knew that the raid had been, by and large, a success. The best gauge of this was the fact that everything below seemed to be on fire.' Searby's Lancaster was attacked two minutes later by a German night fighter but his gunners were alert and drove it off. The Master Bomber and his crew returned safely to their base.

There are many comments available from the men to whom Group Captain Searby had been broadcasting for the past fifty minutes.

Although he and his crew may have experienced some frustration, they certainly made valuable corrections to the marking and the bombing and also gave a boost to the sometimes inexperienced Main Force crews. Squadron records contain many favourable remarks: 'The crew liked this feature', 'A good morale booster', 'It served a very useful purpose', 'A typical Cook's Tour Guide'. Personal accounts would later confirm the feelings of the Main Force over Group Captain Searby's work.

I was most impressed by the professionalism and ability of the Master Bomber. (Flying Officer W. S. Day, 90 Squadron)

It seemed so strange to hear this nice English voice, so calmly telling us what to do. There was an air of English superiority about it. That was very encouraging – it gave the impression that everything was under control – that we had the whole thing buttoned up. It was also a little eerie though. (Pilot Officer D.R. Aldridge, 44 Squadron)

The fact that someone was there, telling us what to do, was a great morale booster. Normally, you felt that it was an individual effort that you were making but, now, you felt as though you were part of a combined force and that everything was more organized. I don't know how he managed to stay so calm; it was just as though he was in the room talking to you – absolutely fantastic. (Sergeant P. S. Crees, 434 Squadron)

The end of the raid was fast approaching. This is the scene as described by one of the last 6 Group pilots to bomb. 24 May – Queen Victoria's birthday – is Canada's Fireworks Day.

I remember that the whole attack was really a very stunning affair. Everyone did a fantastic job. I and my crew were carrying incendiaries only and they caused the target area to look like a 24th-of-May sparkler. Actually, I don't think anyone except the first crews over the target really saw the ground as the area quickly became an obscured mass of great billows of smoke and flames. My bombing picture showed no ground detail at all – it was almost as if we had taken a picture of the inside of a locomotive funnel. Those damned fires must *still* be burning. (Flying Officer J. A. Westland, 419 Squadron)

The German Flak continued to operate to the end, though with ever-decreasing efficiency. A Pathfinder Backer-Up crew of 35 Squadron was probably the only Flak victim of the third wave. The Pathfinders were flying at higher altitudes than the Main Force, and it may have been radar-predicted heavy Flak which picked this one out from the few aircraft flying at that greater height. Flight Sergeant P. R. Raggett and four of his crew died when their Halifax fell in flames just south of Peenemünde. The German night fighters continued to take a heavy toll, and up to ten bombers of the third wave may have been shot down in the immediate area of Peenemünde. However, as mentioned before, the detailed story of the air battle which developed over Peenemünde and on the return route will be more conveniently described later.

Flying Officer Westland's bombing photograph resembling 'the inside of a locomotive funnel' was typical of the results obtained by many crews in the final wave; only a quarter of the photographs could be plotted. It is obvious that much of the final-wave marking and bombing continued to fall too far forward and too far to the left of the third Aiming Point – that is, to the south and east of the Experimental Works. A partial rally occurred towards the end: one load of Pathfinder markers went down very accurately and, because the 5 Group timed runs coincided with them, so did several bomb-loads. At least eight crews bombed after 12.55 a.m., when the raid should have finished. (Bomber Command's record of thirty-five crews bombing after the official end of the third-wave period may be an error.) All the late crews were from 5 Group, undoubtedly determined to make their time-and-distance runs correctly. The Red Spot Fires at Ruden had gone; the Master Bomber and the Pathfinders had gone; Peenemünde blazed fiercely from end to end. Squadron Leader David Balme of 207 Squadron was the pilot of the last but one of those crews over the target who returned to record their bombing times.

We had sculled around for a long time, fifteen minutes or so, determined to find the Thiessow headland on Rügen to start our time-and-distance run; we couldn't find it because of low cloud which had come over it. Eventually we set off to Peenemünde. We had seen the Pathfinder markers and the bombing there. We heard the Master Bomber, ahead, talking about markers being misplaced but, then, heard no more.

Normally at bombing height we saw the bright glow of fires but no details whereas, on this occasion, we could see separate fires – the flames, smoke and parts of burning buildings. I could see the runway of the nearby airfield by the light of the fires. We bombed visually and actually felt the thud of our bombs exploding, each explosion lifting the aircraft a little. I was very pleased about it. I thought we were doing a good job.

Squadron Leader Balme bombed at 1.05 a.m. The final load to go down, carried by the Lancaster of Flight Lieutenant Harry Locke, an experienced Australian pilot of 467 Squadron, was all high-explosive. It fell twelve minutes after the planned end of the raid.

At least 170 aircraft had dropped approximately 670 tons of bombs during this last wave of the attack. During the entire raid, 1,795 tons of high-explosive and incendiary bombs had been aimed at the buildings and at the various groups of people who made up the community of Peenemünde.

NOTES

1. Public Record Office AIR 14/3012.
2. *Bomber Offensive*, p. 123.
3. The 4,500-ton *Undine*, formerly the Dutch naval vessel *Jacob van Heemskerck*, which patrolled this coast regularly. It was armed with eight 105-mm heavy guns, five 40-mm Bofors, and sixteen 20-mm guns. *Undine* was handed back to Holland at the end of the war and became the naval accommodation ship *Neptunus* until sold for breaking up in 1975.
4. Public Record Office AIR 14/3012.

CHAPTER II

Under the Bombs

It is clear that the Peenemünde authorities were not surprised by the raid, but they were woefully unprepared for it. It had become obvious both to the commander of Peenemünde and to his superiors in Berlin that the secrecy which had protected this place for so long could not last indefinitely. General Dornberger has recorded that he received a danger warning from Berlin a few days before the R.A.F. raid, but he had already for some time been putting increased preparations in hand. There had been no intelligence leak from Britain; it was probably the flights of the R.A.F. reconnaissance aircraft that triggered the increased alertness. When the bombers did come, however, the people of Peenemünde would still not be protected adequately. There were several reasons for this. There was probably a reluctance to divert manpower and materials from the rocket programme. There was certainly a lack of appreciation of how destructive a heavy R.A.F. raid could be; a few visiting air-raid officials from the Ruhr or Hamburg would have woken Peenemünde up. Finally, people had lived for so long in the peace of this remote corner of Germany and were so engrossed in their work that they could not believe the blow would ever fall.

Peenemünde had no really substantial buildings which could have provided protection for large numbers of people. The majority of the accommodation, unlike an average German city target, was either light brick housing or wooden barracks. The need for properly constructed air-raid shelters could not have been more urgent. The basements of buildings in the housing estate were converted to shelters, and some reasonably sound communal refuges were provided both here and in the Experimental Works area, but the extensive barracks of the Wehrmacht and of the foreign workers could only be provided with the most primitive, makeshift constructions in the nearby woods. The best of these were '*Splittergraben*', 'splinter-proof trenches', buttressed and roofed with timber and covered with several feet of sand; but many had only concrete paving slabs for head cover or were open zigzag trenches. The big danger with these makeshifts was that they might collapse in the light, sandy soil if heavy bombs fell nearby, and some people were very apprehensive about the safety they would afford. Part of the foreign labour force was still engaged in digging them right up to the day before the raid, and many people would find themselves without proper protection when the bombs fell.

Along with the growing fear that Peenemünde might be bombed had come the realization that the families of the technical men, many of whom had lived here for several years, were in danger. A plan drawn up for the complete evacuation of children and of women who did not do essential work hardly got off the ground. The families clearly could not be sent to their relatives in German cities. The local Gauleiter at Stettin surveyed the many villages and country towns of the area he administered, and some progress was made in listing suitable accommodation, but two factors finally prevented the major evacuation so clearly desirable: many families were reluctant to leave, and, while they dithered, the destruction of Hamburg had produced a flood of refugees which filled most of the spare rooms designated for the Peenemünde people. A renewed effort was made in the last days before the raid, with some of the senior men sending their families away in order to provide an example to their reluctant subordinates, but only a handful of the women and children left before the R.A.F. came.

In this way did the complacent, optimistic people of Peenemünde remain in their flimsy housing and with their often inadequate shelters. There was an official air-raid organization and plans galore, but the fire brigade and medical services were almost non-existent, and the establishment was certainly not ready to face the full fury of a major R.A.F. raid.

Peenemünde was still the 'sleeping beauty'.

The day before the raid was an entirely ordinary one for most of its victims. One event which might have enlivened the routine – the test firing of another V-2 rocket – had been postponed, allowing many people to leave work early. Instead of the test, General Dornberger and the senior members of his team had been forced to hold a meeting to discuss the stepped-up programme for V-2 production being urged by Berlin. Dornberger's scientists did not like being rushed in this way, and the meeting was a difficult one. The whole of the team was present, and all were still at Peenemünde when the bombers arrived.

Most of Peenemünde relaxed in the beautiful Baltic summer evening which followed. Many people remember those last few hours – the clear visibility, the lingering fragrance of pine extracted by the day's sun, the beauty of the beach and the sea. Many people also remember the unusually firm breeze blowing from the land, the same breeze which caused so much trouble to the R.A.F. Pathfinders.

People strolled and chatted. Young men and girls, usually sedately and separately, took a late evening swim. One man writes, with deep nostalgia, of that last evening of Peenemünde's old existence, that the sunset 'was the most beautiful I have ever seen in my whole life.' Inge Holz, a secretary, tells how she and some of her colleagues from the *Ledigenheim* spent that evening.

> Some of us had attended a French lesson at a building some distance away, maybe the school at the housing estate. The lesson was given by a soldier who had been a language teacher before the war. He brought a group of twelve young Frenchmen – forced workers – to meet us and we learnt the text and melody of the *Chanson normande* – the national song of old Normandy.
>
> It was a very happy evening for the girls. As for the French, I think they were proud but sad. At about 11 p.m., we all went home. As we girls walked back to our home, we sang a little as we went – that French song – and we talked of the pleasant time we had had. It was a wonderful moonlight night. There was not another soul on the street. It had been a really wonderful evening for us.

At 11.25 p.m., by Peenemünde's time, the sirens sounded, as they had done so often in recent nights. This alarm was caused, of course, by the flight of the eight Mosquitoes to Berlin. Many people ignored it altogether, and those who did take shelter mostly returned to their beds when no action developed at their quiet haven. 'Poor old Berlin,' they thought. The 'All Clear' did not sound, however; more bombers were approaching. But these, too, were thought to be bound for Berlin and little action was taken. By then, 1 a.m. local time, most of Peenemünde was fast asleep.

When the first bombers did arrive, the silence of the night was broken only gradually. The aircraft which had arrived too early flew away again as soon as they had established their position. But soon a steadily increasing, vibrating growling filled the sky. Czeslaw Bloch, a Polish worker, was sharing a splinter-trench shelter with three Germans near the Experimental Works.

> A morbid silence prevailed. We were all peering into the sky. Then I heard the first German say, 'They must be our planes otherwise the Flak would be firing.' A second German had experienced raids on the Ruhr and he was certain that it was the R.A.F. and he was very annoyed that the guns weren't firing.
>
> My feelings were divided. On the one hand, I really wanted it to be a raid, but, on the other hand, I was afraid of the great unknown. It went through my mind that perhaps the R.A.F. pilots

hadn't discovered the target yet because quite a few minutes had elapsed since we first heard the aeroplanes before anything happened.

When the raid eventually did open, it was the Germans who were most frightened, partly because they had a better idea of what was coming and partly because of the presence of so many of their own or their friends' families at Peenemünde. Most of us foreigners had no idea at all of what was going to happen.

The earliest bombs fell at scattered points. General Dornberger says that the very first fell into the river Peene, west of his establishment; others remember the first explosions as occurring well south of the Trassenheide labour camp. It does not matter much; the bombing soon settled down and progressed from south to north, up the line of selected targets on the peninsula. Although it was never so well directed as to fall exclusively on any one area during any period of time, it will be convenient to describe the experiences of the people on the ground in that same order, south to north.

Because of the difficulties encountered by the R.A.F. Pathfinders, described in the last chapter, many of the bombs dropped in the early stages of the raid – and a few later ones – fell into the area which contained the large camp for foreign workers at Trassenheide. Let us visualize this camp – long rows of wooden barrack-type huts, with tarred roofs, built close together, each hut packed with men tired from a day of hard labour. Surrounding the camp was a high chain-link fence topped by barbed wire, not electrified as some accounts state but still a formidable barrier between the camp and the forested area outside. There was only one main gateway. Many of the men had spent the last weeks digging air-raid shelters in other parts of Peenemünde, but there were few proper shelters in their own camp. It was into this most vulnerable place that 4,000-lb. blast bombs, other large high-explosive bombs, and masses of incendiaries were dropped. It would not be an overstatement to call Trassenheide a death trap.

(I can only record the accounts of Polish workers at Trassenheide because no others could be contacted. Poles comprised the great majority, but their experiences were of course shared by other foreigners – particularly Russians, Ukrainians and some Frenchmen – and by their German guards.)

The opening of the raid found the foreigners under the usual night-time security, the windows of every barrack shuttered, one of the two outside doors of each hut locked, the second guarded by an armed German. The power had been turned off when the alarm sounded.

A few of the guards had allowed the foreigners to take shelter in nearby trenches, but the majority of the huts remained locked and guarded. There was much apprehension when the steadily increasing throbbing of engines was heard, although some of the workers, particularly the young and hungry ones, remained fast asleep. Then, the whole camp suddenly became bathed in bright light; R.A.F. Target Indicators were cascading directly overhead. This was the signal for 'a tremendous turmoil'. More huts were opened up and both prisoners and guards dashed around the open spaces of the camp, looking for any hole in which to take shelter; but many huts remained locked, the men inside banging and shouting to be let out, the guards uncertain what to do and threatening to shoot.

The first bombs fell into the south-western corner of the camp. This is a selection of the many accounts available from the Trassenheide men.

My barrack suffered a direct hit on the end where the sentry was holding us back. He and many of our men were killed. I was dragging my friend to the other end of the hut – my Virgin Mary medal in one hand and my reluctant friend in the other – when there was a tremendous bang and cracking noise as though the earth lifted under our feet and I felt as though somebody had hit me on the head with a thick iron bar which left a ringing noise in my ears. My friend and I both lost consciousness due to the blast of the explosion. The barrack wall started to burn and we were only saved by an older man who shook us to see if we were still alive.

When we came round, he told us to run away or we would burn to death. We got out but heard the rest of the barrack burning with a loud crackling noise and the terrible screams and begging of the dying people. I heard one of the dying shout, 'Oh, mother. You won't see your son again.' There was a terrible panic which it is not possible to describe to anyone who did not live through it. (Feliks Wereszczynski)

One of the first bombs fell near my barrack, pushing it to one side and throwing me to the floor. I picked myself up, rushed into the corridor and then outside. Many other bombs were dropping and bits of metal were flying through the air. I realized that nearby were some holes left when trees had been removed recently. I ran towards one of these. A colleague behind me was running for a second hole; each was just big enough for one man.

I managed to reach my hole just before the next bomb. I was knocked out for a few minutes and came round to find myself covered to the neck in sand. I couldn't get out but I looked around for my colleague; he had come with me to Peenemünde in the same transport. I remember his Christian name, Tadeusz; he was from Warsaw and a few years older than me. I was sixteen. But he had been caught in the open and was dead. His body was torn very badly and the only way we could recognize him afterwards was by the watch on his wrist. My only injury was a damaged eardrum.

Then, I saw that my barrack was on fire. It was so fierce that I feared I might be burnt – I was only about ten metres away from it. It was just like a real good barn fire. Those barracks were all wood, of course, and the weather had been hot and dry. Later, some of my colleagues were found to be missing and I think they may have been inside. I shouted for help and one of those peasant men from the Lublin area, who had only come in a week earlier, helped me. He scooped the soil away from around me and helped me out. (Zdzislaw Chorosz)

I fell several times as I tried to make for the exit gate. Barbed wire and wire netting were all over the place. I thought that the only way out was through the gate – if they would let us out – but I found a hole under the wire fencing after about a hundred metres and people were getting out through there. I think that these men had torn that hole down with their hands. Everyone was using it.

About fifty metres away I saw a German running; he was in a military uniform, of a high-ranking officer I thought because of his cap and because he was wearing glasses. In his panic and, with his poor eyesight, he had run at full pelt and holding his two big suitcases into the wire fence which he either didn't see or he had forgotten was there. He hit the fence and bounced back like a ball, realizing at that moment that he had hit a 'wall' of wire. He put the suitcases down, left his cap which had fallen off and, on his knees, crawled under the fence and ran like mad.

Although it only lasted a moment, this picture has remained in my eyes ever since. (Jan Skwarek)

The German guards ran; we followed them but it was too late, too far to the camp gates. Masses of bombs were falling everywhere. Running people were disappearing – God knows where. The wounded were crying out for help. Crowds of people were squeezing to get through the gate; they were beginning to climb up the wire fence. Some others tried to tear down the wire. Then, another salvo of bombs fell and the explosions blew down the fence and whoever had been climbing up or nearby was killed.

Seeing the death of my friends in front of my eyes, I started running blindly into the forest. The fencing no longer existed.

Three of us were running together; on our way, we found an air-raid shelter in which there were already many people. They screamed at us that there was no more room and some Germans there told us to run deeper into the forest. Next day, I found that four bombs had hit that shelter and we would have perished; everyone inside was dead.

Then there was a new wall of fire in front of us; it forced us to the ground. I got up again but my two friends did not. I fell into a bomb crater after a few steps and decided to go no further. The soil in the bottom was very hot – too hot to stand in – and I climbed up the side and dug out with my hands a little hole in which to put my head so that the fragments of bombs would not hit me. I was alone. The bombing continued but further away and only the earth trembled.

After a while, someone tumbled into my crater; from his speech, I recognized him as a German. I slipped down to him and he grabbed me by my neck and, shouting with all his strength, demanded help but how could I help him at that moment? He was wounded in the head. He didn't seem to feel the heat at the bottom of the crater although it was still too hot for me. The German – whether from pain or fear I do not know – kept banging his head into the loose sand with the result that the area of blood got bigger and bigger and, after a while, he slumped over and lay motionless. I thought he was dead but, after the raid, I found he was still alive.

Then, two Polish boys fell into the crater with a bundled-up blanket. Inside was a torn-up friend who showed no signs of life. The boys started praying loudly and, when the next bombs fell, they rolled up the 'wounded' man in the blanket and ran off again.

There had been sixteen of us in my room, all from the Zarzesce, near Niska in the Tarnobrzeg district. Thirteen of the sixteen were dead, two were wounded and one remained healthy and writes this story. (Jozef Mlynarski)

Several Polish contributors told me that the recently arrived group of their fellow countrymen from the Zamosc region suffered particularly heavy casualties when a large high-explosive bomb – possibly a 4,000-lb. 'Blockbuster' – exploded as they were trying to climb the wire fence to get out of the camp.

Most of the bombs which fell on Trassenheide had been intended for the first R.A.F. Aiming Point. The largest part of that area, the housing estate (*Siedlung*) built just before the war for the families of the research establishment staff, had all the characteristics of a model village, and it was the home of about 3,000 people. Of these, about thirty were key scientists in the rocket programme. Adjoining to the west was the pre-war *Kraft durch Freude* (Strength Through Joy) camp which now housed more than 1,000 technical soldiers. The intention of the first phase of the R.A.F. attack was to kill as many of that group of top scientists and their numerous assistants as possible; the women and children whom the Germans had chosen to leave in such a sensitive place as Peenemünde would just have to take their chance.

When the raid opened, the inhabitants of this area had been allowed a little time to take refuge. A few were still in their shelters from the earlier alarm, and the gathering engine noises and the Target Indicators had persuaded most of the remainder to take cover before the first bombs crashed down. The local Nazi Party officials, who would have to deal with the after-effects of the raid, were gathered at their command post in the basement of the local school; they could do nothing yet. 'We just trembled,' one says. The fire brigade stood ready, so tiny that it was to be overwhelmed by the horror to come. Helmut Graeber, the Protestant chaplain for the whole Peenemünde community under that almost godless régime, could do no more than look after his own family now.

Prompted by some dark foreboding, I had laid out my uniform and boots next to my bed. When the sirens wailed, I quickly put on my uniform – something I had not done for some time during previous alerts – and went outside. There I met an army major, unknown to me, who greeted me with a remark I shall never forget: 'Children, buy yourselves combs; it's going to be a lousy time.'

Soon afterwards, we heard the deep drone of approaching heavy bombers. I dived into the house to fetch out my wife and our two girls. We packed suitcases, grabbed the typewriter and a few personal items and ran down to the shelters on the beach which had been completed only two days earlier and consisted of deep holes in the sand covered by two thick concrete slabs. As soon as the local people had taken cover there, the hellish racket started up all around us ... Suddenly, a young girl from the unmarried quarters opposite us entered in her nightdress and screamed, 'Vicar, why don't you pray for us?'

The following people were all in the housing estate bombing area. Karl Bührer was a civilian engineer.

We were safely in the reinforced room we used as a shelter when we heard the crash of the first bombs and the lights went out. Now they've found us! There was a little window in the room, bunged up with tightly packed paper. Suddenly there was a crash outside and the whole lot of this paper packing flew all round the room. I made my wife and children lie on the floor and I squatted down. I was very worried about the two families occupying the house next door – the Ferenberger family and the Gerhardt family. I found out, later, that the Gerhardts were all down in the shelter but the Ferenbergers – the parents and three children – were all killed. They were our particular friends because Frau Ferenberger also came from Stuttgart. The women had been talking that afternoon and had decided that it would be best to go down to the shelter if there was an alarm. Then, Herr Ferenberger came back from a working trip and told his wife that they would not go down; he said the basement shelter would not be safe enough. He was wrong; those in the shelter survived when a bomb dropped right in front of the house but the blast hit the house and killed the Ferenbergers.

It just isn't possible to describe the rest of the raid. The only thing one could say, 'Lord, let us survive.' It was like hell; hell couldn't be any different from that. There was this continuing crashing of explosions. My wife was very tough and self-disciplined; she had lost her father in the First World War and was quite sure that we would not be killed. By a peculiar coincidence he had been killed on the same day of the year – the 18th of August – in 1917 on the Russian Front and at almost the same minute that our house was hit. She had the presence of mind to remember this when we were in danger of being killed.

But the children, you know what children are, although they were frightened they were very interested in what was going on. After all, their father worked with that kind of thing. They were always delighted when a rocket went off and knew that Papa was helping.

Regina Boy was the wife of a construction worker.

My husband and I were so naive that we never thought there would be a raid here, so deep in the woods. We had gone to bed at 10 o'clock as thoughtlessly as ever and the raid had reached its peak before we woke up. The roof and outer walls of our wooden house collapsed quicker than our minds, drugged with sleep, could understand it. Out of the house – thought we would not manage it – utter confusion – we quickly ducked under an oak-wood table, hoping it will hold. Just a few minutes, phosphorus bombs were dropped and the whole house became a sea of flame. The situation now called for quick action in order to find a way into the open through this hullabaloo. If we have to die, then let us die outside; that's better than burning alive. With scorched hair, burns on hands and legs caused by molten tar from the roof, we succeeded in reaching the open.

It was just as dangerous there. The pine trees were burning like torches. One bomb crater followed the other. We saw bleeding people but we took no notice of them; we had to save ourselves. On through the burning forest, crawling on our bellies from crater to crater, we managed to reach the road to the harbour.

I must say that the airmen did a successful job. They did not forget so much as a crossing keeper's cottage.

Siegfried Winter was a scientist.

We were shaken by huge shock waves. It's not just a matter of the shaking of the ground; it was the realization that for the first time you knew that, if the shelter gave way, then you were dead. I began to realize that here I was, possibly sitting on the end of an English bomb, yet during the day, I was working at preparing exactly the same thing, in rocket form, to send to the English. This struck me more forcibly because I was a scientist and not a soldier who was trained to fight and kill the enemy. It forced me to take stock of what I was doing in my own work – but life took over as normal the next morning.

Dora John was a Luftwaffe girl, living with her parents.

I slept right through the alarm and awoke to find that it was all hell let loose. It took me some time to decide what to do; I was still half asleep. Eventually I decided that I must take shelter. I ran outside in my nightclothes to the cellar which served as a shelter for our little cluster of families. I had to cross some open ground to reach it. I found out later that I had cut my feet on the broken glass from our front door.

Bombs were bursting nearby and I was blown down the steps of the cellar. I was the last one in. A man told us to keep our mouths open so that the force of the blast would not affect us so much. The bombs were so heavy and so close that mother said, 'If we are going to die, we'll die together.' She and father and I held each other very tightly. I had experienced raids in Berlin but I had never experienced such intense bombing and, this time, I felt that we really were going to die. I think that everyone else in the shelter felt the same except Herr Krause and his wife; they started distributing the plum and cherry juice which most German housewives make and store in their cellars. This drink helped soothe our throats; we were very dry with the dust and smoke of the bombing.

We were lucky. The house next door got a high-explosive bomb right through to the cellar and the father and daughter were killed and the mother seriously wounded.

Arthur Rudolph was a works director at the Production Works.

Our shelter shook violently but it held. An unusual noise was caused by the roof tiles of the nearby houses crashing to the ground. From then on, wave after wave of bombing came down on us, violently shaking and rattling us for a full hour. One did not dare to stick one's head out to find out what damage was being done. Two soldiers on leave, who had squeezed into our shelter, said that the raid was an awful experience, much, much worse than being at the front because of the feeling of complete, utter helplessness.

The explosion of heavy bombs was intermingled with the hissing sound of phosphorus and other incendiary bombs. One such incendiary bomb almost came through the roof of our shelter and sparks from it came through the ceiling onto the head of our little daughter, burning her hair. Fortunately, my wife was able to extinguish it.

The final contribution from people who were in the housing estate comes from a lady who was a twenty-year-old girl, living with her family. She was also a junior leader in the *Bund Deutsche Mädchen* – the female equivalent of the Hitler Youth – and she prefers her name not to be quoted.

There were eight of us in the shelter – the two families of the double house we lived in. I got dressed and, after about twenty minutes, it became very hot because the coal in the next cellar to our shelter had started burning. Also, the steel door kept swinging open with the blast. Father and my brother and the other man kept trying to pull it shut but they couldn't and the cellar kept filling with smoke. Father said that we should get out but the two women didn't want to go and we actually had a vote on it. The majority were in favour of going, so we all got ready. The two mothers were the ones who were the most frightened – for their children as much as for themselves.

We had a baby's bath filled with water. We wet all our clothes and hair in the water, put on our gas masks, wet a scarf and put it over our heads. I was thinking of the example I should have given to the girls under my command in the B.D.M. I wanted to behave properly and set a good example. We had been told so often of the strength of the *Deutschesreich* and I had heard so often that Hitler had said that we could not lose that I couldn't really imagine that any of us would die.

I put my gloves on. Then, father opened the door, said, 'One, two, three,' and we all ran towards the sea. The steps of the shelter were covered with the ruins of the house – burning beams and bricks – the bricks themselves were actually burning also, or rather the phosphor on them was. I was the last one out and I tripped over on the steps and fell with both hands forward onto the burning bricks. My gloves started to burn so I took them off. My hands were burnt and also my face where it was exposed between the gas mask and the scarf; the bottom of my trousers and my shoes were smouldering. We had agreed, before we left the cellar, that we would all go to the same place on the beach but, when we did get out, we all went different ways. I think the bombs were still falling in our area at that time; I do know that everything was on fire – all the houses, the pine trees.

I ran straight to the beach in order to put my hands into the sea. The skin was smouldering with particles of phosphor. They weren't really hurting much yet. The sea water made my hands feel better but only for a moment. It was a mistake, because sand got into the wounds. There were a lot of other people on the beach, some of them in the water because their hair or clothes were burning.

Mother burnt her leg, but not seriously. My father and brother were not hurt. I had burns of the third grade and spent three months in hospital. I still receive a 30 per cent disability pension for my wounds and I was awarded the *Verwundetenabzeichen* [wound stripe] while I was in hospital but, when the Russians came, I threw it away because it looked a little like the Iron Cross.

Although some of the bombs intended for the housing estate fell on Trassenheide, many more which should have fallen on the two northern Aiming Points overshot, and the housing estate continued to be battered until the end of the raid. Photographs taken afterwards show large areas of destruction. One young woman, who made a comprehensive search for friends the next morning, estimated that between 70 and 80 per cent of the houses were destroyed. Some streets of wooden houses had virtually disappeared. General Dornberger says that 178 people were killed here, a surprisingly low number and an indication of the virtue of taking shelter in good time.

In contrast to this rule, however, a proper air-raid shelter had not saved the life of one man. Dr Walter Thiel, the engineer responsible for the V-2 rocket propulsion department, lived in an elegant house in the Hindenburgstrasse, one of the streets reserved for Peenemünde's top families. His neighbour Klaus Riedel had urged Thiel to take his wife and young children to a nearby shelter. Riedel was to regret this

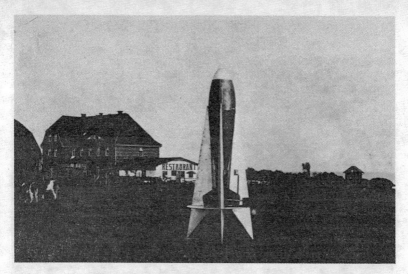

1. A very early German research rocket, the *Winkler HW2*, ready for firing in 1931 on the small island of Greifswalder Oie, 12 kilometres from Peenemünde.

2. General Dornberger and Wernher von Braun, the military and scientific leaders at Peenemünde, read a congratulatory telegram at the dinner celebrating the first successful firing of the A-4 (V-2) rocket on 3 October 1942. Von Braun has just been awarded the War Service Cross, 1st Class, with Swords.

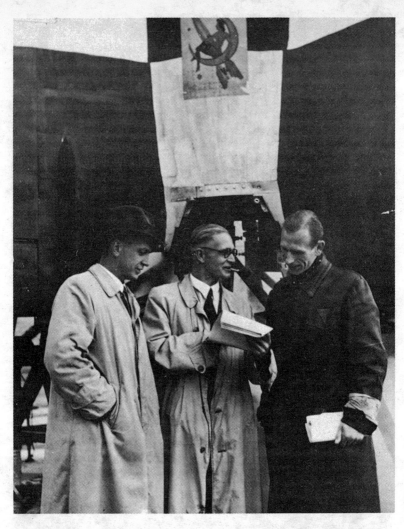

3. Three senior members of the rocket team in front of the first A-4 to be successfully test fired. Left to right are: Werner Gengelbach, an electrical specialist;
Walter Thiel, rocket engine expert; Hans Hüter, senior engineer at the famous
Test Stand VII. Note the 'Moon Maiden' motif painted on the rocket. 'V-4' was
an alternative nomenclature for 'A-4'. Hüter, often working outside on the exposed
test site, wears an official issue leather coat with a triangular H.V.P. (*Heeres-
Versuchsanstalt Peenemünde*) badge.

4. A successful A-4 rocket launching from Test Stand VII in 1943. ▶

5. The checkpoint at the main entrance to the Peenemünde establishment.

6. The Hindenburgstrasse, the road in the housing estate in which those senior scientists who had their families at Peenemünde lived.

7. Foreign workers at wartime Peenemünde – six Poles and one Ukrainian. Five of the Poles are from Warsaw and one from Radom. The Warsaw lad, second from left at back, is only seventeen.

8. The Flak ship *Undine* (formerly the Dutch *Jacob van Heemskerck*), bristling with guns and with its own radar sets, was anchored just off Peenemünde during the night of the attack.

9. Group Captain John Searby, the Master Bomber. He wears the ribbon of the D.F.C. and the Pathfinder Badge. With him are his two flight commanders in 83 Squadron who also flew on the Peenemünde raid.

10. Peenemünde on fire, a photograph taken soon after the bombing ended.

11. Next morning. Serious damage, probably in an office building attached to a rocket assembly hall in the second bombing area.

12 and 13. Deep craters caused by large high-explosive bombs in Peenemünde's sandy soil. Top, a soldier stands in the remains of a timbered air-raid shelter in the woods near the Wehrmacht barrack in the first bombing area. Bottom, the building alongside the second crater is the *R.A.D. Heim*, one of the large dormitory buildings used by female auxiliaries.

14 and 15. Damage caused to one of the rocket assembly halls.

16. Severely damaged buildings in the south-east corner of the civilian housing area. The four large buildings by the beach and the fifth (middle left) were the homes of several hundred young women.

17. Trassenheide. Extensive damage, with many huts completely destroyed, in the foreign workers' camp.

18 and 19. The housing estate. In the top photograph is the Schulstrasse and, in the bottom one, coffins near the Burgermeister's office in the Strandstrasse.

20 and 21. The housing estate. The Brandenburg Tor before the war and after the bombing. Nearly every building at Peenemünde was painted dark green after the outbreak of war for camouflage purposes.

22 and 23. The *Kameradschaftsheim*, formerly a hotel, then the Peenemünde community club, finally a dormitory for young women workers.

24. The communal graves of the Peenemünde dead.

25. The British War Cemetery at Berlin where many of the Bomber Command men lost on the Peenemünde operation are now buried as well as large numbers of airmen killed in the Battle of Berlin fought in following weeks.

26. An American moon rocket – the unbroken chain with the work carried out at Peenemünde. This is the Apollo 17 launched in August 1972. Its statistics can be compared with Peenemünde's A-4 rocket (in brackets): height 365 feet (46 feet), take-off weight 7·67 million lbs. (28,440 lbs.), cost $480 million (approx. $25,000). Compare also with photographs 1 and 4.

advice bitterly, because a direct hit on the shelter killed the entire Thiel family, while the house they had left was only slightly damaged. Dr Thiel and a lesser-known figure, Dr Erich Walther, the chief maintenance engineer in the Production Works, were the only casualties among the team of leading scientists which the R.A.F. had been hoping to destroy.

In the south-eastern corner of the housing estate was a group of four large buildings occupied exclusively by young women doing a variety of jobs. Right by the beach were the *Kameradschaftsheim*, once a hotel and later the club for the Peenemünde community, and the *Mädchenheim*, a large dormitory building. Further along the beach was the *Ledigenheim*, which housed about forty of what one lady called a 'better-class, secretary group'. Just behind the *Ledigenheim* was another large dormitory building used by the R.A.D. (*Reichsarbeitsdienst*) for girls called up for a compulsory period of service in some form of war work. Approximately 400 young women in their late teens or early twenties lived in these four buildings. Photographs taken after the raid show that the upper parts of three – the R.A.D. home, the *Ledigenheim* and the *Mädchenheim* – had been completely destroyed by blast, with a little help from fire; and that the former hotel, the *Kameradschaftsheim*, had been struck by direct hits and was burnt out. The surrounding area, particularly the nearby dunes and the beach, was pitted with the craters of many heavy bomb explosions. This was one of the hardest-hit parts of Peenemünde.

Inge Holz, secretary of one of the top scientists, lived in the *Ledigenheim*.

Suddenly there was a great crash as that first bomb woke us up. It had fallen on the beach. All the windows smashed and the door and the wardrobe doors flew open. The ring and watch which I had placed next to my bed both disappeared. Lisl – the girl who shared my room – and I just had enough time to grab our bags. She had a soldier's water bottle and she brought that too. There was a long corridor leading to the steps down to the basement shelter but the smashed doors at the end were blocking the way. I managed to drag them away and just got onto the basement stairs when the next bomb fell, again on the beach outside the home. It broke the small window near me and I felt a great blast of hot air against the side of my body. Even today, I have trouble with my ear, the sinuses in my face and my throat and all the bronchial tubes on that side of my head. But we were lucky because Lisl's suitcase saved us from the worst of the blast. The suitcase disappeared and she was left holding just the handle.

Bomb after bomb fell then and we could only crouch down on the steps, making ourselves as small as possible. I prayed, very quietly in my soul, that God would look after Lisl and me. There was a lot of dust in the air. I had a white scarf and Lisl took it off me and put some of her water on it out of that soldiers' water bottle. I was astonished that she had the presence of mind to do that; I couldn't have thought of it. We held the scarf to our mouths, side by side. When I looked at it again later, it was green. I don't know why; perhaps the air was filled with phosphor.

And then the bombing seemed to leave our immediate area; it seemed to be going inland a little. I decided that I just had to get out and I started climbing through the broken window of the shelter. I could see that everything seemed to be burning – the roof of our house, the grass, the trees. Then the lady who was our shelter warden appeared; she had her big steel helmet on. She saw my back going through the window and told me to come back; I must stay inside. I did as I was told, Lisl and I crouching down again. The warden had left the iron door open for a few moments and I heard screams and crying from outside. What had happened was that girls in the R.A.D. home were running across the burning street into the side entrance of our shelter. Many of them were wounded.

This account shows once again that people usually survived if they reached a proper shelter before their homes were hit; it is believed that there were no casualties in the *Ledigenheim*. The R.A.D. girls were forced out of their home by fire or possibly by terror – there was a huge bomb crater alongside this building – and some were killed while running down to the beach with bombs dropping around them. Some of the girls in the *Mädchenheim* and the *Kameradschaftsheim* had avoided going down to the shelters when their supervisors ordered them to do so; they had hidden in wardrobes or under beds until the supervisors had checked their rooms and then gone back to bed again. Many of these girls also died, some, in the former hotel, trapped by fire. A number of Russian forced workers from a nearby camp were prominent among the men who tried to rescue the trapped girls, and many people speak of their courage. One Russian died.

There was a tragic loss of life among the girls, and this is undoubtedly one of the horror stories of Peenemünde. One man who described the scene to me kept wringing his hands and had to stop talking at one stage, so emotional was his memory of the scene. It is said that a supervisor had locked one of the buildings in the usual way to keep prowlers out and that she was killed in her room upstairs with the key, but this may be no more than a rumour. Another very emotional event, the alleged machine-gunning of girls running along the beach, will be dealt with in a later chapter.

The final group of buildings in this bombing area, to the south and west of the housing estate and well away from the beach, consisted of the former *Kraft durch Freude* camp, now used for soldiers' accommodation, some newer army barracks, and a group of four wooden huts occupied by foreign labourers. In the labour camp, a direct hit on a hut full of Russians caused many deaths, and some other nationalities also suffered casualties.

Another tiny group of foreigners were here from Luxembourg, drivers in a transport unit, forcibly conscripted for service in the Wehrmacht. Henri Steffen tells a story which, in retrospect, has an element of humour.

When the sirens had sounded, Hauptmann Harris – who had once told us that he had relations in the United States – came round and said that there was no need to worry because there were 200 Flak guns at Peenemünde. We went back to bed but kept our trousers on. So we were still in bed when a shower of incendiary bombs fell around us. We dashed out into the open – there were no shelters – and watched our barrack burn down. There were also some incendiary bombs in the unit office. Hauptmann Harder called me. 'Steffen, throw those bombs out of the office.' I was so furious with him; how could you pick up a burning incendiary bomb? You know those Germans; they just give orders. I said, '*Sie verdammter Preusse, haben Sie den Krieg angefangen oder wir?*' ('You damned Prussian; did you start the war or did we?') I just ran off.

Later, instead of taking action against me over this, I think he respected me for it. There were eleven dead or wounded from the thirty-six men in our barrack.

As Mr Steffen pointed out, this area was not well provided with shelters, and most of the men – soldiers and foreign labourers alike – rushed out of their flimsy wooden sleeping quarters and, 'in a mad, mass exodus of all nations, ran like hell into the surrounding countryside.' Gefreiter Werner Küsters managed to reach a crude shelter with sides made of timber and heaped sand but with no roof cover.

We were right in the woods and the pine trees, about thirty years old, formed a cover over our heads. It seemed to be completely red all above us but we couldn't see the individual Pathfinder markers because of the tree cover.

It seemed as though, just when one wave of bombs was moving

away, another wave came nearer. When you get frightened you start to lose all sense of time. The shelter seemed to be swaying backwards and forwards; that was a terrible feeling, quite terrible.

When bombs dropped near us, I could hear the splinters whizzing through the tree tops just above me. Bits of branches were falling all around us, even on top of us. A large branch fell across my legs. I was lying on my face, steel helmet on the back of my head and hands clasped around my neck. I kept feeling to see if my feet were still there. When you are a twenty-year-old boy, the distance between head and feet seems to be very long.

Rudolf Klaes, a civilian technician, also fled from the camp.

I was running towards some nearby fields when a bomb dropped right near me. I cannot tell you what it was like to be right next to a bomb that explodes. I remember hearing the howling of the bomb as it came down but not the explosion. My mind just went blank at that point. I must have thrown myself over at the same time as the blast knocked me down. I found that I was buried and, to get out, I had to push all this loose earth from on top of me. It was almost like swimming out of it.

I wasn't hurt but there were two men dead – one with his head nearly off. I managed to get myself free. I saw a pipe, four or five metres long and about forty centimetres in diameter; it was lying on the ground ready to be used for something or the other. I felt I would be safe in there and crept into it but it already had some holes in it – splinter holes from the bomb I think. It was as bright as day all around and more bombs were dropping near me. One thing I do remember seeing was phosphorus raining down from the sky – long tendrils one and a half to two metres long and yellow in colour. The splinters kept rattling against the pipe and great waves of air pressure kept shaking it; eventually it became like a sieve but I was not hurt.

Through the holes in the side of the pipe – I used them as peep holes – I watched other men running around all over the place, looking for cover. Some of them were screaming. I saw one man on his knees, praying. The barracks were all burning; like hell it was.

Then my imagination started to work for the first time. I saw, in my mind, my home in Siegen and my wife like an image before my eyes. I remember biting the side of my hand, with regret I think, in emotion. I thought I was going to die. My wife and I had only had two years together. By the end of the bombing, my nerves were so badly shaken that I was crying.

(The 'tendrils' of phosphorus described by Herr Klaes were, of course, the contents of a Pathfinder Target Indicator.)

Ironically, the nearby *Kraft durch Freude* camp, with twelve large accommodation blocks, was hardly touched; one report says that there was only one direct hit, killing eight soldiers. '*Gott sei dank*,' says one of the many men in these buildings.

In human terms, the events at Trassenheide and in and around the housing estate overshadowed all else that occurred at Peenemünde on that night. Although two thirds of the R.A.F. attack was intended to fall on two further bombing areas, there were not many people there at the time of the raid, and the main object was to cause material destruction rather than loss of life. Moreover, the latest phases of the attack had not proceeded smoothly, and no overwhelming weight of bombs fell on either of these two northern areas. But the effects of this later bombing were very important to the success of the R.A.F. plan, and there are enough reliable documents and personal accounts to provide an accurate description of what happened.

The second intended bombing area comprised the two large assembly buildings where it was planned to mass-produce V-2 rockets. Production had already started in one, and the second was almost ready and probably being used as a store for twenty or so completed rockets, without warheads or fuel, to be used for test firings and for the field training of the front-line units which would eventually fire V-2s against England. A small group of technicians may have been on duty, overseeing a night shift, and the large party of concentration-camp men were certainly either working or confined in their usual quarters on the lower floor of one or both of the large buildings which more than a hundred Lancasters, carrying 537 tons of bombs – ninety per cent of them high explosive – were attempting to destroy.

An R.A.F. report[1] based on a photographic reconnaissance flight made immediately after the raid says that only two direct hits were achieved on one of these large buildings, and there must have been much disappointment at this meagre result. But more damage had been inflicted than the photographs revealed. Two direct hits were indeed made by heavy bombs on the newer and more southerly of the two buildings, known to the Germans as *Halle F1*, in which completed V-2s were stored. But seven or eight smaller bombs, probably 500-pounders, had also struck it, as well as some incendiaries. It was saved by the nature of its construction. There was a very high roof, the large main assembly shop with a very strong floor, and, under this, a lower floor with much less headroom, subdivided into machinery shops and the prisoners' living quarters. The bombs had mostly exploded in the

roof, blowing in large areas of if, but then expending their blast effect
through the mostly empty, cavernous spaces of the main upper storey.
The completed rockets and some machinery were damaged and fires
were started among some loose material. The main workshop's
strengthened floor – thick rubber over sixty centimetres of concrete
– had protected the ground-floor compartments, although shock
waves had caused some casualties among the concentration-camp
men: an unconfirmed report by a German engineer says that as many
as seventy may have been injured and a few killed. Near misses caused
some damage to the outside walls of the building but its basic structure
remained intact. No vital machinery was destroyed.

The main weight of this phase of the attack had, through various
factors described earlier, fallen further south and drifted away to the
east towards the sea. A large number of bombs had missed the two
buildings by no more than a few hundred yards. The older assembly
hall suffered minor blast damage but no direct hits. A number of
smaller buildings in the area were however hit; the three-storeyed
wooden offices attached to *Halle F1* were 'nothing but ashes', and
valuable construction plans taken from the drawing tables each night
and locked away were lost when intense heat burst the safes open; but
the plans were probably duplicated elsewhere.

The final target had been the Experimental Works, the scientific
heart of Peenemünde. This was an area approximately 1,100 yards
long and 500 yards at its widest point, containing a mass of mostly
small, exposed, not very substantial buildings – R.A.F. photographic
interpreters had counted seventy-seven of them. Here were the
administrative headquarters and all the valuable, almost irreplace-
able, technical facilities built up over the years of endeavour in the
rocket programme. Here, too, lived the very top men – General
Dornberger and Doktor von Braun – and several other bachelors
and men unaccompanied by their wives. The comparatively flimsy
buildings, with all their valuable equipment, stood every chance of
being swept away by the 180 aircraft and 700 tons of bombs allocated
them by the R.A.F. Again, the main object was to cause material
destruction, although the deaths of Dornberger and von Braun would
have been a crowning success.

Unfortunately for the R.A.F., this final phase was directed against
a target particularly well protected by the smoke-screen, after a lapse
of time which had allowed everyone to take cover in what were
probably the best air-raid shelters in Peenemünde. Moreover the
operation was suffering from the progressive problems encountered by
a force of bombers which had never before attacked a small target,
at a time when German night fighters had arrived and were causing

severe distress. All these factors resulted in the centre of the bombing pattern being approximately 400 yards adrift. In a city, this error would have been nothing; at Peenemünde it was crucial.

Despite all these adverse factors, some serious damage was caused. At least twenty-five buildings were destroyed and nine more damaged, most of them in the southern and eastern parts of the area. Among those destroyed were the headquarters office block, the design office, the Senior Officers' Mess, *Haus 5* where the senior men lived, the steam power plant whose large coal supply burnt for three days, and a group of buildings owned by Baugruppe Schlempp, the contractors who had built Peenemünde. The loss, by fire, of the documents in the design office would have been serious had not precautions been taken to make a copy of every important drawing and to send them away each night to be stored in the vaults of a bank at Wolgast, just over the river Peene. Many important administrative files were also saved through the bravery of Dorothea Kersten, one of von Braun's three secretaries, who went with her chief into the burning headquarters block. She was one of several civilians later awarded the *Kriegsverdienstkreuz*. Another act of bravery was that of an elderly local man, the warden of *Haus 30*, another dwelling block, who remained at his post throughout the raid and saved the building by extinguishing several incendiary bombs with buckets of sand.

The catalogue of destruction, however, does not contain a single item of scientific importance. The wind tunnel, where the Luftwaffe's V-1 flying bomb as well as rockets were tested, was untouched. The vital telemetry block, which could measure by radio signals what happened to rockets during their test flights, also remained intact. The *Einzelbauwerkstatt*, the workshop in which trial parts for rockets were individually made, was 'only scratched'. And what of Dornberger, von Braun, and those of their senior assistants who lived here? The account of Oberleutnant Werner Magirius, General Dornberger's adjutant, shows that the bombing reached this area only slowly.

I couldn't hear anything if I was lying on my left side because of my old wounds; my right ear was deaf. I only woke when I heard the noise of guns and of bombs in the distance. I opened the windows and saw smoke everywhere. I actually saw aircraft against the moonlight and it was only then that I realized we were being attacked.

I had fought in Poland, France, Greece and Russia. I was not surprised but I realized this could be dangerous. I dressed quickly but not in panic. No soldier of four years' service panics. I couldn't find my boots though. The civilian servant who looked after us all in *Haus 5* had taken all of our boots to his room to clean. In spite of the need to get to the shelter quickly, I was determined to be dressed correctly. I eventually found my boots and then I was properly dressed – boots, cap, everything.

The bombing was beginning to move nearer to us by then. I set off to the shelter, a little distance away – a good shelter with double steel doors; I found General Dornberger had reached it ahead of me. There had been nothing wrong with his hearing and neither had he bothered with his boots. He had his full uniform and leather overcoat as well but he hadn't bothered to go looking for his boots. For him, boots weren't the most important thing in life.

Eventually, there were a lot of people in that shelter, possibly more than a hundred. A girl came in quite a few minutes after my arrival. She was the night-time operator on the main telephone exchange. Although she had been fully dressed when the alarm sounded and could have been one of the first in the shelter, she had stayed at her post until the bombing nearly reached our part of Peenemünde. She was out of breath, both with running to the shelter and with excitement. There was some admiration for the way she had stayed at her unprotected post until the last minute. There was no air conditioning but we had large double-skinned barrels which contained some of the liquid oxygen we used for the rockets. They had cotton wool on top but, through this, beautiful fresh air came.

Then the bombing seemed to be all around us; we could feel the shock waves through the ground of the nearby hits before we heard their explosions. We were all very anxious for the obvious danger to our lives but there was no panic. We were all very calm but that quietness could mean different things to different people. I know we were all waiting for the end of the bombing and hoping for the best.

It eventually diminished and finally stopped altogether. We opened the door and found that there were no more aeroplane engines to be heard. We went out of the shelter and saw many of the surrounding buildings on fire. I shall always remember exactly what General Dornberger said: '*Mein schönes Peenemünde!*' – 'My beautiful Peenemünde!'; he said it with great sadness. I thing he meant not just Peenemünde but all the fine work that had been done there and with which he had been associated – the spirit of Peenemünde. Of course, we had no idea yet of the extent of the damage.

The top men had been lucky. A similar shelter nearby which was penetrated by a heavy bomb was nearly empty, and not many people were killed. Fate had more work in store for Peenemünde's top men, particularly for Wernher von Braun.

Except for the major mistake of attacking the foreign workers' camp at Trassenheide and the bombs which fell into the woods and the sea, the R.A.F. loads had not fallen beyond the areas selected for attack. The airfield at Peenemünde West, where the V-1 programme carried out its test flights, received not a single hit. The famous Test Stand VII, in the woods north of the Experimental Works, was not damaged, although a few bombs did fall nearby. (Photographs showing this area pitted with craters sometimes attributed to this R.A.F. raid were actually taken after an American raid in 1944.) On the western side of the peninsula, the liquid oxygen plant was also untouched. If the bombing had drifted west instead of east, this important installation might have gone up in a spectacular explosion. A few bombs hit the original Peenemünde village: the bakery was destroyed and four people – two women and two children – killed.

Large numbers of people outside the immediate bombing area soon emerged from their shelters to watch; 'You became a little braver when you realized that the bombs were not for you.' Most of them knew exactly how important the outcome of the raid would be both for their own future and for that of their country. They had looked on, fascinated. 'There was a tremendous cloud of smoke, clearly visible in the night sky, lit by the glow of fire – a veritable sea of flames.' 'Looking over the edge of my hole, I could see great fountains caused by the bombs which landed in the water.' 'The noise of seemingly hundreds of aircraft and of thousands of explosions seemed to go on for ever.' A fifteen-year-old boy who had watched the raid from his naval training school at Wolgast, five miles from the bombing, says that the sight of the burning establishment was 'almost spectral – a ghostly apparition', and, when the raid ended, 'there was suddenly this eerie silence'.

NOTE

1. Bomber Command Night Raid Report No. 404, Public Record Office AIR 14/3410.

CHAPTER 12

The Air Battle

Earlier chapters have described how the first two waves of bombers over Peenemünde were very little troubled by German fighter action. It is true that two Halifaxes of the first wave reported attacks by night fighters in the target area, and other crews said they witnessed a small number of further combats or heard 'excitable enemy R/T'. But the two Halifaxes evaded the attacks successfully, and at least two of the further 'combats' were actually nervous Halifax gunners firing at each other. In one such incident, crews of 51 and 77 Squadrons opened fire on each other; in subsequent reports each accused the other of firing first. No harm was done. In the second incident, a 76 Squadron aircraft received a burst of fire in the nose from a Halifax ahead, and Sergeant K. R. Parry, the navigator, received a serious bullet wound in the arm. The 'attacker' was later identified as an experienced crew from 158 Squadron.

There were virtually no German fighters over Peenemünde during the first thirty minutes of the raid, despite the fact that there was a night-fighter airfield at Greifswald only eighteen miles away. It is possible that a few of the Greifswald aircraft – from the 4th and 9th *Staffels* of NJG 5 – were patrolling local boxes; if so, they had little success. NJG 5 was not an experienced *Geschwader*; it was the first night of action for the 9th *Staffel*. One German report says that these aircraft were looking for the bombers at the R.A.F.'s normal operational height of 18,000 to 20,000 feet, when they were in fact flying at less than half that height. Most of the local fighters had been at Berlin.

The final German instruction directing all fighters on the Wild Boar operation to go to Berlin was issued at 11.35 p.m., just before the last of the diversionary force of Mosquitoes left the city. There was no further development for thirty-five minutes. Some of the Berlin Flak continued to fire, to a restricted altitude, and the night fighters went on with their monotonous circling, waiting to pounce on the main bomber force whose flight over the Baltic was being tracked by the German control organization. Many of the fighter crews became anxious: the fuel tanks of some would soon be empty, and a few of the old hands began to think that the small number of Target Indicators and bombs, which is all they had yet seen of the R.A.F. over Berlin, bore the hallmark of a decoy operation. The suspicion began to dawn in some minds that the Luftwaffe had been comprehensively tricked, and that the main attack would develop elsewhere. Then, at ten minutes past midnight, new R.A.F.-type markers had been seen cascading, far away to the north but still visible in the clear conditions of that night.

Before proceeding, comment should be made upon certain aspects of the Luftwaffe's prolonged presence over Berlin.

Over Berlin there was chaos, terrible and complete: the ill-trained day fighters were making daring attacks on every twin-ruddered aircraft in sight. The anti-aircraft gun crews, aware of the presence of hundreds of aircraft over Berlin, were opening fire on everything within range; and the night fighters assumed that the guns would hardly be shooting unless the enemy were really present in force.

The sky was a wild mêlée of air battles, tracer shells, signal flares, searchlight beams and shell bursts.

Thus wrote David Irving in 1964,[1] and his widely read account has been repeated many times. There is no doubt that there was some confusion over Berlin – the R.A.F. had intended that there should be – but, after meeting many of the German pilots who were present, it is my opinion that Mr Irving was provided with an over-dramatized version of events. He carried out his research comparatively soon after the war, during a period when wartime jealousies were still very much alive and when some former Luftwaffe personalities were trying to score historical points off old rivals. Loss of reliable Luftwaffe records gave unscrupulous men much opportunity to sow exaggeration and untruth. There were certainly strong feelings about, and much criticism of Major Herrmann's single-engined night-fighter units by former members of what might be called the 'conventional' night-fighter force.

There may have been isolated instances of single-engined fighters firing on their twin-engined colleagues, but not one of the nine twin-engined Luftwaffe men flying over Berlin that night who made contact with me could remember anything untoward. Most did not fly over the city but stood off waiting to come in when the R.A.F. arrived. In the surviving War Diaries of three twin-engined *Gruppen* there is no mention of any trouble. The records kept by the two central Luftwaffe departments of casualties to personnel and lost or damaged aircraft have also survived,[2] and although it is now believed that up to 10 per cent of the relevant documents were never received, a reliable general picture emerges. There is no record of any Luftwaffe man being killed or hurt over Berlin that night. There is no record of any twin-engined

German fighter sustaining damage over Berlin. One Focke-Wulf 190 of I/JG 300 was hit by Flak but was able to fly almost to its home airfield before having to land with damage later assessed as '30 per cent'.

Similarly, when many of the night fighters at Berlin were forced by fuel shortage to come down nearby, the story became established that too many tried to land at one airfield, Brandenburg/Briest, thirty miles west of Berlin, piling into each other on the runway; thirty aircraft are supposed to have been written off. But this description, too, seems to have been exaggerated: the German records show that just one Focke-Wulf 190, of the 4th *Staffel* of JG 300, was destroyed, and, its pilot, Feldwebel Walther Schu, killed, when it hit a radio mast at Briest. There is no other record of accidents at this airfield. Perhaps a pile-up at Briest occurred on another night.

No criticism of David Irving is intended, for I have the advantage of being able to concentrate on this one night while he had to cover the whole of the German V-weapon saga. The passage of years is also an advantage in clarifying these matters. But it is now time to return to the description of the main events.

Although Peenemünde was only twenty minutes' flying time from Berlin, the German fighter pilots were not ordered on their way to the true target even when the R.A.F. markers and bombs were seen to the north and reported to the ground controllers. The Germans' own secrecy over Peenemünde and their continuing obsession with the danger to Berlin were further compounded by a failure to get a message swiftly to the capital from the Peenemünde area. Although the German pilots could quite clearly see the raid to the north developing fast, they received only the order to continue waiting where they were. The attack to the north, they were told, was a British decoy. The failure of the Luftwaffe's senior officers in Berlin to assess the true situation was complete.

No order has been found which finally released the German fighters from Berlin and sent them to Peenemünde. The limited success eventually salvaged was due entirely to the initiative of individual pilots and of more distant and more junior control rooms. One of the pilots to leave Berlin early was Oberleutnant Friedrich-Karl Müller, whose take-off from his airfield near Bonn had been delayed because he had been out hunting.

While I was actually circling a little south of Berlin, I saw a new lot of searchlights to the north. I thought that they must be at Oranienburg; I knew that there was a big aircraft factory there and

I thought that that must be where the raid was. I flew north across Berlin. I must say that there was the most wonderful visibility on this night – no fog, no cloud, a full moon – you could read a newspaper. I remember that I was flying on a heading of 10 degrees, altitude 6,000 metres, but I was surprised that, as I flew along, the searchlights seemed to get no nearer. I crossed Oranienburg and flew on for about twenty to twenty-five minutes.

I tried to call the R/T station at Berlin – code-name *Berolina* – but got no answer. Then, I made contact with another station, code-name *Heuberg*, located at Münster. I heard it very clear, five by five. I told this station that I was on the Baltic coast, west of Swinemünde. Those searchlights I had seen had been the Swinemünde defences. I had never heard the name of Peenemünde and I had heard nothing of the V-weapons.

Leutnant Peter Spoden, II/NJG 5, had come to Berlin from Parchim, only eighty miles away. '*Kakadu*' (Cockatoo) was the call sign for the whole of his *Geschwader*; *Funkfeuer Berta* was a radio beacon just west of Berlin.

I heard the orders, '*Alle Kakadus warten über Funkfeuer Berta,*' repeated many times. There must have been many of us there; I didn't see the others but I felt the prop wash.

Then I saw markers and fires on the ground, an estimated 200–300 kilometres to the north. I didn't report this; we younger pilots didn't do such things, we left that to the big shots. I thought it was Stettin and I knew that the raid would soon be over if I could see fires on the ground already. The radio orders were still to stay over Berlin but I wanted to get my first shoot-down so badly that I set off on my own – a twenty-one-year-old pilot, training for this for three years.

I was at 6,000 metres. I put the nose down and went flat out, full throttle – an extended dive. I didn't know that the bombers were flying low on that night; I just needed that dive to get there before the raid was over.

Many German pilots acted as Müller and Spoden had done, but for others it was too late; they were nearing the end of their fuel supplies and they had to land near Berlin. Others again continued to ignore the activities to the north and followed instructions to remain where they were. One pilot later told his more successful colleagues that he had deliberately stayed over Berlin to protect his mother who lived in the Adolf Hitler Platz! None of the crews who flew to the north realized that the R.A.F. target was a rocket research centre at a place called Peenemünde. One radar operator – whose first and last operational flight this would be, for he was wounded on it – remained convinced that the raid had been on Stettin until interviewed in 1980!

Oberleutnant Müller's Focke-Wulf 190 arrived at Peenemünde.

When I reached that bit of coast north-west of Swinemünde, I suddenly realized that one area of land seemed to be covered by fog; this seemed very strange because there was no fog anywhere else. About five minutes later, the *Heuberg* station told me that heavy bombers were bombing a position on this coast; their altitude was 6,000 metres.

About one minute later, I saw markers – green and red – but the bombers dropping them were not at 6,000 metres. Then I saw the bombers; they were well below me at 1,500 to 2,000 metres. I reported to *Heuberg*, '*Negative in 6,000 Meter; keine dicke Autos. Dicke Autos greiffen in 1,500 bis 2,000 Meters an.*' I repeated this maybe three or four times and *Heuberg* sent every fighter which still had fuel to that area just west of Swinemünde.

Oberleutnant Müller's 'fog' was the Peenemünde smoke-screen; '*dicke Autos*' (big cars) was the German jargon for 'heavy bombers'.

The immunity from serious fighter attack for the British bombers at Peenemünde ended at approximately 00.40 when a Lancaster flying at the end of the second wave was shot down into the sea.

After our bombing run, we made two complete circuits of the area – no indication of fighters or Flak – when, suddenly, aircraft began to go down. The night fighters had arrived. Our excitement at a successful operation was immediately squashed as Lancs began to fall out of the sky. We turned for home in a silence only to be broken by the voice of the rear gunner, 'There goes another.' It was a perfectly clear night and the Lancs made perfect silhouettes against the brightly lit target areas – a hazard well known to experienced crews. (Pilot Officer F. J. Wilkin, 156 Squadron)

The one thing that stands out very clearly in my memory is that, on our arrival in the target area, the German fighters appeared to outnumber our bombers considerably. Standing up in the astrodome, fighters seemed to be above and below us and on either side. My immediate thoughts were that this was going to be my last flight and that our chances of getting out of this tight corner were remote. (Sergeant A. F. Anderson, 49 Squadron)

There is no record of how many German fighters reached Peenemünde and joined battle. Oberleutnant Müller's fast flight from

Berlin, in his Focke-Wulf 190, probably meant that he was one of the first to arrive, and his late take-off and the extra-large American 'drop-tank' which he had fitted would enable him to remain at Peenemünde for the remainder of the raid and still fly back to land near Berlin. Not so fortunate was one of Müller's colleagues, Ober-leutnant Ertel, who had earlier landed at Berlin, taken on more fuel, taken off again and reached Peenemünde only to have his engine fail. Müller heard Ertel reporting 'a nice soft landing' in a large wheatfield. Of the three single-engined night units, these were the only two aircraft from Bonn/Hangelar to reach the Peenemünde area, although others from II/JG 300 at Rheine and III/JG 300 at Oldenburg also arrived. A scattering of crews from every one of the twin-engined *Geschwader* sent to Berlin also caught up with the battle. A few may have heard the Münster station broadcasting details of the raid, but most had used their own initiative and sped to Peenemünde when they realized that Berlin was a lost cause. The total number of German fighters of all types to arrive on the scene may have been no more than thirty or thirty-five.

Many of the Germans were at first confused by the R.A.F.'s unusually low bombing height and wasted time before realizing where the attackers were. It is said that one German pilot who, earlier in the evening, had had a few drinks because he did not think the R.A.F. would come on this moonlit night, became 'uncomfortable' while looking for them at their normal height and descended to find himself in the bomber stream. He wasted no time and shot down four bombers. The few Germans who started operating to the north, on the approach to the target, found particularly easy victims among the 5 Group Lancasters making time-and-distance runs. Most of the Germans, however, found it more fruitful to go hunting to the south and west, where the bombers were turning west to fly home.

Conditions for the night fighters were particularly favourable. First, the glow of fires from below and the moon shining above made the thin cloud which had formed at about 3,000 feet like a sheet of illuminated frosted glass against which the bombers were starkly outlined. Second, the R.A.F. flight plan, unusually, called for the bombers to climb out of the target area, and this slowed them down while crossing the dangerous cloud. (The area covered by the air battle is shown in the inset to the map on pages 240–41.)

The scene was thus set for what was to be the most intense night battle of the war to that date.

The following quotations will give an idea of what it was like for the German night-fighter crews. Oberleutnant Müller was soon in action.

I attacked at once. It was so easy; I could see fifty bombers. I was a bit nervous – I seemed to be alone. I chose a Lancaster. The tail gunner fired back, of course. His first hit was actually in the middle of the spinner of my propeller; then he knocked a piece out of my engine cowling. It was a quick combat. He didn't take any evasive action. I tried to hit the tanks between the engines in the right wing, and I think I must have hit both engines on that side because I saw the propellers windmilling and he kept swinging to the right. I think he cut the power in the left engines but then he couldn't maintain altitude. I didn't see any parachutes and I watched him make a forced landing among the breakers a few yards off the shore. There was a great cloud of spray.

I flew back to the target area and found another Lancaster, easily visible against the smoke. I attacked again but this tail gunner was not so well trained or else he was very nervous. His first shots went past me on the left. He swung his turret and fired again but I had moved to the left and I easily avoided his fire which passed to my right. The right wing caught fire and, then, about a minute later, the wing fell off and he spiralled down. I couldn't see any parachutes again. It was very difficult to bale out when an aircraft was spinning. It fell into the sea.

My ammunition had all gone by then. We had orders to fire only the shortest of bursts – to save the rifling in our cannons – but I had my own system. My reasoning was that I only had one engine; the bombers had four engines. I thought it was good business sense to make sure of getting the bomber even if it meant putting in new cannons. It had cost Churchill more to build that bomber with its four engines than it had cost Hitler to build mine with only one.

I never saw a raid at such a low level and in such clear visibility. I think I saw your Master Bomber going round once or twice.

Oberleutnant Walter Barte II/NJG 1 had flown his Messerschmitt 110 all the way from St Trond in Belgium.

There were two four-engined bombers right in front of me, only fifty metres apart and both flying to the west. We did not need to do any radar work; it was so light that the operator was helping me with visual sightings. Also, when it was so light, you felt you had to keep a good watch in case you collided with someone. I decided to attack the left one; it was flying slightly in front of the other. In this way, the tail gunner of the one on the right could not fire at me. I always fired at the left side of my targets and that is what I did this time. I hit it in the wing between the engines. We had a friendly contest in our group. We each tried to use as short a burst as possible. I only needed a few rounds. There was no evasive action and no return fire. I don't think he ever saw me. There was a large fire at once and the plane on the right veered away quickly. I watched the first one go down but I don't know whether it crashed in the sea or on the land.

I flew back to the target area, turned west again and picked up another bomber straight away – a Halifax. I attacked it in exactly the same way and the wing exploded and broke off. The bomber went straight down and exploded in the air above a forest west of the target.

My fuel had started to run low by then and the bombers appeared to have all gone home. I could have landed at Greifswald but I wanted to get down at Neuruppin because that was my home town and because my wife, who was pregnant at that time, was there. I was home, by bicycle, half an hour after landing.

Obergefreiter Helmut Hafner was the radar operator for Leutnant Dieter Musset, another of the enterprising pilots of II/NJG 1 who had reached Peenemünde. It was Hafner's first operation and probably Musset's too. Seldom could a night-fighter crew have had such a hectic baptism.

We picked up the first one by radar but the rest were all spotted visually by Leutnant Musset. His method was to climb after each attack, because the Messerschmitt 110 was comparatively slow, and make the next attack in a shallow dive. He was able to see the bombers' exhausts from above. We got the first one in the fuel tanks between the engines. One burst was enough and it went down.

We saw the second one while the first was still going down, fifty metres below us and to the right. We were going too fast and I asked the pilot to reduce speed; I was frightened of a collision. We slowed down and one burst of fire caused the bomber to explode. In the whirl of events, I thought we were finished too but we turned out to be all right.

We climbed again and could see the target burning seven or eight kilometres away. We saw the third bomber below us. This one needed two or three bursts before it burned. We watched it hit the ground. Only a minute or two later, we made another attack; I believe this one went down but we didn't see it crash. I don't remember much about the next two attacks except that the pilot says that neither of our cannons was working properly [the unit War Diary says that a barrel had burst] and the sixth attack had to be made with machine-guns and only three out of the four of these were working properly. I definitely saw the fifth bomber spinning down but I don't know about the sixth – a Lancaster. It hit us and we were in too much trouble to watch it. We had been hit by a burst of machine-gun fire which started a fire in our port engine and I was hit by an incendiary bullet in my shoulder. We turned away from the bomber stream and tried to reach Güstrow airfield. We were fired on by our own light Flak at one place and hit by a few splinters but they stopped when we fired the colours of the day. But the fire spread, we lost control and had to bale out. I got out all right; I had no feeling in my injured shoulder and I just slid over the wing but Leutnant Musset broke both legs when he hit the tailplane and made a very painful landing. We met in hospital at Güstrow.

I never flew on operations again and all the radar operators in the *Gruppe* wanted to take my place and crew up with Leutnant Musset when he recovered because of his instant success on that night.

The details of the combat report submitted by the 619 Squadron Lancaster crew of Sergeant R. T. Hughes – on their eighth operation – coincide neatly with the time, location and manner in which this German fighter was hit. The tail and mid-upper gunners – Sergeants J. B. Crisp and R. Atkinson – had fired 1,000 rounds of ammunition. Leutnant Musset was killed in a flying accident on 9 February 1945.

Leutnant Peter Spoden was the young pilot who was so anxious to achieve his first success.

When I got to the target area, I saw an overcast – smoke or cloud, I don't know. Instinctively I went to the west because I felt that the bombers would be leaving the target in that direction. I kept looking everywhere and kept asking my radar operator to keep his eyes open.

Then I saw it, ahead of me and below. It was very small, just like a moth. I dived down on him and then I realized that I was overshooting. I throttled back and gave left and right rudder to get rid of the speed. I knew I had to act fast because the visibility was so perfect and, in a matter of seconds, they would see me and open fire. Those fellows were not asleep, you know. I pulled up my nose and, as it came up, I fired one good burst – a careful aim because I knew that I had to get him before he got me. I hit it in the left wing between the engines. We had been taught, in training, that this was the most effective place but I was also pleased that it gave those fellows in the fuselage a better chance.

There was a fire at once and a small explosion but he kept on flying. I slid well away to the right in order to keep out of his fire – he never did fire – and to continue watching him. He flew on for half a minute or so. I was afraid the fire would go out but then I saw that it got fiercer and he started to go into a shallow dive. I was so excited with my first success that, when I followed him down, I did not realize that his dive was becoming steeper and steeper, and the next thing I knew was that he had crashed in a forest and I had to pull up hard to avoid hitting the ground myself. Of course there was a big explosion – red and yellow, a terrible sight – then that typical column of smoke.

I saw a house nearby, by the light of the fire, and asked my radio operator for our position; he had been able to fix it by bearings from Greifswald. I was so excited that I didn't bother about any more bombers. The war was over that night for me. I wanted to land and go and see my shot-down bomber.

Oberleutnant Paul Zorner was one of the few pilots to join the air battle who had not first been to Berlin. His *Staffel* had been delayed by local thunderstorms in their take-off from Kastrup airfield, outside Copenhagen, and he had been well away to the west when his radar operator received news that the raid was on the Baltic coast.

I turned south-east to put myself on to a better course to find the bombers. Then I saw, a long way away, an aircraft shot down and I knew that the raid must be in that direction. 'Stettin', I thought; it was difficult to estimate the distance. I flew in that direction, seeing more bombers shot down on the way. I think it was all happening about 100 kilometres away.

Then I realized that I might be too late to catch the bombers over the target so I decided to fly a slow zigzag course on what I thought was the bombers' return route and the radar operator soon said that he had a contact, moving across in front of us and very fast.

We had to get behind him somehow so we flew in a half-circle. Of course, the radar operator lost him in the turn, but I got into the approximate position and we soon had a contact again. It may have been another bomber this time, of course, but we certainly picked one up again. I soon saw it. I got right behind it. The target was burning behind me and I didn't want him to see me against the glow so I kept well back – perhaps 400 or 500 metres – and as low as I could, but keeping him in sight all the time and keeping my aircraft against the dark background of the sea. I closed up on him carefully and recognized it as a Lancaster. At about 120 metres, I opened fire, just one burst. I hit him in the right wing between the engines; that was the most sensitive point. It started to burn –

not too fiercely at first – and it went into a shallow dive for perhaps three or four minutes. I flew off to the right-hand side and watched. He certainly hadn't fired at me and I don't think he took any evasive action at any stage.

I saw two or three parachutes open, one of the few times I ever saw parachutes in all my combats. Then the nose of the Lancaster went over and it went straight down into the sea with a big explosion and a fire remained for a little time.

Then I saw several more aircraft being shot down and knew that I had to try to get at least one more bomber. I kept thinking it would be too late but I flew on towards the target area and soon saw the second one against that mist or low cloud. I turned quickly and attacked him from behind, from a little above this time. I remember that it was a very quick attack. I think I was further back than the first time and my hits were all over him. The combination of moon and that ground mist or cloud made it very easy. It was almost like a daylight attack. The bomber started burning and, soon after, exploded in the air. As before, there was no return fire and no evasive action. I don't think he ever saw me.

I continued to circle round, trying to find another bomber, but I think I was a little too far south and I think the bombers had nearly all gone by then.

These two successes were the eleventh and twelfth of fifty-nine in Oberleutnant Zorner's long night-fighting career.

From a reading of the German fighter crews' accounts, it is obvious that many of the R.A.F. men met swift and violent deaths; the combats were rarely lengthy. But there were some British survivors, and a selection of their experiences can also be quoted. Nearly all the victims of the air battle were the aircraft and crews making up the third wave of the attack – Lancasters of 5 Group and Halifaxes and a few Lancaster IIs of the mostly Canadian 6 Group – but two Stirlings, which should have bombed and been well on their way home by this time, had been badly delayed and also fell victim to the night fighters.

Sergeant Ron Scandrett was the man ordered to take the place of a gunner under threat of court martial at Mildenhall airfield. There had been a major navigational error, and the Stirling had wandered well to the south of the target before the mistake was realized. It was now flying north, towards the fires of Peenemünde. Sergeant Scandrett, on his first operation, was in the Stirling's rear turret, and he was in trouble. His intercom to the rest of the crew was as 'dead as a doornail', and the button for the emergency light-signalling system was not in the same place as in the type of Stirling in which he had just finished his training. Men's lives often depended on such minor details.

It was then that I spotted the Focke-Wulf 190. It was a hunter's moon; it really was as bright as day and, with those big cowlings, you could identify the Focke-Wulfs easily. I tried to raise the others by intercom but it was still dead. In the back of my mind there was this wishful thinking that he wouldn't see us but he'd spotted us and started closing in fast and we were still flying straight and level.

Then something happened for which I always blame myself – it led to the death of three of the crew. I watched the fighter closing in on us, my left finger on the trigger for the four guns, my right finger by my shoulder ready to press the button – which wasn't there! Basic training had overcome reason. I should have thought it out carefully but I didn't and that's what I blame myself for. It never even entered my head that the button was in the top of the turret. He closed in to about 300 yards and I fired first but my fire went high because these guns had been set at 400 yards and I had always trained at 200 and, all the time, I was trying to press this button that wasn't there.

I think his first burst went too low but he certainly got us with his second or third. There was no panic or fear; training took over and you became a machine. I thought I hit him because my tracers appeared to be hitting his engine and, as he passed under us, diving under our starboard side, I thought I hit him in the body. But he was moving very fast and he was a dead shot and I couldn't stop him hitting us. He got us in the starboard wing, between the engines, and the petrol tanks there caught fire.

I heard the pilot say he was going to dive and he put the nose straight down and came down at least 3,000 feet but it had no effect whatever on the fire. Then he told us he would try to gain a little height and we were to bale out. His was the only voice I heard. I carried out the normal procedure. The flames from the burning tanks were streaming within inches of my hatch. I had to dive through those flames but I knew that it was all or nothing and I had to do it. It was over twelve months later that I remembered leaving the aircraft and, to this day, I never ever remember pulling the rip-cord.

The pilot, Sergeant Robert Grundy, was one of the three men who died in this crew. Sergeant Scandrett later added, 'I have nothing but admiration for the way he was determined to get to the target.'

The second Stirling, from 620 Squadron, had been delayed by several factors. This crew were without their regular pilot – who was sick – and his place had been taken by Squadron Leader A. D. Lambert, a newly arrived, second-tour flight-commander. A new 'second pilot' was also on board. Sergeant Chris Leeming was the mid-upper gunner.

Squadron Leader Lambert had called us to his office and asked us if we minded going with him. We were happy enough. We thought it was another one for the book; the sooner we got them over, the sooner we finished. We were to find out that he was an excellent pilot, an ideal R.A.F. type, full of the joys of spring, one of the 'nothing can hurt me' types. He had thrown that kite about like a Spitfire on the air test.

On our second bomb run, we got hit by Flak which made a big hole in the side of the aircraft. It holed a petrol tank, or a pipe to it, and petrol was running down the floor of the fuselage. Then the rear gunner, Thompson, saw a fighter and called out to me, 'On the beam, Chris!', but he didn't say which beam. I was facing forward. I swung round to the port, and then my turret was hit by a cannon shell. I got a few cuts from the perspex and bits of cannon shell and, although I lost a lot of blood, I wasn't seriously hurt. I never did see the fighter.

The intercom went dead then. I got out, wobbled past the Flak hole in the fuselage and through the petrol on the floor. I reached the cockpit, tapped the skipper on the shoulder and he pointed down at the open escape hatch. It was open and the bomb aimer had already gone. I sat on the edge and looked up at the second dicky; he was only a young lad. I touched him, to draw attention that I was going. He reached out, put his thumb up, grabbed my hand and shook it to wish me luck.

The air battle was being fought over rapidly alternating areas of land and water, and two of the six men who baled out from this aircraft came down in the sea and were drowned. The story of how Squadron Leader Lambert and the second pilot ditched the Stirling will be told in a later chapter.

Many crews from the Canadian squadrons of 6 Group were caught in the battle. Pilot Officer R. W. Charman was the navigator in this 427 Squadron Halifax.

I had never seen such a sight before or since. All over the sky, R.A.F. planes were going down in flaming infernos. The great German fighter armada, poised for the expected raid on Berlin, had all been brought into service and had arrived in time to catch the last wave into Peenemünde.

I recall asking the captain, Frank Brady, to get down on the deck and break the order to climb on track as we wouldn't have a chance against the waves of fighters. He refused, said if everyone did that it would screw up the whole mission. What an unselfish, dedicated person; they didn't come any better.

I had barely given Frank a course for home when Jimmy Fletcher, the tail gunner, broke in with evasive action. A Junkers 88 was bearing down on our tail.

We went down in a dive, trying to avoid the fighter. Then the aircraft quivered, like in killing poultry you strike the brain with a knife and the feathers release – that is the way the aircraft felt. A horrible smell of gunpowder enveloped the aircraft and the wireless operator beside me lay dying, with his entrails exposed.

Then Frank issued the order, 'Abandon aircraft . . .', a cut, and that was all. I rushed back and he was wriggling the controls without effect. They had been severed and we were spinning down. The centrifugal force was enormous and I crawled along the floor to get my parachute. I lifted the floor hatch and the night air rushed in. My maps and navigational aids were all sucked out immediately. I put my hand on the rip-cord of the chute. I remember thinking to myself that I had better know where the cord was or it was going to be hard finding it travelling through the air.

Only one man followed Pilot Officer Charman through the escape hatch.

Another Canadian Halifax to be attacked, from 434 Squadron, was captained by Sergeant G. M. Johnston. Sergeant Keith Rowe was the young English flight engineer. The Halifax had already corkscrewed away from one German fighter.

We straightened up, got our breaths back and into some semblance of order but, immediately, literally within moments, we were attacked again.

Doug Labell, the rear gunner, was very good – a tough, husky, French-Canadian who seemed to be absolutely impervious to cold; he had cut all the perspex out of his turret to improve visibility. He also had good eyesight – a bit of a 'cat's eye'. He was one of the most manly of men I had met so far in my young life. He was very emphatic in his 'Dive port!', and we took really violent evasive action – a very steep dive to port but, almost instantaneously, I saw tracer – whitish-orange, I think – going into our port wing-tip. I watched the tracer travelling rapidly right across the port wing and then into the starboard wing but, somehow, it missed the fuselage. That German was a super shot, and the thought went through my mind that he had done this before. I have the feeling that it was a single-engined fighter but I can't be sure.

Both wings were burning fiercely within seconds. It must have been the fuel tanks, and I remember thinking so much for the self-sealing fuel tanks about which we had been told there had been great developments. We were losing altitude rapidly. 'Johnny' Johnston was struggling to regain control but the engines soon caught fire. The roar of the fire was so fierce – well above the noise of the engines – it was quite frightening; all that fuel was burning. I can also remember seeing the wings literally melting towards their leading edges – both wings.

Very soon, 'Johnny' said, 'We're not going to save it; bale out. Go!' I clipped my parachute on, then leant across to hold the control column to let him get up. He took off his safety straps. I remember seeing the altimeter; we were losing altitude fast and were down to 3,000 feet. We still had intercom and 'Johnny' told me to go and he would follow. I took two steps, was into the nose and at the hatch. I half turned and saw 'Johnny' standing, out of his seat but with his left hand out, obviously still on the control column which was out of my sight. I just dived straight out.

Six men escaped from this aircraft, the nearest to a complete crew to do so in the whole Peenemünde operation; Sergeant Gregg Johnston, son of a large prairie farmer near Moose Jaw, Saskatchewan, paid the price so many Bomber Command pilots had to pay, carrying out their final duty of remaining at the controls to enable as many of their crew to bale out as possible.

Sergeant Peter Crees was an English flight engineer in another 434 Squadron Halifax.

The French-Canadian rear gunner, Micky Lapointe, told the skipper that a fighter was coming in – level and a bit higher and from our starboard rear quarter. We broke away to starboard straight away. I was in the astrodome; the flight engineer's position was immediately under this, and it was my normal look-out position. All I saw was the three lots of tracer – yellowish-red – our two turrets' and the fighter's. I would have expected the fighter to have stood off and pumped shells into us, but he must have kept coming right in. I was surprised at that. No one was saying much except the rear gunner; there was quite a lot of excitement from him. I don't know what he was saying – it was all in French.

He came in so close that both gunners were right on him and the fighter took quite a pounding from us. That's when I first saw him. You could see its outline quite clearly because it was so bright. I was sure that it was a twin fin and ruddered aircraft which I assume was an Me 110. He was on fire between his starboard engine and the fuselage, quite a furious fire. We lost him after that and we all assumed he went in. He had hit us but not too seriously. All the controls were working; none of us had been hit and, when the fighter peeled off, we thought we had a chance of getting over to Sweden.

Then, when we were pulling ourselves together and summing up the damage, another lot of cannon shells came in without any warning at all. The first lot passed underneath us, but he must have lifted his nose because the next lot got us. It must have been a very long burst, the first shells hitting the rear turret, killing the gunner I suppose, then, watching from the astrodome, I could see more shells working their way along the fuselage, the tracer entering the fuselage with a little burst of sparks; I watched it reach the mid-upper turret, killing the gunner there as well, I think.

I saw the aircraft which was firing at us – just briefly. It seemed bigger than the other and I believe he only had one fin. He stood off and kept firing; he didn't come right in like the first one. At that stage, I decided to get out of the astrodome and stood alongside the pilot. Then a shell burst in the cockpit; I think it had come straight down the fuselage. It burst behind us and the pilot got the worst of it. He didn't have an armour-plated seat. I got pieces of shrapnel in the back, left leg and buttocks. I've still got some of them there. They work their way to the surface sometimes; my wife often digs them out.

The port wing was now burning furiously and we were obviously going down and the pilot had told us to get out. Jimmy, the navigator, had got the hatch opened but it was twisted and jammed in the opening. I got the axe, knelt on the floor, chopped and it fell away more easily than I expected.

The two gunners were dead and the pilot, Flying Officer Ian Colquhoun, a doctor's only son from Edmonton, Alberta, was probably dying. Sergeant Crees last saw the Canadian bomb aimer, Flight Sergeant Charles Fitzpatrick from Toronto, in the nose, 'blazing away with the single machine-gun there, seemingly unconcerned about getting out and surrounded by the stink of cordite.' Fitzpatrick also died.

The losses in the 5 Group squadrons were just as heavy. Flying Officer Philip Duckham was the navigator of a 49 Squadron Lancaster.

Almost immediately after taking up our new heading, after bombing, we were attacked from the rear. The rear gunner was able to give avoiding instructions of about two 'Turn ports' before the 'Go!' He discharged his guns at about the same time as the enemy fighter discharged his. How successful our shots were, I cannot say. We were hit but, in view of what followed, I do not know the full extent of the damage to the aircraft from this attack. The last words uttered by the rear gunner were, 'The bastard's got my sights.' The bastard had also got him!

At almost the same time as the attack from the rear, we were again attacked, this time from the starboard beam. The starboard wing was set alight and, as the flames would reach the petrol tanks in a few seconds, causing the aircraft to explode, the pilot gave the order to abandon aircraft.

Sergeant Charles Robinson was the pilot.

I heard the various crew members acknowledge the order and three of them went. There were only the two gunners and the navigator left. The mid-upper said something like, 'Jack is no good' or 'Jack is no go'; I don't know which. There was a lot of crackling of the burning wing. The air from the front escape hatch was blowing bits of paper and all sorts of things up through the space on my right. I assumed the mid-upper gunner had gone to look at the tail gunner and then baled out himself through the rear door.

The other three engines were running normally but the two on the right were making the aircraft tend to yaw to port, with the port wing dropping, and I thought that it would soon drop off when the fire got into the main spar so I was virtually standing on the starboard rudder bar to bring the nose back round to the right and trying to pick the wing up by turning the control wheel to the right. All the time, I was looking out at that fire sizzling away just outside my window and thinking, 'God, when's this lot going to go up?', thinking about the tanks, and hoping they would all get out quickly. Phil Duckham went past me on his way out; as he did so, he undid my seat harness and this left me sitting on my seat-type parachute pack. That saved my life. I watched him go. As far as I knew, I was on my own then, assuming that the tail gunner had gone or was dead, but I couldn't do anything about him.

Now it was time to get out myself. I put full starboard trim on the rudders; that's all I could do to set the controls. I had just started to ease myself out of my seat when there was this hot blast on the left-hand side of my face and I remember feeling rather than hearing an explosion. The next thing I knew, I was outside in the air, hanging from my opened parachute. It was quiet and cool and I could feel a bit of blood dribbling down my face.

I found out later that my D-ring was still safely packed and had obviously never been pulled. My theory is that the parachute had needed repacking and parts of it may have been bulging a little and these had caught the air when I was more or less ejected by the explosion or had caught in some broken part of the cockpit perspex as I went through it. How lucky can you get!

44 Squadron lost three Lancasters near Peenemünde. Sergeant Bill Sparkes was the bomb aimer in one of them when it was hit by cannon fire.

We kept on going down and, at that time, I thought we were still trying to evade by a straightforward dive but we continued on – down, down, down. It was then that we got instructions to prepare to abandon the aircraft. My job was to get the front hatch open and, to do this, I had to get the bundles of Window off the hatch. It didn't take me long, not the way I moved; I tossed it all forward on to the bomb sight. I opened the hatch and, almost immediately, heard the command to abandon the aircraft.

Because I had been so busy, I had stopped taking note of the altitude of the aircraft and what the rest of the crew were doing. I just don't know what the damage had been or whether any of the others had been hit. I do know that there was no doubt in my mind about getting out – there was no hesitation – so I suppose that I must have known the situation was rather dire. Normally, in training, the crew was always lined up behind me, waiting to get out, and it has always puzzled me why there was no one there. When the prisoners of war were collected at Greifswald, I kept trying to find more of my crew and, when none of them turned up, I began to wonder whether they had got away after all and returned to England. It never occurred to me that they were all dead.

Sergeant Sparkes was the only survivor from the three 44 Squadron crews lost. In more than half of the bombers shot down, there were no survivors at all.

Such scenes of combat had been seen many times in Germany's night skies – though not always in such intensity – but on this occasion there was one method of destroying bombers which had not been used before. Sergeant R. Garnett, the rear gunner of a 467 Squadron Lancaster, who, with the mid-upper gunner, had beaten off a conventional attack by a Junkers 88, goes on to describe a second attack which destroyed their Lancaster.

We settled down again, climbing steadily. Then we were hit, just a very gentle judder, but the speed of the aircraft was affected. The sensation was as though the aircraft had hit a big cloud of cotton wool. We saw no tracer. That was a complete mystery to we gunners; we couldn't see how an aircraft could be hit by invisible fire like that.

Then, immediately, a real stream of fire and sparks came back past my turret from the port wing. It was just like a real gunpowder plot night, just like a bonfire being lit. The pilot told us to get out at once. I heard him asking for someone to pass him his parachute.

The unseen burst of fire which had hit this bomber had struck the wing root area almost vertically from below.

The reader will remember that the 5th *Staffel* of NJG 5, at Parchim airfield, had fitted two of its Messerschmitt 110s with twin cannon adjusted to fire almost vertically through the cockpit roof. The two fighters were both making their first operational flights with these new weapons – named *schräge Musik* ('slanting' or 'jazz' music) – and both had arrived from Berlin. The new device had naturally been fitted to the aircraft of senior and experienced pilots. The first was Leutnant Peter Erhardt, the *Staffelkapitän*. Erhardt – a swashbuckling character – shot down four bombers in thirty minutes with his *schräge Musik*. He identified two as Lancasters, but two were recorded only as 'four-engined bombers'. The identity of all Erhardt's victims is not known, but the 467 Squadron Lancaster whose destruction has just been described was probably one of them. Erhardt's fighter was presumably never seen by any of the bombers he shot down and no defensive fire was ever directed at him.

The second *schräge Musik* aircraft was normally flown by an officer whose turn it was that night to be on duty in the local fighter control room; his place was taken by Unteroffizier Walter Hölker, a typical 'new boy' whose own fighter – the oldest in the *Staffel* – had a technical defect. Hölker had never seen an R.A.F. bomber at night and never piloted the *schräge Musik* aircraft before. Here he describes his exciting flight.

We were over 8,500 metres high by the time I reached the target area. We always needed good height when in a waiting position. I saw, much lower, a whole lot of bombers flying east to west against the fire and smoke over the target. They looked like ants, crawling over the ground. I dived, but too quickly, far too fast to aim and shoot, and flew right past the bombers. I had to circle back again.

Then Werner Zahl, my radar man, said he could see a Halifax ahead and above. I reduced speed and let it come over us. But then

I found that the sight in the roof of the cockpit had fallen off on to the floor so I flew right up under him, so close that I couldn't see the sky, only this huge aeroplane. Then I pressed the button aiming as best I could at the left inner engine. I only fired four or six shots and the petrol immediately came pouring out on fire and the bomber started to go down. I slid out from underneath it and we flew alongside it as it fell because it was our first success and I was determined to get the credit for it. Suddenly, light Flak, like strings of pearls, came up and nearly hit us, so I got out of the way but I was able to see the bomber hit the water. I didn't see any parachutes but might have missed them because I was well to the side as it came down.

We climbed up again and found another one immediately – a Lancaster this time. I think this one had seen us because he started his weaving, evasive manoeuvre. It was difficult to get under this bomber when he was flying in this way so I maintained a steady course and waited for him to cross over the top of me. I fired when he did so but my first shots went behind him. I corrected by dropping my nose a little and the next burst started hitting him in the left wing. But he responded by putting his nose up and his tail gunner opened fire on me. He was a really good shot. One of his first bullets hit one of the portable oxygen bottles that our third man – the extra lookout – needed. The bottle exploded. I don't know much what happened then. I wasn't able to think very clearly. I found later that I had got three bits of metal in the back of my head and about forty in the rest of my body.

We were in a dive and fell from about 3,000 down to 1,500 metres; only then was I able to pull out of the dive. The cockpit roof had all gone in the explosion. I couldn't speak to the others because the intercom had gone and I couldn't see them because of the radar set between me and them.

Hölker decided not to bale out himself in case any of his crew were still aboard. His subsequent flight will be described later.

Unteroffizier Hölker was later told that observers on the ground had verified that the second bomber he had attacked had crashed. If this is true, it had been a successful debut for *schräge Musik*. Six bombers had been destroyed. The damage to Hölker's fighter was probably due more to his own inexperience than to any failure in the tactical use of the new weapon. Hölker was not destined to join the ranks of the great; he was able to claim only three more successes in the next twenty months of night fighting.

Despite the excellent visibility, none of the R.A.F. bombers which returned safely to their bases submitted reports which might have triggered off a warning that the Germans had this new and lethal weapon. The tracerless ammunition used in *schräge Musik* gave no hint that the fighter was attacking from underneath instead of from the normal rear position. Many R.A.F. men had seen the sudden explosions or bursting into flames of stricken bombers without previous tracer fire, and their observation of these unexplained phenomena led either to the creation of a new legend or to a reawakening of interest in an old one.

> I cannot agree with you that 'scarecrows' didn't exist. The answers to the questions regarding these will undoubtedly come to light when material will be forwarded to you by those who took part in the Peenemünde raid. This was the only raid during my tour that I came into contact with them, mainly as the raid was carried out at the low level for us of 8,000 feet. As we neared the target area, I first spotted these explosions with their pyrotechnic displays and asked the pilot what they were. He said, 'Scarecrows, to put the wind up you.' I said, 'Hell, they don't need those.' Over the target area there were far too many to be aircraft exploding.

So writes Sergeant F. G. Miller of 467 Squadron. The squadron's records contain this observation about the defences at Peenemünde: 'Flak – light stuff and sundry scarecrows.'[3]

Very many ex-Bomber Command men still believe that the Germans fired large pyrotechnic shells which burst in imitation of an exploding bomber. But the unusual, vivid shells that the Germans did fire from time to time at various places were navigational aids to their own fighters or, occasionally, experimental missiles. No doubt such explosions often frightened R.A.F. bomber men nearby, but it remains my contention that there was no such thing as the purely 'scarecrow' shell; what the R.A.F. thought were 'scarecrows' were often bombers blowing up after being hit by the tracerless cannon fire of a *schräge Musik* fighter.

The combats were not completely one-sided. Some bombers were able to drive off the fighters, inflicting various degrees of damage; others withstood the effects of German fire and managed to struggle home. The following accounts are from men who did get back to England.

The 460 Squadron Lancaster of Flight Sergeant Danny Rees, an Australian, with three other Australians in the crew, bombed in the second wave and must have been one of the first aircraft to be caught by a night fighter. Flight Sergeant John Venning was the tail gunner. The 'Boozer' in his account was a device which warned the pilot when a German fighter behind was using radar.

On our way out of the bombing run, we were being followed by several Lancs coming up behind. Then Danny called out, 'Boozer in operation.' A frantic search began for our adversary. He eventually came to light when a Lanc about 300 yards dead astern banked out suddenly and the Ju 88 was sitting under his wing. I immediately opened fire from the rear turret as the Ju 88 decided to follow my way of thinking. Our mid-upper, 'Chook' Harris, joined in the fray, and after a brief encounter the Ju 88 was last seen heading for the deck followed by a bright red glow.

We suffered considerable damage to the tail section and elevators and the main petrol tank was holed, from which I received an unwelcome shower in petrol.

The Lancaster lost 580 gallons from the damaged fuel tank, but it reached its base. Flight Sergeant Venning says that 'we treated the operation as just another job well done,' but Flight Sergeant Rees was awarded the Conspicuous Gallantry Medal for his handling of the aircraft.

Pilot Officer Lindsay Vogan was the Canadian bomb aimer in a 427 Squadron Halifax with five other Canadians in the crew. After leaving Peenemünde, the Halifax was attacked by a single-engined fighter, believed to be a Messerschmitt 109. The pilot, Sergeant W. H. Schmitt, was a squadron 'character'. Vogan says:

By the time of Peenemünde, we were a seasoned and senior crew on the squadron roster, but it is easy to understand why 'Indian' Schmitt was still a sergeant. He was a real wild man, a real daredevil.

The night, of course, gets its halo as the years go by. We had lost our place in the gaggle and were a sitting duck for enemy fighters hovering around the edge of the pack. We got right down on the ground, heading west as fast as we could go, fighting our way out. Why we didn't slam into some pylon or something like that remains a miracle to this day. Sure, it was easy to spot the fighters. I had no trouble alerting our gunners from my belly position in the nose. That's how we got at least one Me 109F for sure; it blew up on its fourth attack. When the 'hot stuff' cooled off a bit, we wriggled our way north-west as best we could.

When we reached England, we had the option of baling out or of riding the craft down to a belly landing. We all chose to remain aboard, and I can still feel the jolt on my back when we skidded in.

This crew completed their tour with this operation, the first on their comparatively new squadron to do so. Their Halifax was a 'write-off'.

It was believed to be another single-engined fighter which attacked the Lancaster piloted by Warrant Officer W. L. Wilson, nicknamed 'Pluto' from earlier gambling successes on a troopship which had made him 'a filthy plutocrat'. Although this aircraft was from an Australian squadron, only Wilson and one other man were Australians. Sergeant Patrick Barry, the Southern Irish tail gunner, is the first of three members of this crew to describe the attack.

He came up from below and behind, intending, it would appear, to knock out my turret. He was successful. I believe I got in one short burst at his exposed belly before the hydraulics went 'for a Burton', but my recollections are hazy and, indeed, it was an explosive time and there was a lot of confusion.

We were going down in a rather steep dive and, after a moment of convulsive panic or rebellion at what seemed inevitable, I remember distinctly that a feeling of peace or acceptance came over me and I calmly awaited the end.

Of course, the lads 'up front' pulled her out. I became aware that the tail was afire with ammunition exploding. My turret doors were jammed with the turret askew and, as I discovered later, my parachute had been shot to ribbons. I wasn't immediately conscious of my injuries but, as I became so, I called for help. I still don't know if the intercom was working.

Sergeant George Oliver, the mid-upper gunner, had fired on the German fighter but then found that there were flames all around his turret.

I dropped out of my turret and grabbed my parachute. Just as I was getting out, I had looked out and seen water underneath me. I couldn't swim but that wasn't going to stop me going. I couldn't get to the back door because the fuselage behind my turret was full of flames. I went up the front and opened the bulkhead doors. My intention, at that stage, was survival. I just wanted to get to the emergency hatch. When I opened those doors, the first person I came to was the wireless operator. I tapped him on the shoulder and pointed back. As soon as he saw the fire, he grabbed his parachute and was off in front of me. The navigator soon followed but our way was blocked when we reached the pilot and engineer's position.

The pilot told us that the plane was still flying properly and ordered us to go back and try to put the fire out. He was the boss – we trusted him – and, if he said the plane was all right, then it was all right and we got on and did what he said.

The main cause of the fire were the hydraulic pipes burst by the fighter. You know what burning oil is like in an enclosed space; it was just thick and choking and there was all the ammunition exploding. I can't actually describe it any further; we just got on with it. It was just something that had to be done. It seemed an eternity. We used up two extinguishers and they certainly quelled most of the flames, but the padding over the tail spar was still smouldering. I presumed the tail gunner was dead; we hadn't had any contact with him at all.

The crew later agreed that the pilot's decision to fight the fire had saved the aircraft and the life of the tail gunner. The flight engineer, Sergeant C. A. Cawthorne, had earlier reported the inferno in the fuselage to the pilot, 'who had coolly remarked, "Well, go and put the bloody thing out." Had it not been for those cool, calculated words, we would have abandoned the aircraft.' The mid-upper gunner, together with the navigator, the flight engineer and the wireless operator, eventually extinguished the fire and then, very laboriously, chopped open the jammed door to the rear turret and released the gunner, who was badly wounded in the ankle.

This Lancaster found its way safely to England, and the flight ended with satisfaction all round. The crews' bombing photograph showed that they had obtained an 'Aiming Point'. The injured tail gunner recovered. Mid-upper gunner and pilot were given 'immediate' awards of the CGM and DFC respectively; the other crew members were all decorated later. After two more operations – both to Berlin – the crew completed their tour.

The final quotation in this group illustrates so well the outlook of a good, steady English bomber pilot. Pilot Officer Deryck Aldridge of 44 Squadron and his crew were on their twenty-sixth operation. After bombing, Aldridge formated upon another bomber so that mutual support could be given if either were attacked, but the other aircraft was soon shot down, perhaps by the same fighter which now attacked Aldridge's Lancaster.

The rear gunner reported the fighter but he went on to say, 'He's not in range yet, skipper. I'm keeping an eye on him.' He probably meant that the fighter wasn't in range of his guns, but I took it that the fighter couldn't hit us. I told him to keep me informed and I took no avoiding action. But, almost immediately, I saw these sparks – tracer – coming up from behind us and disappearing away in front of us and then the bangs and shudderings as he hit us. I dived quite a long way – several thousand feet – before I realized that we weren't still being attacked. I levelled off and turned back on to course so that we were not still charging off into unknown territory. We always had the feeling in Bomber Command that high was safe; you couldn't get over it. So I started climbing again. The intercom had gone in the attack, and I often wondered what the crew had thought, going into that great dive and not hearing anything on the intercom. I think they were very frightened. I remember looking at the flight engineer and he looked very apprehensive. We hadn't got our oxygen masks on then and I gave him a big grin. I felt I had to do that to let him know that I thought we were going to be all right.

It was then that this face appeared and, there, behind me, stood Sammy Holmes, the rear gunner. I was very surprised to see him. He had climbed over that great main spar and, I found out later, had slipped up on some hydraulic oil on the floor outside the wireless operator's position and gone flat on his back. The wireless operator thought that Sammy had come up front to die, but he'd only come to tell me that his guns were no good. The automatic rotation and training had gone and he could only do all this manually. I knew that this was a very cumbersome way. We shouted into each other's ears and I told him to go back and man his turret again. That arrival of the gunner came as a bit of light relief in a hairy situation.

I continued climbing and, within a very few minutes, we were attacked again. It was very similar to the first one – the tracer going past, then the aircraft shuddering when it was hit. I repeated the same manoeuvre, turning and diving. This time I decided that I wouldn't climb again but keep diving. I remember that my first trip as second dicky with another pilot had been to Stettin and, on the return flight, this pilot had put the nose down over the Baltic and come home at really low level. He obviously knew that there was no high ground in Denmark and had come back at about 200 feet. I decided that this is what I would do this time.

It was then that we realized that an engine had failed, and we feathered it. We went down until we could see the sea clearly in the moonlight and knew we were just a few hundred feet above it. We flew the whole way across Denmark like that at two or three hundred feet. I do remember clearly that we were doing 230 knots and I was so proud of the old Lanc that she could keep that speed up on three engines. We had been very lucky to get away with it.

We couldn't face that sort of thing, uncaring, at our ages now the way we did in those days when we were young.

The main air battle had taken place on the bombers' final approach to Peenemünde and over the alternating areas of land and sea of the first thirty miles of the return route between Peenemünde and the town of Stralsund. The few German fighters which hung on to harry the bombers for another thirty miles were eventually forced to break off for lack of fuel. The battle had lasted for less than fifty minutes. The further fighter action that occurred on the return to England was to be produced by entirely different conditions.

Many of the R.A.F. men who emerged unscathed had been close witnesses to the violent loss of their comrades. The navigator in each crew was supposed to record details of every combat seen so that Bomber Command could later make a résumé of what had happened. Here are two such 'sightings':

Report No. 19. Greifswald, 2 miles S of, 00.50. Aircraft seen falling on fire but managed to get down and make forced landing, finally bursting into flames on the deck after what appeared to be the third bounce.

Report No. 109. Peenemünde area, 00.52. Lanc seen attacked by E/A [enemy aircraft]. 4 engines on fire. Gunners continued firing until aircraft hit ground and exploded.[4]

It is not known which Lancaster was the subject of the second report, but the pilot attempting the forced landing was probably Wing Commander Leslie Crooks, DSO, DFC, the English commander of the Canadian 426 Squadron, going down on the eighth operation of his second tour and flying his first operation since the squadron had converted from Wellingtons to Lancaster IIs. His bomb aimer baled out safely, but Crooks and the rest of his crew did not survive.

The men who returned home still have memories of that scene. Flight Lieutenant G. Whitten was a Pathfinder navigator.

Because of the perfect visibility I was free to spend quite long spells away from the chart on the way home when all we had to think about was ourselves. That was the trouble though. On a night when even those like pilots and gunners who were used to it saw more one-sided air battles than ever before, the grandstand view was more akin to the gladiatorial arena or bull-ring than a happy day at the races. There hardly seemed to be a minute when we did not have in sight some aircraft in flames or exploding – and, clearly, most of them were ours.

Not once were we ourselves fired on or even menaced by an enemy fighter, but I think it was an experience that convinced most of the crew that there was something to be said for being in our usual place at the front of the stream after all.

It had indeed been a night out for those German crews who had reached Peenemünde. In combats between night fighter and bomber, the odds were always in favour of the light, fast, manoeuvrable fighter with its 20-mm cannon rather than of the large, lumbering bomber with its so-dangerous fuel tanks and puny .303-in. machineguns. The bombers' best chance of escape was always to corkscrew away into the darkness rather than stand and fight; the bright moonlight conditions which the British had risked for the chance of destroying Peenemünde increased the odds against them. The unseen and unsuspected *schräge Musik* attacks from underneath had further stacked the odds.

It can be calculated that forty-six combats took place in the air battle around Peenemünde, a 'combat' being whenever one side or the other opened fire, however briefly or inconclusively. Twenty-eight R.A.F. bombers – eighteen Lancasters, eight Halifaxes and two Stirlings – were shot down in the area, but the German losses cannot be calculated with quite such accuracy; five fighters – four Messerschmitt 110s and a Dornier 217 – although there may have been more. From the above figures, once fire had been opened, the bomber had less than a four-in-ten chance of escaping destruction, while the German chances were more than nine out of ten. The bombers that did survive were usually manned by a more experienced crew than average; very likely, too, the German pilot involved was raw. It is probably significant that the crews of the four damaged bombers described above who did make it back to England were all nearing the end of their tours.

It was said earlier that approximately thirty-five German fighters reached Peenemünde. It is believed that just seventeen of them were responsible for the twenty-eight bombers shot down here. Predictably, the recognized German aces had added to their scores with less than usual difficulty: Majors Walter Ehle and Günther Radusch each claimed three bombers; Hauptmann August Geiger and Oberleutnants Friedrich-Karl Müller and Paul Zorner had two claims each. Apart from a few bullet holes in Müller's aircraft, these men and their machines survived the night without a scratch.

(Radusch, Müller and Zorner survived the war, but Ehle and Geiger both died in the next few weeks – neither of them the victim of the bomber gunners they had so often faced. August Geiger's fighter was shot down over the Zuider Zee on 29 September 1943 by Wing Commander Braham, the Intruder ace met earlier in this book, and Geiger was drowned. Walter Ehle crashed while attempting a landing at St Trond when the airfield landing lights were doused, possibly because an R.A.F. Intruder was in the area.)

NOTES

1. *The Mare's Nest*, pp. 108–9.
2. The War Diaries of II and III/NJG 1 and III/NJG 5 are now in the Bundesarchiv, Freiburg, references RL 10/540, 10/620 and 10/604; the Luftwaffe personnel files are at the Deutsche Dienststelle (WASt) in the Eichborndamm, Berlin, and the Luftwaffe Quartermaster General's Return of Aircraft Losses is on microfilm at the Imperial War Museum in London and at various other places.
3. Public Record Office AIR 27/1930.
4. Public Record Office AIR 14/3219.

CHAPTER 13

The Homeward Flight

As most of the German fighters fell away, the bomber-stream pressed on north-westwards. It was 220 miles from Peenemünde to the North Sea, about eighty minutes' flying time with the existing slight head-wind. The first quarter of the flight was over Germany, the remainder over the Baltic and the narrow mainland of Denmark. Most of the bombers quickly regained the 14/15,000 feet shown in their flight plans; of the few that decided that it was safer to fly low-level all the way, one Pathfinder navigator remembers, 'I was delighted with the peaceful and well ordered Danish countryside, clearly seen in the moonlight.' Conditions stayed clear, and the glow of burning Peenemünde remained visible in the sky behind the bombers until the North Sea was reached.

Once the main body of German fighters had left, most of the bombers had an uneventful flight, at least over the Baltic. There are several reports of combats, but conditions were no longer so favourable to the Germans. The few night fighters in action here were probably flown by crews who had not been clever enough to reach Peenemünde. The bombers were no longer silhouetted against low cloud but were flying into the darkest part of the sky, with the moon behind them. No R.A.F. bombers were lost before the mainland of Denmark was reached; the report that one German fighter was destroyed is unconfirmed. What is sure is that there was again much nervousness among the air gunners of the first and second waves who had earlier watched the air battle behind them. Several bombers opened fire on each other, and a 100 Squadron Lancaster slightly damaged in this way is believed to have been the only R.A.F. casualty during this part of the flight.

But the bomber-stream still had to cross Denmark with its night-fighter boxes – if the Germans had kept back any aircraft to man them – and its Flak and searchlights; moreover the 'hot spots' of Kiel and Flensburg just across the German border were ready to pounce on any bomber straying within reach of their defences. The crews of 3 and 4 Groups, making up the first wave, negotiated these hazards without too much difficulty, but the Lancasters of 1 Group, the second wave, were not so lucky: one strayed only a few miles to the north of its correct track and was picked up by Esbjerg's searchlights, while a second went twenty miles too far south and flew into Flensburg's defences. Flying Officer E. J. Densley, of 103 Squadron, was watching from the north.

> A Lancaster was flying over Flensburg and half a dozen searchlights were seeking it. At last it was picked up by them, and I could see the aircraft frantically corkscrewing to avoid disaster. Flensburg was one of the very large Flak areas, and the Lancaster exploded in an awe-inspiring mass of flame. None of the crew could possibly have escaped.
>   One of the strategies of Bomber Command's mass raids was that there was safety in numbers and the lesson one had to learn very early was to keep on track at all times. The unfortunate crew of the bomber I had seen had paid the penalty of ignoring this essential element of night bombing over Germany. The night was clear and I remember wondering how they had got so far off track ... I do not recall any casualties on our own squadron but I was fairly new and would probably not have known many people.

It is again ironical that the witness of a bomber's destruction was a man from the same squadron, despite Densley's failure to remember his squadron suffering a casualty. The crew, captained by Pilot Officer P. J. O'Donnell, were on their third operation. There were no survivors. The Lancaster had not been destroyed by Flak, however; Oberleutnant Gerhard Raht, of II/NJG 3, had spotted the bomber in the searchlights, fired off a signal flare to silence the Flak, and then swiftly dispatched the Lancaster. The outcome at Esbjerg had been almost identical. The searchlights had held the bomber for a night fighter, probably a Junkers 88 piloted by Unteroffizier Günther Liersch, to shoot down into the sea. The crew of the second Lancaster was probably that of Squadron Leader F. B. Slade, a flight commander of 12 Squadron well into his second tour. Again there were no survivors.

An even worse blow was to befall the third and final wave of the bomber-stream which had already had such a harassing time. Leutnant Hans Meissner and his radar operator, Unteroffizier Josef Krinner, had been delayed by slight engine trouble in their take-off from Schleswig/Jagel and had been only halfway to Berlin in their Messerschmitt 110 when they had seen the glow of fires at Peenemünde. Krinner describes subsequent events.

> Then came new orders. I had been in touch with Oberleutnant Riedel, a fighter-control officer I had often worked well with; we

had achieved three shoot-downs with him in box *Kiebitz* in the past. He told us to give up flying to Berlin and go to *Ameise* – a box on the east coast of Denmark – so we flew back to that area. We had no more contact with him after that and, when I tried to get into contact with *Ameise*, I could get nothing from them either.

It was a wonderful full-moon night. Suddenly I picked up a lot of contacts with my *Lichtenstein* radar. There were at least five contacts, all clear ones. I guided the pilot to the first and, at about 200 metres, he told me he'd got it. He'd seen it. It was a Lancaster. He saw the eight flames of the exhaust. I looked back at this stage, for safety's sake. I wanted to make sure that there was no Intruder behind us or even a German who might mistake us for a bomber.

Meissner closed up to within about fifty metres of the bomber – below and behind – opened fire and hit the right inner engine. It exploded after just one burst of fire, and large chunks of that engine broke off. We banked and watched it falling down in flames and saw it explode on the ground.

I got into touch with Jagel and reported a shoot-down in the normal manner so that they could get cross bearings. We had been flying north while making our report and, while doing so, picked up another contact straightaway, about 1,000 metres away. Exactly the same thing happened. We shot him down and reported it.

Then we flew in a large circle and, while doing this, I picked up several more contacts flying towards us. The closing speeds were very fast. Meissner turned quickly and I picked up one of them from the rear and got right up to it – forty or fifty metres. Those great wings were spread out right across the front of us; we were too near really. After one burst of fire there was a huge explosion in the engine we had aimed at. Parts flew past us on all sides. None of them hit us but our cockpit was covered with oil. I think it must have been oil and not petrol because we couldn't see. That Lancaster went straight down, fast, not slowly like the other two. We felt our engine might be in trouble so we landed at our home airfield. Meissner had to slide open the side panel of the cockpit to see the ground because of that oil on the windshield.

Not one of those three bombers had fired a shot at us or tried to evade us. I don't think they had seen us at all, and I don't think any of them were using what you call Window, either; there was no interference on my radar.

Meissner's and Krinner's three successes had taken just nine minutes. The victims were all 5 Group Lancasters. The first and second were captained by Pilot Officer T. E. Tomlin and Flying Officer H. J.

Randall, of 49 Squadron, the third by Wing Commander I. J. McGhie, the commander of 619 Squadron. These aircraft had not strayed from their correct track, but there were no survivors to tell why the German fighter was not spotted, particularly after the first Lancaster had gone down and should have advertised the presence of danger. These were all experienced crews.

There are several personal aspects of these losses. The sister of one of the dead R.A.F. men writes of her brother's tail gunner, whom she had once met, as 'pretty terrified of his job, poor lad,' and a Danish contributor writes, 'The war in the air was tough. From a police report near one of the crashes we read that the heart of a human being was found in the field near the aircraft.' By coincidence, Wing Commander McGhie's wife and family had come close to death earlier in the night from enemy action at the quiet little town of Woodhall Spa, near her husband's airfield, where a bomber had dropped two parachute mines. The resulting explosion destroyed a hotel, a block of flats, and eight other buildings, and caused damage to nearly 300 more. Three people were killed and sixty-six injured.

A few German fighters followed the bomber-stream out over the North Sea, but most of the remaining combats reported were brief and inconclusive. There was one exception. The reader may remember, from an earlier chapter, a German pilot, Unteroffizier Benno Gramlich, and his crew with 'miserable morale' over their failure to secure their first success; a bomber they had made contact with earlier in the evening had easily given them the slip. Gramlich's Junkers 88 was still on box duty, controlled now from Heligoland, when the first bombers returning from Peenemünde flew nearby.

> We had been listening endlessly to those monotonous instructions: 'Course 90 degrees. Course 270 degrees. Circle,' when there came the excited voice of the control officer. 'I have a contact for you. Range 30 kilometres. Height 2,600 metres. Come on to 260 degrees. Top speed.'
>
> We had to get to 2,800 metres to find the bomber. Then we had him on the *Lichtenstein* radar. He burnt immediately. Blinded by the jet of flame, we nearly rammed him. When we circled back over the sea, it was already lying on the water. It was uncannily quiet in our cockpit, and then one of us said what we were all thinking: 'Those poor chaps; none of them got out.'
>
> When we landed at Westerland, we had to work the wheels and flaps by hand. They had hit our hydraulics; they could have hit us! This relentless, merciless 'you or me'.

Gramlich was credited with the destruction of a 'Short Stirling', but the only two Stirlings lost that night were definitely shot down near Peenemünde. His victim was probably one of the two Halifaxes of 4 Group which were lost without trace. The location of the combat was seventy miles south of the bomber-stream's track; it is possible that the aircraft had been disabled earlier and forced to take this lethal short cut. Gramlich's night-fighter crew had thus gained their first success; on their nineteenth operational flight. They spent the rest of the war collecting five more night successes and one daylight one.

German fighters had been landing all over northern Germany for some time. Those pilots who had obeyed orders and stayed over Berlin were furious when they heard what easy pickings there had been near that strange target on the Baltic coast. They had no idea why the British should have bombed a remote little place called Peenemünde.

There were the usual difficulties for those German pilots whose aircraft had been damaged or had technical problems. Oberleutnant Henseler, of II/NJG 1, found that the supercharger of one of his engines was in trouble, and decided that his trained crew was more useful to the Luftwaffe than a fighter. He and his radar man baled out safely and let the Messerschmitt 110 crash. Unteroffizier Hölker, who had had such an exciting time with his new *schräge Musik* weapons until hit by a bomber's fire, found himself flying with his cockpit roof blown away. Because the intercom had failed and he could not see behind the radar set against which he sat, he did not know whether his two crew members were dead or wounded inside the plane or whether they had parachuted. He managed to land his aircraft at Güstrow but found the rear of the plane empty. The other two men must have baled out over the sea. The body of one was washed ashore a few days later; that of the second was never found.

A second wave of R.A.F. Intruders was trying to catch the Germans landing. Ten Mosquitoes were patrolling various airfields. Squadron Leader A. W. Mack, of 605 Squadron, nearly crashed when his aircraft lost three feet off the end of a wing and most of its aileron after running into a 'parachute and cable' projectile near Schleswig/Jagel airfield – a remarkable shot in the dark for the patient German operator of this weapon. Mack returned safely. The only Mosquito contact with German fighters was made by Flying Officer A. G. Woods, also of 605 Squadron, who had been sent to patrol Parchim airfield. Woods had watched two German fighters land but had been unable to position himself for attacks on them. His planned patrol time ended at 2 a.m. but, in view of the obvious activity at this airfield only seventy-five miles from the bombers' return route from

Peenemünde, Woods decided to carry on. He was rewarded by the sight of another fighter landing and, being in a good position, was able to give it a long burst. Although many strikes and small explosions were seen, the German plane did not burst into the flames which the Mosquito crew needed to claim a 'destroyed'. Unfortunately, no German documents have been found to identify the German plane or the amount of damage inflicted. All the other Mosquitoes operated over non-active airfields without success or loss.

The shorter-range Beaufighters of 141 Squadron also flew a second wave of sorties. The activities of one of their crews completed a most successful night's work for their squadron. Flying Officer H. E. White was the pilot and the Serrate set operator was Flying Officer M. S. Allen. Flying Officer Allen describes their encounters.

We saw another aircraft stooging alongside us but couldn't believe that it was a German so early in the flight. We both thought it was another 141 Squadron Beau. We only identified it as an enemy after we had let it pass. He was quick enough to turn in behind us. I knew he was close. I remember looking hard into my set, trying to pick it up again, when I looked up through the astrodome which was just above me and saw the lines of tracer passing just over us. I could actually hear the sound of his cannon above our engine noises. I reckon that he was so close behind and going so fast that he couldn't get his nose down. There was just that one short burst. Harry immediately put the wing straight down and we fell out of the sky. We must have dropped several thousand feet.

I expect we were kicking ourselves that we hadn't carried out a proper interception. We certainly realized that we had taken things too casually when we first saw him.

Twenty minutes later, the crew gained a classic Serrate contact with another German fighter. This time, the Beaufighter turned and came up behind it, identifying it visually as a Messerschmitt 110. There was only time to fire a brief burst before the German dived away and was lost, but several hits were believed to have been scored and the fighter was later claimed as damaged. This combat took place over the Dutch coast, and the Beaufighter crew now flew deeper inland, into Germany, in the hope of getting a firm success. Half an hour later, another radar contact was made. Flying Officer Allen again:

Having made a mess of the first contact and having failed to catch the second, we were determined to get this one properly and make no mistake. We went in as close as possible. I kept my eyes on my two radar displays – even when Harry opened fire – so that if the German moved away and Harry lost him, being blinded by our own gun flashes, I could regain contact. This wasn't necessary and the German blew up on our second burst.

Our immediate feeling was that of sheer elation, and then the feeling of wanting to get home and tell the others all about it.

This German was reported as a 'Junkers 88' and claimed as destroyed.

Flying Officers White and Allen had actually destroyed two German fighters. The Messerschmitt 110 which had dived away on their second contact was a IV/NJG 1 aircraft which crashed into the sea just north of its home airfield at Leeuwarden; both crewmen were killed. This made three aircraft lost and five men killed from this élite *Gruppe* which had spent most of the night chasing 141 Squadron's Beaufighters instead of flying in the more profitable operations at Peenemünde. The third contact had also been with a Messerschmitt 110 (not the Junkers 88 recorded), flown by Hauptmann Wilhelm Dormann of III/NJG 1, a pre-war Lufthansa pilot and a veteran night fighter who had been sent up from Twenthe to patrol a local box. His fighter control officer kept vectoring him on to 'stray British bombers' – the wandering Beaufighter.

My radar man kept on obtaining firm contacts but none of them led to a visual sighting. The bombers were flying faster than we were. They knew this area well and were diving through it fast. I was sent higher so that I, too, could dive on the next contact, but that didn't work either.

Then my operator got another contact on his screen. I went after it, but the next thing that happened was that we were hit by well-aimed defensive fire from its rear gunner. My plane started burning and the rudders wouldn't work. We were going straight down. I couldn't contact the radar operator because the intercom had failed. I was pulled out of the plane by strong suction. I made a hard landing and lay in a field until a farm worker found me the next morning.

Hauptmann Dormann suffered severe head injuries and burns and never flew operationally again. He was most interested to be told, nearly forty years later, that there never had been a bomber and that he had been shot down by an Intruder. The body of his radar operator was found near his half-opened parachute.

This action concluded what is believed to have been 141 Squadron's most successful night of the war, with four German aircraft destroyed from two of the best units in the Luftwaffe's night-fighter force. 141 Squadron's old Beaufighters had not suffered a scratch. These actions also represented the last contact between the Luftwaffe and the R.A.F. during this action-packed night.

The return of the Peenemünde bomber force from Denmark to the English coast entailed a two-hour flight over the North Sea. There were no navigational difficulties; the weather remained fine and clear, and for most crews it was an uneventful, even boring passage. A Stirling had this encounter.

> When about half way across the North Sea, our rear gunner identified a Mosquito approaching (from the Berlin diversionary raid). It formated on our starboard wing for a few minutes – about twenty to thirty feet away. We exchanged signs – polite ones – then he got into top gear and walked away from us. Most probably he had breakfasted and was in bed by the time we got home. (Flying Officer G. W. Ingram, 90 Squadron)

This Mosquito was almost certainly a returning Intruder.

The bomber force suffered one more casualty. A distress signal was received from a 419 Squadron Halifax, and two good 'fixes' were obtained before it ceased to transmit; but despite the last fix being only twenty miles from England, and a big search the next day, no trace was ever found of Sergeant John Batterton, a Canadian, and his mostly Canadian crew. It is recorded that 'heavy seas were running'. It is not known whether this aircraft's difficulties were caused by enemy action or by technical trouble.

The honour of being the first aircraft back from a raid usually belonged to the Pathfinders, but not on this night. The crew of Flight Lieutenant Keith Eggleston of 115 Squadron were flying a fast Mark II Lancaster on the last operation of their tour. Having the best aircraft on their squadron and plenty of fuel, they had ignored the ordered speeds and, 'opening up the boost and revs,' had touched down at Little Snoring airfield at 3.25 a.m., only three hours and ten minutes after bombing Peenemünde. Next morning they were 'mildly reprimanded' by the squadron commander for using too much petrol and went on their end-of-tour leave. Eggleston's crew were down eleven minutes before the first of the Pathfinders.

Many of the early crews back had seen little evidence of the action experienced by the later bombers and would be most surprised when they heard the news of the heavy casualties suffered by the 5 and 6 Group squadrons. A 1 Group pilot says that 'as far as our crew was concerned, the whole Peenemünde trip was an interesting doddle', and Pilot Officer Gerry South, a new Pathfinder pilot, writes:

We returned uneventfully to Gransden Lodge and I think my general impression was that, perhaps, this pathfinding business wasn't going to be so bad after all. I little realized that the next operation for which we would be briefed was to be Berlin, the dreaded 'Big City', and that on that raid the two Canadian pilots with whom I joined the squadron would be lost, one never to be seen or heard of again.

The squadrons based in Lincolnshire and East Anglia found clear conditions for their landings, but the Yorkshire airfields had become affected by a sheet of low stratus cloud during the night, and a large-scale diversion was ordered to bases all over southern England; however those Yorkshire-based crews who had not received, or pretended they had not received, the diversion instructions flew straight home in safety. Some damaged planes made 'dodgy' landings at other airfields, but there were no serious casualties. When a 427 Squadron Halifax piloted by Captain C. A. Taylor, an American flying with this Canadian squadron, was diverted to Newmarket, a 2,000-lb. bomb which had 'hung up' over Peenemünde fell on the runway and rolled away ... without exploding.

Another fortunate crew was that of Flight Sergeant W. B. Lambert of 102 Squadron. Their Halifax had been damaged over Peenemünde and the bomb doors had refused to close. The resulting drag had caused most of their fuel to be gone by the time they reached their diversion airfield at Ashbourne in Derbyshire. The response for extra lighting from this non-operational base was poor and, with fuel tanks almost empty, Lambert had to land in semi-darkness. Flight Sergeant W. A. Rice was the wireless operator.

The landing seemed normal until I saw the chequered caravan at the end of the runway go past in the wrong direction and we still hadn't touched down. I rapidly lay flat on my back, feet braced against a cross spar, with my hands clasped behind my head.

We touched down with a thump, bounced, touched down again, continued with the plane rocking violently from side to side until a further thump coincided with the plane dropping its port wing and slewing round. The last impact caused a top hatch to break open and, as the plane slewed to port, a shower of apples came in through the open hatch.

The Halifax had run through the airfield boundary, across a main road along which a convoy of American army trucks drove a few seconds later, through a brick wall, and had come to rest in what appeared to be a kitchen garden.

While we were waiting for transport, a senior officer arrived and was furious to see that we had prematurely dug up his potatoes and picked his apples. As he bemoaned his bad luck, a fireman was adding to his misery by squirting foam all over the aircraft.

When the crew reached the Sergeants' Mess, the duty officer sent out to a local farm for some fresh eggs so that the traditional 'operational' breakfast of bacon and eggs could be provided.

The last aircraft to return from Peenemünde was the Halifax of Sergeant J. McIntosh, of 419 Squadron, who landed at Bassingbourn airfield, home of an American Flying Fortress unit, at 5.53 a.m. McIntosh and his crew had been flying for eight hours and forty minutes.

CHAPTER 14

The Aftermath

The bomber crews were debriefed – with more than usual care – and went to bed, extremely anxious about the outcome of the raid. If it had not been sufficiently successful, they quite expected to be going to Peenemünde again the next night – and the German fighters were unlikely to be fooled again. There was regret on some airfields over missing faces at breakfast, but squadrons had suffered heavy losses before and would do so again. This was a routine part of life. Preliminary reports were rushed to Bomber Command Headquarters, to the Air Ministry and to the War Cabinet. Winston Churchill was attending the Quebec Conference, but he would know the results of the raid within hours.

At 10.00 a.m., a Mosquito piloted by Flight Lieutenant G. E. Hughes flew over Peenemünde and returned safely with photographs showing a heavy concentration of bomb craters in the selected target areas, many shattered buildings, and some fires still burning. The good news flashed around the bomber airfields that Peenemünde could be considered 'dealt with'. A return visit would not be necessary. Congratulatory messages were soon on their way to the squadrons from High Wycombe and from the headquarters of the various groups. Men turned their backs on the Peenemünde operation and thoughts turned to the future. It would be nearly a year before they learned exactly what they had bombed, and that their work on that night had given Britain a breathing-space from rocket bombardment.

No operations were ordered for the next night. The Australian 460 Squadron, at Binbrook, which had been forced to postpone a party to celebrate the squadron's 1,000th Lancaster sortie, had sent 168 men to Peenemünde, and every one of them had returned unharmed. The delayed celebration took place at the Pier Dance Hall at Cleethorpes. Sergeant W. L. Miller was there.

Last memories. Came out of the dance-hall heat and confusion to get some air and tripped over some of my crew and other cobbers collapsed on the pier with a red fire bucket full of beer and, before I could speak, a glass was pushed into my hand. The rest is vague but it was a grand finale to a heavy period of raids.

I understand that the Mayor of the town sent a letter to the C.O. that we would not be welcome in the town again. I wonder what his reaction would have been if he had been with us on the night before.

Back at Peenemünde, the survivors had emerged from their shelters when the bombing ceased. In the housing estate, people 'greeted each other as if we had returned from a long journey'. For many the first instinct, in this mainly civilian area, was to locate their families and flee from the blazing village. Gertrud Pawehls, the daughter of the chief of civil police at Peenemünde, had run into the nearby woods when her home was hit.

I was worried about my parents because the wall between two houses had collapsed and I had seen my mother fall. There was the crackling of the burning houses – all the surrounding houses were on fire – and the street itself, recently tarmacked, was burning in places. I heard the cries of people from the direction of the beach, nothing from the direction of the houses; I think they had all fled or were dead. Then I saw my father guiding my mother; I was delighted that they were both safe. He had dragged her out through a hole in the wall. He left mother with me and went back into the burning houses to help other people.

Mother and I set off through the woods in the direction of Trassenheide. We just wanted to get away from the bombing. On the way we passed a parachute on the ground. There was no body on it. I wanted to go and have a look at it; perhaps someone needed help. I wasn't afraid. I had nothing against the English; both sides were in it together. Mother was frightened though; she was always afraid something would happen to me – I was the only daughter. I never heard what happened to the airman.

We went on through the trees. I could see people streaming along the beach – a whole exodus of the population, mothers pushing prams – all sorts of people. We thought they must have lost their homes like us.

Eventually, we reached a tent where some Russian soldiers gave us a drink. Then I saw my first wounded, a girl who had lost part of her face and a man without an arm. He told us he had only just come from Hannover two days earlier. I was very surprised that such badly wounded people could still stand.

Father found us after this. He was crying from the reaction – the loss of our house and the worry about us. My mother had dark brown hair till then but it turned grey immediately after that night.

Inge Holz, a secretary, and her friend Lisl, from the young

ladies' home, the *Ledigenheim*, were among those escaping along the beach.

> We went back to our room quickly but there was nothing there so we left, crawling out of another window, still carrying our bags; Lisl only had one now. The grass in the dunes was burning and what we did was to take a blanket and use it to make a series of stepping stones across the dunes to the beach.
>
> When we reached the beach, we could see a lot of bomb craters. There was one German soldier standing there and he was shouting at the top of his voice, very angily, 'What are you doing? That's not right!' There were unexploded bombs everywhere and we had to be very careful. He made us all line up in single file and we were told to thread our way carefully, right on the edge of the sea.

One 'terribly shocked' girl, dressed only in a fur coat over her nightdress, was seen running down the road away from the housing estate shouting out, over and over again, that she wanted to go home. Her home was a little town on the shores of Lake Constance in southern Germany. Apparently, she did manage to reach her destination by train, screaming out at every station that she wanted to go home. One of her male colleagues says that she had always been nervous; she was a radar operator at the rocket firing site and had invariably fainted when there had been a test firing.

The survivors in other parts of Peenemünde and in the foreign workers' camp at Trassenheide started to pull themselves together. No plan had envisaged such widespread destruction, and the early recovery work was all done on a makeshift basis by local initiative. The Peenemünde fire brigade, never very large, was hardly to be seen; some of its units had been hit in the bombing, and the remainder had been unable to move far because of cratered roads. Only primitive fire-fighting took place for some hours, and many wooden buildings burnt to the ground, only the brick chimneys remaining to stand, gaunt, above the ashes.

At Trassenheide, an army officer with soldiers in lorries arrived from outside Peenemünde and took command. An eyewitness says, 'There were cries for help in many languages.' The camp and the surrounding woods were searched for wounded men. Control in the housing estate was provided by the leaders of the local Nazi Party – many of them men who normally worked as scientists in the rocket establishment. Helpers who arrived found the estate 'a sea of fire'. There were plenty of leaders at the Experimental Works. General Dornberger's adjutant, Oberleutnant Magirius, says that after Dornberger's first reaction, 'My beautiful Peenemünde!', his chief 'immediately started commanding Peenemünde again'. The head-quarters building had not been hit – there were only a few tiles burning – and Dornberger got down to work at once. After issuing his preliminary orders, he left von Braun to take command of recovery work in the Experimental Area and set off on a bicycle to see what was happening elsewhere. The bicycle soon had to be abandoned and, on foot, the general continued his tour of what had once constituted his fine command.

News that Peenemünde had been raided and had suffered seriously soon reached the German leaders in Berlin and elsewhere. It was too much for one man. Generaloberst Hans Jeschonnek, the long-serving Chief of Staff of the Luftwaffe and the man who had to face Goering and Hitler when things went wrong, heard the news at his headquarters in East Prussia. A few hours earlier, Jeschonnek had been forced to endure a blasting over the telephone from Goering over the confusion caused to the Luftwaffe defences by the Mosquito diversion raid. A few hours before that, Hitler had given him a verbal dressing-down, presumably over the Luftwaffe's declining ability to protect Germany from such disasters as the destruction of Hamburg by the R.A.F. and the precision bombing that very day by the U.S.A.A.F. of the factories at Schweinfurt and Regensburg, important targets previously considered beyond the effective range of the Americans. It was all too much for Jeschonnek. He wrote a note: 'I cannot work with Goering any more. Long live the Führer!' Then he shot himself.

Full daylight came late to Peenemünde that day; the smoke from the smouldering or still burning fires shut out the sunlight. Many people speak of the great shock experienced with their first clear view of the worst-bombed areas. Great bomb craters were everywhere; people could sometimes only clamber with difficulty over the tumbled ground. Trees and houses were shattered or swept away completely by the R.A.F.'s 4,000-lb. blast bombs. Everywhere there was the stink of explosive and fire. People found it difficult to realize that this was their old familiar Peenemünde; one person says that 'at times we lost our way because it all looked so different.' And, in those early hours before the working parties had completed their tasks, there were bodies, or fragments of bodies, to be encountered at every turn. A Polish man says that the worst areas 'were really something to see – the ruins and the human meat'. There is no doubt that the dawn of 18 August saw Peenemünde at its grimmest. Helmut Graeber, the Protestant chaplain, had these chilling encounters.

A man I knew very well sat outside his destroyed house, holding one small child in his lap; another was wrapped up in a towel in a parcel. I asked him, 'Herr — how did you get through this night and where is the rest of your family?' They were a family with four children, two of whom I had christened and confirmed. He merely pointed with his hand behind him and said – and I will never forget it for the rest of my life – quoting from the book of Job: 'The Lord has given and the Lord has taken away. Blessed be the name of the Lord.' I don't know whether even the writer of these lines could have quoted this sentence in a similar situation, however strong and enduring his faith.

Then I managed to get through to the school building, which was not damaged. Soldiers were carrying the recovered bodies into its basement. The area leader of the Hitler Youth was also there and he greeted me with the raised arm salute, saying, 'Vicar, do you *still* believe in your God about whom you preach to others?'

But the Germans are good at recovery and regrouping under pressure, and Peenemünde started to pull itself together quickly. It had always been an intelligent and disciplined community. Some of the first arrivals from outside were the workers who lived in nearby villages and had escaped the bombing. Because the electric railway was out of action and the roads were cratered, the only way in was on foot; to reach their old places of work, they had to walk through the horrors of the housing estate where so many of their colleagues and their families had lived. They soon found out which of their friends had died. Important personalities from Berlin also arrived quickly; the sensible ones flew into Peenemünde West airfield.

Soon after dawn, General Dornberger and Wernher von Braun took off in a Fieseler Storch and inspected the whole of their establishment. It was a sobering sight. Dornberger was 'struck to the heart by this first comprehensive view of the destruction'.[1] At 11 a.m., the energetic chief called a conference of all his senior men to organize both the immediate task of recovery and the swiftest possible re-establishment of 'normal work'. This mid-morning conference would be a daily feature throughout the recovery period. Dornberger's men often found themselves doing unusual jobs: Professor Wierer, a scientist, was ordered to oversee the collection of all the dead bodies, and a message soon came back that he needed twenty lorries. Probably within thirty-six hours of the bombing, someone – it is not known who – brought into use a new title as a *Deckname* or 'cover name' for the establishment. Instead of '*Heeresversuchs Anstalt, Peenemünde*', 'HAP' for short, this military unit was now to be known as '*Heeres Artillerie Park Nr 11*' (Army

Artillery Depot No. 11); this innocent-sounding title with the same initials was henceforth used on all correspondence.

Zinnowitz, the first village outside the bombing area, became the base for the treatment of the wounded and for evacuation. The main hospital there found itself with only one doctor, and he was not a surgeon; the rest were attending a conference at Stettin. Fortunately, a military doctor who was a patient at a nearby hospital had had experience of field surgery in Russia and was able to deal with the worst casualties until surgical teams arrived. Only Germans were treated here. Some of the lightly wounded and most of the foreign wounded were taken further afield; one Pole says that, although the foreigners had to wait until the Germans in his party had been looked after, the medical treatment he did receive then and in ensuing months was excellent. The school at Zinnowitz became the organizing centre for evacuation. All reports say that this proceeded smoothly. Those who had been bombed out were soon found homes in the surrounding area, and even families whose homes had not been hit were now willing to leave Peenemünde. Another group to depart was a party of army apprentices, sent to their homes on leave.

We were mothered along and shown a lot of sympathy because we were so young and we were excused the clearing-up work after the raid. But you know what feelings were like at that time; we were almost offended by this consideration. We were, after all, fourteen to eighteen years old. (Gerhard Rühr)

The bombing of the workers' camp at Trassenheide posed a severe accommodation problem. Although there was much heavy work waiting to be done, it was decided that those men whose huts had been destroyed and others whose huts were needed for bombed-out Germans must be sent away. Long columns of Poles, Russians and others were thus to be seen tramping down the road to Zinnowitz in order to be put on trains to Swinemünde. Some would soon return to a temporary camp erected in the woods, but many had seen their last of Peenemünde. All these movements, of the wounded, of civilians being evacuated, of labourers being moved out, signified the beginning of a prolonged rundown in the size and importance of the community.

Back at Peenemünde, a large number of men of many nationalities were carrying out a variety of tasks in the smoking ruins. Matthias Kempkens, one of a party of sailors brought in from a naval Flak training unit at Ueckeritz, was now working at Trassenheide.

It was a gruesome scene. The large forest around was burnt into charred remnants. The same applied to the wooden barracks of the forced workers. There were only the chimneys and fireplaces made of brick remaining now, and sometimes these had one or two burnt bodies stuck into them – human beings who, in their crazed condition, had not been able to escape from the flames and had tried to find refuge in the chimney. We took them out of there as charred puppets. There were masses of burnt and smashed bodies lying around. There seemed to be thousands. We ought to erect monuments to these people.

We received our meal at the lunch break from the field kitchens and, because the air was full of stink and dust, I and many of my comrades were ill. It was easier to vomit than to eat. At 3 p.m., those of us who were sick were collected and taken back to Ueckeritz.

By contrast, Siegfried Winter, a scientist, was performing an unusual job at the other end of Peenemünde.

I was in a group of men formed very hurriedly and ordered to do two kinds of work in the research area.

We got black and white paint and climbed on to the roofs of some of the undamaged buildings and painted black and white lines to simulate the charred beams of burnt roofs. We had plenty of buckets but were a bit short of paint. At the same time, men with spades were removing all the grass and shrubs and top sand from circular areas, thus exposing new light-coloured sand in the shape of bomb craters. This work was done around the vital wind-tunnel area to create the impression of greater damage in this important area before the expected R.A.F. photographic plane.

It is also known that some minor undamaged or lightly damaged buildings were deliberately blown up to create the same impression.

Everyone working at Peenemünde at this time remembers the random explosions of delayed-action bombs. A proportion of the loads, usually 1,000-pounders, had been deliberately fitted with delayed-action fuzes to hamper the work of recovery and prolong the effects of the raid. The 'delays' were set by the R.A.F. for between six hours and three days after the time of release. In addition, the many bombs whose fuzes had not worked properly were likely to explode whenever disturbed. All these were a source of acute anxiety to everyone. Stefan Janowski, a Pole, was working in or near the housing estate. His 'tanker lorry' appears in another report as a 'fire engine'.

We were ordered to push a damaged tanker lorry. Not far away was a hole in the concrete roadway with a notice saying that there was an unexploded bomb. While we were working, the bomb exploded. The lorry went up in pieces, bits of the concrete road flew all over the place, and some of my Polish friends were hit and others crushed by lumps of concrete. There was awful screaming by the wounded and a terrible scene of flight by the rest of us and a cloud of drifting, yellow smoke. A soldier who had been passing by lay screaming terribly; I think he had broken his spine.

After lorries had taken away the wounded, I felt very strange – stiff legs, trembling knees, and I couldn't walk for fear and shock.

Robert Czech – despite his name, another Pole – also witnessed an explosion.

Our job was to mark the positions of the dead for later burial by placing sticks with white flags attached and then covering the bodies with hay or sacking until other parties came to take them away. We were also collecting together the many small unexploded incendiary bombs, but we were warned by an officer not to touch the larger bombs or a jelly-like substance which was likely to burst into flame.

One German in our group, a chap in his early twenties who had been kicked out of Sweden for petty crime – a very jovial chap, always up to mischief, stealing from the kitchens etcetera but always friendly and chatting – found an orange-coloured bomb. He picked up a stick and poked at it from behind a tree. Nothing happened, so he came out, but just then the bomb burst with a spluttering sound and immediately showered this man with a flaming substance. He became a human torch. He covered his face with his hands and ran off blindly. Someone tripped him to stop his flight and rolled him in the sand to put out the flames.

His skin was badly burnt, although his face seemed to be all right, but he died later. We were very sorry because we had lost such a lively character.

Many of the unexploded bombs had fallen into the sea, and these, too, would continue to detonate in following days. A German girl also reports that it was not safe to swim at Peenemünde for several weeks for fear of contact with the phosphorus from some of the larger incendiary bombs.

Jean Degert, a French forced worker, has recorded several interesting events he witnessed that day.

I put my suitcases on the edge of the road with those of my friends. The Hitler Youth go to work, clearing up; they are singing. The naval firemen from Swinemünde are already here. A German officer, proud of his find, shows off the parachute of a shot-down airman. Lorries full of blankets arrive. Dead bodies are wrapped up and taken to be laid out in rows in the main canteen.

We are not closely supervised now but we think it best to keep well out of the way. They pick on the foreigners for the dirtiest and most dangerous work.

Curiosity draws us to the factory area – but carefully. We can't get further than the level crossing. Although the Germans don't say anything, I recognize some who used to work in the woodwork shop and, seeing their empty look, know that they must have been through a veritable hell. They are very excitable and I do not persist.

I look to see if I can find the crossing keeper – a young German Labour Service girl who had always worn proudly the black uniform of the German railways. She is dead in the ditch which runs alongside what one can only guess was once the railway track. An army lorry comes along, two soldiers get down, pick up the body, one by the feet and one by the arms, and swing her up into the lorry in which there are already other corpses. You cannot be surprised that these people, who had so little respect for their own, could behave with such little humanity to other nationalities.

One of the saddest sights at Peenemünde was the collection of the bodies of the German girls killed in the group of buildings near the beach which had been their homes. Czeslaw Bloch, a Pole only eighteen years old, was there.

It was the first time in my life that I had seen so many people killed in one place. It was a terrible moment; I was completely taken by surprise. For a long time I just stood motionless, almost paralysed and unconscious, and it was only the shouts of 'murderers' and 'bandits' of the distraught Germans that brought me out of this trance. I stepped aside and cried bitterly – not only me; we were all affected alike; we were only children yet. With great pain and grief, we removed all eleven dead girls and three men to one place from where they were taken to the cemetery.

That was a hard day for me. I could not understand why so many young people had to die – for what and why? We Poles hoped that the bombing would lead to the end of the war but we were all sorry that so many innocents died. I would dearly love to have seen those torturing Gestapo in Poland bombed. They were the ones who should have paid the penalty.

But life had to carry on as usual although, even today, I still have nightmares about that scene.

Peenemünde buried its dead on Saturday 21 August, three days after the raid. A clearing had been made in the woods between Trassenheide and Karlshagen and long communal graves prepared, although a few of the more prominent dead had individual graves. One man had come from Stettin and asked to take his daughter's body home for burial. The Party official in charge, knowing that the girl had been burnt beyond recognition, told him that, because she and her friends had died together serving Peenemünde, they must be buried together there. The father seemed satisfied.

The burial ceremony was a sad reflection of the conflicts inside the Germany of those times. Chaplain Helmut Graeber describes what happened.

My Catholic colleague from Swinemünde and I were asked to conduct the religious ceremony for the burial. Even before we arrived at that cemetery, we were suddenly confronted by the district leader of the Party – naturally dressed up in the uniform of a Luftwaffe major – who said, 'Gentlemen, if you try to preach about that Jewish lout, Jesus, I will immediately order the troops to march off.'

We decided that my Catholic colleague would read the liturgy and I would preach the sermon. We agreed that the sermon would be based on Romans, Chapter 14, Verses 7 and 8. Naturally it would be related to Christ, and naturally it would refer to the Christian belief in Resurrection.

And then that major really did give the order, 'Soldiers. Attention! Right turn! Quick march!' But the Commanding Admiral, Baltic Area, was standing next to me. His louder voice rang out. 'Soldiers. Stand fast! Vicar, please continue!'

There were many people present and all of them had come together here to attend the ceremony and I will never forget how most of them including the loud voice of that admiral standing next to me – said the Lord's Prayer at the end of the ceremony. Thus ended a chapter at Peenemünde.

There were others on the move around Peenemünde – the R.A.F. men who had managed to survive being shot down. The swift transition from being a member of an operational crew to being a lonely hunted fugitive in enemy territory was one that every bomber man knew that he might have to face.

Opening the hatch had saved my life because the glare from the burning engine illuminated the interior and I was able to spot my 'chute. One half second later I had it snapped on and was diving out the hatch.

I hung up there, seemingly for a long time, watching the aircraft circle down, flaming, and crash. I watched the fires and listened to the battle still going on. Then the ground came up and I was on German soil and, suddenly, a very lonely man. (Flight Sergeant L. G. Christmas, 434 Squadron)

It was a very depressing time. I was pretty sure that only the navigator and myself had survived the attack. Our career on the squadron had been short; my parents would be informed that I was missing in action and the chances of getting out of Germany would be pretty slim. (Sergeant R. T. Johnson, 427 Squadron)

Several bombers had crashed near Peenemünde itself; one was found next morning, almost intact, in a shallow lake between the Experimental Works and Peenemünde West airfield. This has been tentatively identified as a 44 Squadron Lancaster from which there were no survivors. Parachuting airmen from at least two crews came down very close to the bombing area. Sergeant L. C. Wood of 15 Squadron landed next to a German Flak position and heard the gunners' shouted fire orders and the gun firing. He slipped away unseen but was captured later. Sergeant C. S. Carter, of the same crew, came down in the water near the shore of what may have been one of the inland lakes south-east of Peenemünde. He was able to float easily in his lifejacket.

For the next twenty-five minutes I just lay back watching the raid. I recall feeling no fear of being hit because of the accuracy of the Pathfinder flares and subsequent bombing. I had often wondered what the effect was of virtually being underneath a concentrated R.A.F. raid and, that morning, I knew. It was deafening with bombs dropping, almost spectacular with the immediate fires and flames – and interspersed with aircraft going down on fire.

Sergeant Chris Leeming, of 620 Squadron, came down just west of Peenemünde and found himself directly under the air battle. He could see 'the tracer of the dogfights above me; that tracer was a beautiful sight – lovely patterns in the sky.' When he decided to move, he had to hold the back panel of his parachute harness over his head to protect him from the empty cartridge cases falling all around. Two members of a 35 Squadron Halifax came down in the river Peene and were rescued by rowing-boat. After being landed in the harbour of the old Peenemünde village, they were taken into the establishment. Next morning they were marched right through the areas which had been bombed. Sergeant P. H. Palmer was 'not much impressed with the moderate damage' in the two large assembly buildings, more so by the destruction in the housing estate, and very upset by the sight of dead children there. A German soldier who had lost some of his friends in the bombing of the housing estate tried to attack him with a rifle and bayonet but was restrained by other Germans. These two men were later flown out of Peenemünde in a light aircraft. One Canadian airman, not identified, wandered through the woods around Peenemünde for three days but could not find his way off the peninsula; he therefore approached a 'German' soldier and asked to be taken prisoner. The soldier was actually one of the Luxembourg conscripts – but he could do nothing to help the Canadian, who was taken into custody.

Some of the R.A.F. men were captured very quickly.

As I looked down on the little village which lay beneath me, I could quite easily discern the local population making a circle for me to fall in and I became very concerned as to what was going to happen to me once I landed. No sooner had this thought entered my head when I hit the ground and I experienced a sharp pain in my right leg which I thought I had broken. By this time, the first of their Home Guard was on to me and, with a cry of jubilation, shouted, 'For you the war is over,' and promptly gave me a kick in the ribs. I was roughly pulled to my feet; it was then I realized what the pain in my leg was – I had broken my foot on landing without my flying boot. I was led away to a barn and locked in.

I could hear the last notes of our other aircraft as the lads turned for home and their bacon-and-egg breakfast which, to me, just then seemed to be the most important thing in the world. (Pilot Officer W. J. Lowe, 49 Squadron)

I set off but soon heard voices and I was caught. There were three Germans – a soldier with a gun, a policeman with a revolver, and a civilian with a stick. It was the soldier who spotted me. I was very conscious that the next thirty seconds would be my most dangerous period. I ran straight down and stood right next to him so that he couldn't get his gun up. I don't know whether he would have shot me but I was pleased it was the soldier and not the policeman because, later on, the policeman wanted to beat me up and it was the soldier who stopped him.

After that, things quietened down. I stopped being frightened and even began to feel cocky – reaction I suppose. I had some sweets and even offered them some. It was just cheek; that's all it was. (Sergeant W. Sparkes, 44 Squadron)

Much of the air battle had taken place over the Greifswalder Bodden, a large stretch of sea to the west of Peenemünde where many R.A.F. men lost their lives when they landed by parachute. This is the account of one man who was fortunate enough to survive.

I remembered a little bit from the service manual about judging your height from the size of the waves, getting out of the parachute harness and dropping out of it about twenty feet up. The idea was that, when you landed, you went one way and the parachute another. If you got covered by the parachute you could drown.

I could see the waves and I thought of all this but I couldn't make up my mind whether they were big waves seen from high up or little waves from low down. Actually, they were small waves and I hit the water unexpectedly with my parachute still on. I was surprised to find that it fell to one side and didn't collapse over me. There must have been a breeze from the land. This kept the parachute full of air, and I actually started to go out to sea on my back. I managed to get rid of the parachute and my other flying boot and started to swim to land.

I swam and swam until I could go no further. By that time I think shock was setting in, and I just had to rest. I let my legs down and found I was standing on firm sand only knee deep in water. From my subsequent walk ashore, I decided that it was a gently shelving beach and that I had been needlessly swimming for much of the time. (Sergeant C. A. Bicknell, 467 Squadron)

Squadron Leader Tony Lambert, the 620 Squadron second-tour pilot, remained at his controls while six of his crew baled out – two of them drowned – and then found that his Stirling was too low for himself and his new second pilot to follow. Lambert decided to attempt a 'ditching' near the coast.

The Stirling was the only heavy bomber with two sets of controls and it was useful to have the second pilot helping me.

I could see the surface of the sea easily. In the final few seconds I cut the engines and kept it straight in my approach by using the rudder and eased the nose up to lose as much speed as possible to ensure that we hit the sea tail first. We had been taught all that in flying training and it went according to plan. There was only a gentle impact and the nose didn't dig in. I wasn't even strapped in; I had been ready to bale out earlier and had no time to restrap.

The dinghy opened automatically and was floating, tethered to the wing, but I decided I wasn't going to sit there and await capture. Our orders were always to try and evade capture and return to 'get on with the war'. I decided to swim to the shore, which I could see about half a mile away. I just managed it, although I was quite exhausted when I crawled ashore. I do remember seeing other aircraft falling, some quite near me, but I was really concentrating on my own survival.

I last saw the second pilot about halfway to the shore, but after that I was aware that he was no longer in sight. I was sorry when you told me that he had died; he could have stayed in the dinghy and been saved.

All R.A.F. men were ordered to evade capture for as long as possible and to attempt to reach a neutral country. Most of the men on the run turned westwards and started walking towards the port of Rostock, sixty miles away, or Denmark, two hundred miles distant. Their eventual destination was Sweden. Sergeant R. Garnett, of 467 Squadron, met up with two other members of his crew and they set off on the evening of the 18th.

We happened to meet a man on the other side of the hedge. The German greeted us with '*Guten Abend*' and we muttered something back and got away with it. After that, we thought that it was going to be easy; all we had to do was avoid serious conversation, just greet people like that and we would manage. We really felt we might reach Sweden that way. Talk about being naïve!

Then, within twenty minutes, we came to a large farm with many outbuildings on the road we were taking and decided to walk right through it rather than skirt it. But we came face to face with two old men in uniform with shotguns. I think they were more frightened of us than we were of them until I saw their guns waving about. I was definitely the most frightened of the five then.

Flight Sergeant R. W. Charman, a Canadian from Calgary, was equally optimistic.

Wow! Alone in enemy territory, 6,300 miles from home! Where do I go from here?

I thought of the lectures on what to do in enemy territory. Number one, bury parachute; check rations and water purifier, maps etcetera. I checked the maps, hoping for a detailed one of the area, but no such luck. Whoever had packed the maps thought the operation was Italy or North Africa for that was all the maps there were. I became angry and searched the heavens for the North Star. It was quite easy to locate, so, with a bearing on it, I began skirting the Baltic coastline westward. Even in those days, Sweden had the reputation for beautiful blondes. That would be a lot more fun than dropping bombs on the Fatherland.

Charman was captured a few hours later.

A large-scale manhunt across the farming countryside to the west of Peenemünde was taking place, and many of the would-be evaders were rounded up by the German *Landwacht*, the equivalent of the Home Guard, or by farmers armed with sporting guns. Not one R.A.F. man reached Rostock, Denmark or Sweden. The men who were captured in these country areas were rarely harmed. Once it had been established that they were unarmed and unlikely to be violent, the German civilians often showed their prisoners much kindness. One man, taken to the home of a large landowner, was asked to sign the visitors' book, and 'the ladies of the house showed much sympathy for my poor mother who would be worried about me.' Another man found that he was in the home of an English-born lady, now married to a Luftwaffe officer. 'She was too scared to elaborate. She came from Berlin and I told her not to go back there; it was next on our list.'

Sergeant Bill Sparkes had an interesting encounter soon after he was captured.

> A young German pilot came to see me. He looked a typical, clean-looking German, square cut, trim and blond. I remember that he had no hat on. He treated me with great respect. He spoke to me in English and told me that he had shot my plane down. I felt amazed that I was talking to someone who had shot me down. I don't remember my answer. I do know that I didn't tell him anything much but I did ask someone what had happened to my crew; it was probably that pilot I asked.

The German pilot was Leutnant Peter Spoden, who had just shot down his first R.A.F. bomber and, being anxious to see the result, had landed at Greifswald and travelled by motorcycle to the crash site about twelve kilometres away.

> They told me that they had a prisoner from that bomber, so we drove to see him, and soon I was talking to him. He was a tall young man, good-looking, with a white sweater.
>
> I tried talking to him in my English – which wasn't too good then – and I asked him if he was from that bomber. He refused to answer and just kept on saying that he was 'Sergeant Sparkes, number so-and-so' – I forget what it was, and that he came from Portsmouth. I told him some of the details of the combat but, again, he would only give me his name etcetera. Then, after I had told him some more, he suddenly became more interested and friendly.

After that, I went to see the smouldering wreckage of the bomber. I wanted a souvenir like Baron von Richthofen in the First World War, but the officer in charge said that it was not allowed. I was shocked when I saw the bodies of the dead R.A.F. men and I must confess that the whole matter affects me very deeply when I think of it now. Those young men, in their early twenties, were just the age of my four boys today. It all seems like nonsense now.

Otto Beisswenger, then a fifteen-year-old 'boy sailor' at Wolgast, was also moved by the sight of a dead R.A.F. man whose identity is not known.

When we found the plane, we were told that we were not allowed to look around the wreck, but I went and spoke with my immediate superior about this and he arranged that a few of us could satisfy our curiosity. What I saw next, in conjunction with what I was to see in the following days when we were sent to work at Peene-münde, was so to make its impact upon me that it changed my whole attitude to life – at first not consciously, but already in noticeable fashion. That is why I can remember these events so well.

The pilot was still sitting in the cockpit holding his controls. Externally, he didn't seem to be very badly hurt. His face was not disfigured by the heat but, rather, he gave the impression of being asleep, that is if the position of the head hadn't made such a thing impossible. His head was bent over at an angle of about forty-five degrees but without any sign of injury. All the same, it was a gruesome sight. He was young, certainly handsome, and probably tall and slim.

At this moment, I thought of two of my brothers who, after being wounded, had died in field hospitals in Russia. I asked myself why young people had to lose their lives in this way and imagined that, perhaps, the same might happen to me.

Most of the bodies of the R.A.F. men who died in the area west of Peenemünde were buried at Greifswald. Those found in the immediate Peenemünde area were either laid properly to rest on the airfield there or buried in the most casual fashion in the sand dunes where they had drifted ashore. Only one of these graves could be traced after the war.

The R.A.F. prisoners were mostly collected at Greifswald, some in the civilian gaol, some at the airfield. Their experiences from that time on, though interesting, are little different from those of men shot down on other raids, and I shall not go into them here – with one exception. That story starts with Oberleutnant Friedrich-Karl Müller, who had shot down two bombers near Peenemünde. A few days later, Müller flew to visit the commander of the Luftwaffe's central interrogation centre, *Dulag Luft*, at Oberursel near Frankfurt. When he asked if any of the recently arrived R.A.F. men had been in the bombers he had shot down, he was introduced to an R.A.F. sergeant who, it was said, 'had been very helpful'; Müller was even allowed to fly him back to Hangelar airfield for a short 'holiday'.

The identity of the 'helpful' airman is known: it is almost certain that he was not in either of the bombers shot down by Müller. Believed to have given information freely at Oberursel, he may have acted as a 'stool pigeon' there; he certainly broadcast for the Germans. After the war, he was court-martialled by the R.A.F. and served a term of imprisonment. Fellow crew members were most surprised to hear of his behaviour, for he had acted with great courage when his bomber was attacked and shot down; but one of them says, 'he was always very volatile and excitable.'

NOTE
1. *V-2*, p. 179

CHAPTER 15

The Reckoning

This examination of the results of the Peenemünde operation will begin by detailing the casualties of all the parties involved and the immediate material effects of the bombing. The long-term results, a less easily judged but more important subject, can follow later.

Of the 596 four-engined aircraft dispatched by R.A.F. Bomber Command to Peenemünde, it is believed that 560 – including twenty-eight later shot down – bombed the target area. The bomb tonnage loaded in England totalled 1,924; the 1,795 released at the target were made up of 1,528 tons of high explosive and 267 tons of incendiaries. Further analysis yields the following approximate totals:

Type		Number dropped
High Explosive	4,000 lb.	232
	2,000 lb.	120
	1,000 lb.	1,423
	500 lb.	1,510
	40 lb.	1,912
Incendiary	30 lb.	9,606
	4 lb.	77,530

The 4,000-pounders were the High Capacity blast bombs – 'Block-busters' or 'Cookies' to the R.A.F., '*Luftminen*' to the Germans. The 40-lb. high explosives were anti-personnel bombs dropped by some of the Pathfinder aircraft on Flak and searchlight positions. The 30-lb. incendiaries contained some phosphorus, much disliked by the Germans, and the 4-pounders were 'stick' incendiaries, called by the Germans '*Stabbrandbomben*'.

The R.A.F. lost forty bombers – twenty-three Lancasters, fifteen Halifaxes and two Stirlings – with a further Halifax written off because of damage after landing in England. The table on the next page gives the group performances. In addition, eight Mosquito bombers were sent to Berlin as a diversion and thirty-eight Beaufighters and Mosquitoes dispatched as Intruders, each force losing one Mosquito; another Mosquito was written off when it crash-landed on return to England.

The R.A.F. lost 290 of its highly trained aircrew – 288 from Bomber Command, 2 from Fighter Command. 245 were killed – a high propor-

Group	Dispatched	Bombed	Missing
I	113 Lancasters	106 (93.8%)	3 (2.7%)
3	66 Stirlings and Lancasters	61 (92.4%)	3 (4.5%)
4	145 Halifaxes	137 (94.5%)	3 (2.1%)
5	117 Lancasters	109 (93.2%)	17 (14.5%)
6 (R.C.A.F.)	61 Halifaxes and Lancasters	57 (93.4%)	12 (19.7%)
8 (Pathfinder)	94 Halifaxes and Lancasters	90 (95.7%)	2 (2.1%)
Total	596	560 (94.0%)	40 (6.7%)

tion of fatalities, due to the fact that so many bombers had been shot down over the sea. The dead came from the following countries: United Kingdom 167, Canada sixty, Australia ten, New Zealand three, U.S.A. two, and one each from Rhodesia, Trinidad, and Southern Ireland. Of the forty-five men who became prisoners of war, the highest-ranking were Squadron Leaders F. N. Brinsden and A. D. Lambert, who, coincidentally, both landed planes on the sea, Brinsden a Mosquito off Sylt, Lambert a Stirling near Peenemünde.

The heavy casualties suffered by 5 and 6 Groups came as no surprise; it was always expected that the later phases of the attack would be particularly dangerous. In fact these groups lost six times as many men as the rest of the Peenemünde force. Perhaps because they knew their crews had the toughest job, no less than two thirds of the 5 and 6 Group squadron commanders had decided to take part in the raid themselves. Four out of the ten who went were shot down; all four were killed. 5 Group suffered the loss of a particularly high proportion of experienced crews because the group commander had ordered that only those who had practised time-and-distance bombing were to take part. This had excluded most of the group's new crews.

The mainly Canadian 6 Group sent only sixty-one aircraft to Peenemünde, but its losses, at nearly 20 per cent, were proportionally the highest of all; not one Canadian squadron escaped unscathed. Particularly disappointing to the units concerned were the experiences of the brand-new 434 Squadron, which could send only nine aircraft on its first operation to Germany and lost three of them, and 426 Squadron, flying its first operation since converting to Lancaster IIs, which could also send only nine and lost two, including that of the squadron commander.

So the R.A.F. lost forty-four aircraft and forty-two crews in what had always been considered a hazardous enterprise. The missing rate of 6.7 per cent for the main bombing force was far heavier than the casualty rate which Bomber Command could afford to sustain over a long period of operations. Were the results worth it?

To begin with, the immediate *tactical* outcome of the operation can be summed up. Bomber Command was justifiably satisfied with the apparent results. Every aircraft which reached Germany and was not shot down dropped its bombs inside or very close to the confines of the Peenemünde establishment. The three selected target areas had all been struck many times, and the housing estate was particularly heavily hit. It is true that there were two major blemishes: the bombs dropped, so tragically from the Allied point of view, on the Trassenheide workers' camp, and those which fell in the sea to the east of the target areas. It will never be known exactly how many bombs missed their proper target because so many photographs did not contain enough detail – it may have been between 15 and 20 per cent. But it should be stressed again that the attacking force had never before been presented with so small a target. In this sense, Peenemünde was an outstanding success, to which at least four factors contributed.

In the first place, the ordinary crews of Bomber Command had been so impressed by the importance of the target that they were prepared to devote every effort and to take extra risks – for which many paid with their lives – to ensure that their bomb-loads achieved the best results. Secondly, the use of a Master Bomber mitigated the effect of some of the Pathfinder marking errors and did much to concentrate the bombing in the right areas. Group Captain Searby and his crew did well in the testing circumstances of the very early use of a difficult technique. In particular, Searby's swift detection of the major bombing effort developing at Trassenheide, well south of the true target, and his prompt corrective orders were indispensable; without John Searby and his crew, the whole operation could have been a ghastly failure.

Discussion of sophisticated techniques leads to the third favourable factor – the use of time-and-distance bombing by some of the crews of 5 Group, which is one of the most interesting aspects of the Peenemünde operation. It had certainly been a good test for Air Vice-Marshal Cochrane's theories. 5 Group bombed in the last wave, when the German smoke-screen was at its most effective and the Pathfinder marking was overshooting. The reader will remember that Cochrane's view had not been given full support by Sir Arthur Harris and that, although the 5 Group crews had been ordered to carry out their time-and-distance runs, they were to obey the Master Bomber's instructions at the end of that run providing they were satisfied that the Pathfinder markers were not drastically misplaced.

It is unfortunate that the German smoke-screen did not permit the full plotting of the resulting bombing photographs. Approximately 120 crews from 5 and 6 Groups, all in the third wave, returned with photographs, but only forty could be plotted (see the map on the opposite page). The photographs of twenty-five crews – from both 5 and 6 Groups – who had bombed on the instructions of the Master Bomber, showed a spread of three and a half miles, with some bombs up to two and a half miles from the Aiming Point. Twelve further photographs from 5 Group crews who had ignored the Master Bomber's advice and bombed on time-and-distance alone showed a spread of only two miles, with no bomb more than one and a quarter miles from the Aiming Point. Because two thirds of the photographs had not shown sufficient ground detail to be plotted, this test could not be regarded as conclusive; but it did seem that the purely time-and-distance bombing had been significantly the more accurate. Ironically, the remaining three plottable photographs came from crews who had ignored both methods and bombed visually; these were the most accurate of all!

Air Vice-Marshal Cochrane was most annoyed when he saw the results of these pictures the next day. He had always felt that 5 Group alone, or a limited part of the Main Force using 5 Group tactics alone, could have destroyed Peenemünde; instead, the attack had been based mainly on a modified standard Pathfinder technique. Squadron Leader John Beach, Cochrane's Group Bombing Leader, was with his chief that morning.

> He was furious that more 5 Group crews had not stuck to time-and-distance ... I'm sure he was convinced that, instead of major damage, virtually total destruction would have been effected had 5 Group been left to carry out the operation alone.

A passing thought may be given to what might have happened if the U.S.A.A.F. bomber force in England had been asked to carry out a daylight attack on Peenemünde. The Americans could only have carried a much lighter bomb-load than the R.A.F. had delivered, but it is quite possible that they would have bombed more accurately. The German smoke-screen would have been a factor but, forewarned, the Americans could have used 'off-target' reference points for what would have been, in effect, a daylight time-and-distance bomb run. It is significant that the R.A.F. never raided Peenemünde again and that the U.S.A.A.F. did so three times in 1944. The American Official History makes this comment on the first of their 1944 raids.

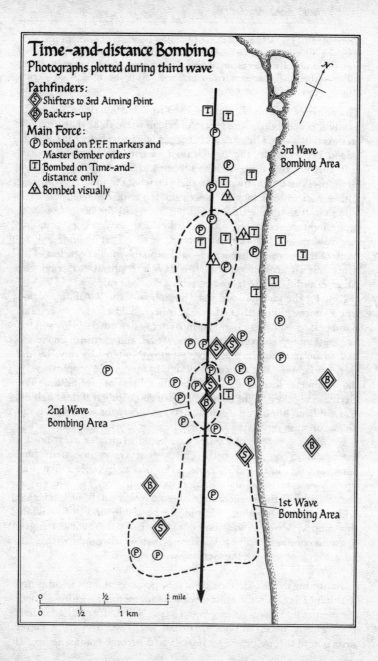

The raid of 18 July was one of the outstanding examples of daylight precision bombing during the war in Europe. Three hundred and seventy-nine heavy bombers, with full fighter escort, dropped 920.6 tons on eight separate aiming points within the concentrated target area, with the result that Peenemünde was seriously damaged.[1]

The figure of 379 bombers dispatched to Peenemünde in July 1944 – only a proportion of the great American strength at that time – is an interesting one. On 17 August 1943, a few hours before the R.A.F. raided Peenemünde, the Americans had sent 376 bombers – their entire force at that time – to Regensburg and Schweinfurt in southern Germany. It is fascinating to speculate on what might have happened if they had instead tackled the virgin target of Peenemünde. It is true that at that time they would not have had the benefit of long-range fighter escort; but although they lost sixty planes bombing Regensburg and Schweinfurt, the loss against Peenemünde, on the flank of the German defences, would probably have been less. This is not just an academic point; two days after the R.A.F. raid, the Americans did offer to follow up with a daylight raid.

Now for the fourth – and last – reason why the R.A.F. operation was a success. Sir Arthur Harris had been bold enough to commit Bomber Command to a flight far into enemy-defended territory in the brightest moonlight conditions he could find, and the use of that moon had to be paid for in bombers shot down, often so easily, by the German fighters. But the cost was kept to reasonable proportions by the complete success of the Mosquito diversion to Berlin. The Germans say they might have shot down 200 bombers if their fighters had not been lured to the capital and kept there for so long. It is not an unduly rash estimate.

Finally, the success of Fighter Command's Intruder effort on this night should be mentioned. Thirty-eight crews operated. One Mosquito was lost, and its crew taken prisoner; at least five, and probably six, German night fighters were destroyed. The effect upon the outcome of the Peenemünde operation was small, but, together with the heavy-bomber raid on Peenemünde and the brilliant diversion at Berlin, it was another example of the growing strength, aggressiveness and skill of Allied airpower which would eventually pose such problems for the German war machine.

In turning to the German side of the operation, it must be admitted that it had not been the most glorious of nights for the Luftwaffe; but the verdict that it was a fiasco is too harsh. The Luftwaffe had indeed been grossly deceived, but they had been deceived by a clever diversion at a time before such ploys had become commonplace. It should be remembered, too, that few in the German fighter control service knew that there was a potential target of such importance at Peenemünde for which the R.A.F. would risk its bomber force on a moonlit night – a target more important to the British than Berlin. In a way, it can be said that Peenemünde fell victim to its own need for secrecy. When they did arrive, the German night fighters took a heavy toll, but most of their successes were against aircraft which had already bombed. The charge that the Luftwaffe completely failed to protect Peenemünde is justified, but the circumstances were exceptional.

Bomber Command would have been given much cause for anxiety had they known where some of the German night fighters had come from. Occasional mention has been made of II/NJG 1, the 2nd *Gruppe* of the 1st Night-Fighter *Geschwader* whose home airfield was at St Trond, in eastern Belgium, and whose normal scene of operations was in the closely controlled local 'boxes' on the approaches to the Ruhr. Thirteen Messerschmitt 110s from St Trond had been directed to Berlin in the Luftwaffe's first comprehensive Wild Boar operation. Five crews then flew on to Peenemünde and, between them, claimed the destruction of thirteen bombers. Although the true figure may have been slightly smaller, it was still a remarkable achievement: ordinary German night-fighter crews, flying standard aircraft, used to operating near their base and under close control, had, without any special training, struck hard at a British bomber force near a target 430 miles away, despite the fact that their main running commentary was completely mistaken about the British intentions.

The performance of II/NJG 1 was not matched by any other German unit on this occasion; but if the R.A.F. had known what the German night-fighter force might achieve in coming months with increasing experience in these new tactics – to say nothing of the successful introduction of another unsuspected feature, the *schräge Musik* upward-firing cannon – they would have had many bad dreams.

The documented Luftwaffe casualties (there may have been a few more) were twelve night fighters destroyed – eight Messerschmitt 110s, one Dornier 217, two Focke-Wulf 190s and one Messerschmitt 109 – and twelve aircrew killed.

The Flak and searchlight defences supposed to give direct protection to Peenemünde were – apart from the naval Flak ship offshore – also the responsibility of the Luftwaffe, but there was little glory to be found here either.

The land-based heavy Flak may have consisted of no more than three or four batteries – twelve or sixteen of the famous 88-mm guns – all outside the immediate bombing areas. The colourful light Flak – 20- and 37-mm – was scattered through the target area, often mounted on the roofs of large buildings. All were under the control of Flak Untergruppe Karlshagen commanded by Major Lauterbach, a promising officer reputed to have once been in charge of the Flak on Hitler's private train.

For nearly an hour Lauterbach's command had more than 500 heavy bombers cruising over their heads at steady speeds and courses. There was a standing order that no battery was to fire until it received orders to do so from the central control, and one battery commander, who apparently blindly obeyed that order even after the telephone line to his position was cut by an early bomb, is supposed to have successfully defended himself against subsequent disciplinary action by claiming that he was only following orders. The men serving with the 1st, 2nd and 5th Batteries of the 337th Heavy Flak Battalion later received certificates showing that they had shot down four R.A.F. bombers – three Lancasters and a Halifax – on this their first night in action at Peenemünde, but it is believed that their successes numbered only three, all Halifaxes, two by heavy Flak and one by a 37-mm gun. The poor Flak performance was chiefly due to the use of Window and to the fact that the barrage was fired too high because the bombers were flying at an abnormally low level. The deeply held conviction of many at Peenemünde during the raid that a lot of the heavy Flak guns had recently been moved away from the establishment is not based on fact. These guns had simply been moved to new positions not long before.

The Peenemünde smoke-screen, manned by elderly home service troops and Russian volunteers, had been the establishment's most effective form of defence.

As so much of the ground has been covered before, only a short summary of the damage and casualties at Peenemünde will be needed here before dealing with two unusual aspects of the raid and, finally, the important subject of its overall effect on the German rocket programme.

Airmen have often found to their dismay that a seemingly devastating raid has not caused as much damage as expected, and that targets believed to have been 'knocked out' were functioning again in a surprisingly short time. Peenemünde conformed, in part, to this experience. Seeing the mass of fires, the billowing clouds of smoke, the continuous flash of explosions, the R.A.F. crews could be excused for thinking that little would be left to function after the height of the raid;

surely nearly 1,800 tons of bombs could not have failed to knock out this small and comparatively fragile target. But two factors had combined to rob Bomber Command of the complete destruction so fervently desired.

The first factor has already been described. The technical difficulties of maintaining the accurate marking of three Aiming Points for nearly an hour in a cross-wind had been too great: too many bombs had either missed completely or had fallen on the wrong targets. The second factor was the nature of the soil. The main weight of the R.A.F. bomb-loads, more than four fifths of the total, was comprised of high-explosive bombs fuzed to detonate on impact. In the soft, sandy soil at Peenemünde, this resulted in exceptionally deep craters; but most of the force of the explosions went harmlessly upwards. Bomber Command planners had clearly hoped that the attack would be so accurate that enough of the high-explosive bombs – over 3,300 were dropped – would score direct hits to ensure that the establishment of Peenemünde would completely cease to function. This had not quite happened.

In the two northern Aiming Points, the object was the destruction of buildings and the equipment inside them. But neither the Experimental Works nor the Production Works suffered crippling damage to their most important parts. In the Experimental Works there was an element of sheer bad luck because, while many non-essential parts were destroyed, most of the more important buildings such as the vital wind tunnel and telemetry block escaped. Because of the German policy of daily dispersal of important technical drawings, these, too, had survived.

The housing estate, the first of the Aiming Points, had, by contrast, received more bombs than intended, and photographs showed its devastation. But the object here had been to kill people, not to destroy buildings. The only figures available are those of General Dornberger. According to David Irving, Dornberger informed American interrogators after the war that the raid had cost the lives of 120 'of the regular German staff', the rest of the dead being foreigners. In his own book, Dornberger states that 178 of the 4,000 people in the housing estate were killed.[2] It is thus probable that the number of Germans to die was somewhere between 120 and 178, the rest of the dead being foreign workers known to have been killed in the small labour camp near the housing estate (not the large Trassenheide camp). On these figures, it would appear that although the civilian housing was comprehensively blown up or burnt down, only about one in twenty people were killed; the rest survived in their shelters.

Some Germans have harsh things to say about the bombing of the housing area.

The raid would have been understandable if it had been limited to the military targets which were situated far away from the housing estate. I was of the opinion at that time and I am still of the opinion that a raid upon a built-up area with hundreds of women and children is a crime.

Thus – understandably – writes Karl Schreiner, an engineer. But it must not be forgotten that Britain and Germany were locked in a deadly conflict which had developed, by 1943, into total war. The British knew that weapons were being produced at Peenemünde for use in an indiscriminate bombardment which would give no warning and against which there could be no defence. In this context, every technical man at Peenemünde was a legitimate target, and the lives of accompanying loved ones must naturally be at hazard, too. The slow approach and gradual assembly of the bombers had at least given these civilians time to take shelter. The V-2 rocket would give no such warning to the civilians of London and other cities.

The death of civilians opens up a new subject. Any German who was at Peenemünde on that night in August will tell the story of the machine-gunning on the beach by low-flying aircraft which took place towards the end of the raid and which killed some of the people – young women are usually mentioned as the victims – who were fleeing from the burning housing estate. Here are two German comments.

The only view open to me is towards the sea. I can see, there, how screaming Luftwaffe female auxiliaries try to seek salvation in the water. Almost at once, low-flying aircraft appear and are opening up with their guns on the girls. I cannot see it in detail because it is too far away in the semi-darkness, but the noise is clearly revealing.

This demonstration given to me by skilled warriors filled me with the utmost nausea. (Heinz Menschel)

I hope that some of the German wives will respond to your call and write to you. Most of them were right on the spot, under the descending 'presents', and a few were in the water of the Baltic Sea, trying to extinguish the phosphorus you brought as 'spices' when you 'christened' them with machine-gun fire. (Ernst Seiler)

But both these men were at Zinnowitz at the time of the raid, and neither actually saw a low-flying aircraft machine-gunning people on the beach and in the water. General Dornberger refers to 'the rattle of machine-gun fire from the direction of the beach'[3] but he does not infer that it was British fire deliberately aimed at the people there.

This is my third book covering R.A.F. raids on Germany. I am used to the normal exaggerations. Every burn is claimed as a 'phosphorus burn' – they were not. Allied fighter-bombers had strafed the streets of Hamburg after the firestorm – they had not. My experience is that people who have recently been subjected to such a harrowing experience as a heavy air-raid are all too willing to accept rumours as truth. The German authorities did little to stop the spread of such accounts of British 'terror tactics'. When I started to hear the 'beach strafing' story at Peenemünde, I patiently explained that there had been no R.A.F. fighters present, and that for a heavy bomber to have come down from the bombing height of 8,000 feet to machine-gun the beach area would have been operationally very difficult and potentially suicidal. Perhaps a burst of spent bullets from the air battle overhead had come down here. Perhaps a light Flak gun in action had been hit by a bomb and had sent a stray burst into this area. But these explanations were not accepted.

I shall always remember an incident at the annual reunion, at Friedrichshafen, of people who had once worked at Peenemünde. One lady agreed to be interviewed while the party crossed the Bodensee by lake steamer for a day out in Switzerland. The whole of the trip across amid such beautiful surroundings was taken up by a tense discussion of the supposed strafing incident. When I explained that it could not have happened, the lady first became very angry, and then burst into tears. She had definitely heard a low-flying aeroplane, had counted five bursts of fire, and she had a bullet wound in her shoulder to prove the point. Another lady remained calmer and could be pressed harder with questions. Yes, she was absolutely sure that she had heard 'low-flying, zooming aeroplanes and bursts of machine-gun fire,' and had actually seen lines of '*Spritzer*' – 'squirts of spray' – in the sea. She was not wounded but claims to have met people in hospital who had been hit.

I eventually accepted that something unusual must have happened. Perhaps it was no more than the random firing suggested earlier. Perhaps a German fighter pursued a bomber down to this lower altitude and bursts of fire from one or the other struck the beach and sea – several bombers of the third wave did crash in the water near here. Perhaps one doomed bomber, its gunners too low to escape by parachute, did machine-gun the beach; after all, they had been sent to Peenemünde to kill scientists, and the sex and age of the people seen on the beach would not have been distinguishable. Perhaps, even, a daredevil bomber did circle back and make a strafing run: the crew of a Lancaster of 100 Squadron told me that they had machine-gunned prominent buildings, not near Peenemünde, but after they had decided to lose height and fly the first part of the homeward route at low level. In any case it is unlikely that the full truth will ever be known.

The German rumour-mongers were presented with another gift – the bombing of the forced labour camp at Trassenheide. The circumstances can be repeated quickly. Because the small island of Ruden did not show up clearly on the radar sets of the Pathfinders, the first markers went down at Trassenheide, two miles south of the correct Aiming Point. The subsequent bombing caused serious casualties to defenceless men taken forcibly from their homes in the German-occupied countries. The loss to the Germans of easily replaceable, unskilled labour was little compensation for this tragedy. A diligent R.A.F. photographic reconnaissance interpreter tells us that twenty-three of the forty-five large barrack huts at Trassenheide were destroyed.[4] General Dornberger's casualty figures would suggest that at least 500, and possibly as many as 600, men were killed. A large proportion of the dead were Poles, but there must have been many Russians and Ukrainians, a few Frenchmen, and a sprinkling of other nationalities. An unconfirmable report says that a few concentration-camp men in their small camp nearby died too, including two Luxembourgers. Some German guards and administration personnel were also killed. The number of wounded must have been considerable.

The bombing of Trassenheide seems to have been so accurate that it was assumed by many Germans and by the foreign workers that it was all part of the plan. Some German accounts take pleasure in castigating an 'inhuman' R.A.F. for trying to kill everyone at Peenemünde, even their own friends. General Dornberger did not help to dispel this myth when he wrote that maps from shot-down bombers showed four main target areas, the fourth being 'the construction workers' camp at Trassenheide'.[5] In fact, Trassenheide was never an R.A.F. target, and no captured map could have shown anything to the contrary.

The foreigners were naturally dismayed by what had happened. Their lot in life had not been happy even before the bombing, and the loss of their friends was a tragic blow from which some have never recovered; they, too, believed that the R.A.F. bombing was according to plan. Even after the most detailed of explanations, with sketches, to a group of surviving Poles, one man still refused to accept that the bombing was accidental. Another Pole, Jan Marzynski, says:

When we had looked after the wounded, it was time to collect up the dead, and that was the time for bitter thoughts. Various answers suggested themselves. We could not understand how it was possible to make such a mistake – missing the target by such a distance – because it was seven kilometres between the rocket factory and our camp. Instead of aiming at the other end of the peninsula, the English were bashing our camp. We assumed that some terrible mistake had taken place but it was very difficult for us to understand it.

The Germans scoffed at us, telling us, 'Your friends did this,' and they laughed. Some of those who supervised us said that the English had botched the job. They had been so scared of the Germans that they had flown over without taking proper care of what they were bombing. They dropped their bombs and ran away as fast as they could . . . The pain was so much harder to bear when we heard that the factory had hardly been touched.

The memory of this will last a long time.

The final judgement on the success of the Peenemünde raid will not be found in a catalogue of buildings and equipment destroyed or in numbers of people killed. The sole object was to delay the development, production and operational use of the V-2 rocket. Are these two views, from men who bombed Peenemünde, valid?

I have often thought that this was probably one of the most important and successful raids of the war as it did put back the flying bomb and rocket offensive several months.

I shall always be proud of participating in that Peenemünde operation, described by one commentator as 'the raid which won the war'.

There were many such enthusiastic opinions on the Allied side, although to call it 'the raid which won the war' is an exaggeration, and the reference to the flying bomb a popular misconception. A statement by General Eisenhower in his book, *Crusade in Europe*,[6] is often quoted in support of the claim that the raid set the rocket programme back by six months or more; but Eisenhower's opinion that the invasion of Europe might have been 'written off' had the Germans been able to use V-weapons six months earlier, particularly if they had bombarded the Portsmouth–Southampton port areas, referred rather to V-1 flying bombs than to V-2 rockets – and it must be emphasized once more that the R.A.F. operation had nothing to do with flying bombs.

It is difficult to calculate the time lost by the Germans in the rocket programme, largely because of the action taken over Peenemünde's future by the authorities in Berlin. Immediately after the raid,

Dornberger and his team worked furiously to get the establishment back to normal; but a top-level meeting between Hitler, Speer and Himmler, only four days later, altered matters dramatically. Peenemünde was not to be rebuilt, except for a few lightly damaged buildings. The establishment was deliberately to be left with a ruined appearance. A large part of its activities was to be moved to more secure locations – the test firing of rockets to Poland, experimental work to caves in Austria, the mass-production of rockets to huge underground caverns and tunnels in the Harz Mountains. In the event, the experimental work did not move to Austria, and Peenemünde carried on to a limited extent almost to the end of the war.

It is said that some of these moves had been under consideration for some time, so that the influence of the raid on the firm decisions of 22 August cannot be calculated. It can safely be claimed however that the R.A.F. operation precipitated this drastic action, which would take time to implement and would result in massive disruption at all levels in the rocket programme, producing a major gain for the Allied cause.

Informed opinions on the actual length of the delay are remarkably similar. Goebbels has been quoted as saying that it amounted to 'six to eight weeks'.[7] The British Official History states that the raid 'may well have caused a delay of two months'.[8] David Irving and Professor R. V. Jones both say 'at least two months'. If this figure is accepted – and these estimates are the best informed likely to appear – it can be seen that the attack had no effect upon the initial success of the invasion of Europe. The first rockets were fired operationally on 8 September 1944, three months and two days after D-Day. The last German estimate made before the raid for the opening of their rocket operations had been 'the summer of 1944',[9] which fits in well with the two-month setback opinion expressed by others. But all these analysts also conclude that the R.A.F. operation achieved not only a setback in the V-2's experimental programme, but also a reduction in the eventual scale of its production.

If one accepts the two-month delay – and sets aside for the moment the reduction in scale, which cannot be estimated – it is possible to put a mathematical figure on the raid's success. When it did start, the V-2 campaign lasted just under seven months, and 370 rockets were launched in an average month. The R.A.F. can thus claim to have prevented the launching of at least 740 rockets. Again on average, 155 V-2s would have fallen on London, causing 809 fatal casualties, 155 more on less densely populated parts of England, and 370 on Continental targets, mostly on the port of Antwerp then being used to supply the Allied armies fighting in Europe. These estimates are perfectly valid, and to them can be added the unknown quantity of the reduction in scale of rocket production.

There were other benefits. The general dislocation produced by the raid, and particularly the death of Dr Thiel, the propulsion specialist, also affected the development of the *Wasserfall* anti-aircraft rocket projectile and of the two-stage A-9 rocket, which was designed to reach any part of Britain as far as Glasgow. The *Wasserfall* never reached the production line and the A-9, although tested in 1945, was never put into action. In fact it is debatable whether the A-9 would ever have reached operational status; it was a very ambitious project, and the end of the war would have come too soon for its fruition.

Finally, the morale aspect of the raid should not be forgotten. The confident, contented Germans, engrossed in their interesting work at remote and beautiful Peenemünde, and their leaders in Berlin had been given a dramatic demonstration that the R.A.F. was capable of reaching and hitting hard any target in Germany. The morale and willingness to fight on of many people were affected, from the young woman with a fur coat over her nightdress who had run away from Peenemünde screaming that she wanted to go home, to the Luftwaffe general for whom the raid on Peenemünde was the one burden too many and who committed suicide.

NOTES

1. W. F. Craven and J. L. Cate, *The Army Air Forces in World War II*, vol. III, p. 537.
2. Irving's statement comes from *The Mare's Nest*, p. 119, Dornberger's from *V-2*, p. 180.
3. *V-2*, p. 174.
4. Public Record Office AIR 14/3410.
5. *V-2*, p. 180.
6. Published by Doubleday, New York, 1948, p. 260.
7. From a quotation by Oberst Max Wachtel, who served at Peenemünde, in a *Sunday Mirror* article, 18 August 1968.
8. Vol. II, p. 285.
9. Craven and Cate, *op. cit.*, vol. III, p. 89.

CHAPTER 16

The Years that Followed

Bomber Command went back to its normal methods of waging war. There were no major operations for four nights after Peenemünde. The next was on the night of 22/23 August, when 462 aircraft were sent to Leverkusen, an industrial town in the Ruhr. Heavy cloud reduced the effectiveness of the normally accurate Oboe marking, however, and bombs were scattered over a wide area. The poor weather also prevented the Luftwaffe from achieving anything dramatic, and only five bombers were lost.

Peenemünde made its mark as a most unusual operation – it was undoubtedly a milestone in the air war – but it never became the turning point it might have been. There were those within Bomber Command, and there were certainly those at the Air Ministry, who hoped that the sophisticated techniques used to attack the three small targets at Peenemünde – the Master Bomber, the moving of the Aiming Points, the time-and-distance bombing – would form the basis of a more advanced and selective approach to tactics and choice of target. For more than eighteen months the 'Area Bombing' of cities had been judged the only effective use for Bomber Command, but some senior officers felt that it was time to be moving on. To them, the techniques imposed by the special needs of Peenemünde must have seemed the basis for future improvement. These techniques – used by moonlight – were not of course all suitable for immediate employment by the whole of the Main Force on the darker nights in which Bomber Command would have to operate: it was more a hope that the recent experience would stimulate further developments in bombing techniques and lead to better things.

It did not happen. That dominant personality, Sir Arthur Harris, in whom the Air Ministry still had sufficient confidence not to impose an outside will, had other intentions. Early in 1942, Harris had taken over a dispirited force, on the verge of possible failure and disbandment. In that first year, he had patiently nursed along the sickly command, introducing the major new tactics of the bomber-stream and fire-raising, and establishing the Pathfinders. The first seven months of 1943 had seen continuing success. The new devices of Oboe and H2S had dramatically improved marking, although only on certain types of target. Bomb-carrying capacity had also improved, and Harris was now on the verge of having a completely four-engined command. The undoubted success of the Battles of the Ruhr and Hamburg had been achieved by this growing force, using the now established techniques of 'standard pathfinding' and Area Bombing.

I have written at length, in an earlier book,[1] of what might be called 'the bomber dream'. Briefly, this was the hope by certain R.A.F. leaders that air power could win the war by causing the collapse of Germany before the land invasion of Europe. Various paths to this object had now crystallized into two schools of thought: the selective target school and the massive general destruction school. The Air Ministry, with the positive co-operation of the U.S.A.A.F., was moving steadily towards the first; hence the desire to employ more refined bombing techniques. Sir Arthur Harris, however, was convinced that the second method was the way to success. Moreover, in the autumn of 1943, he believed that he was on the verge of that success. In the coming weeks, he intended to mete out to other German cities the fate he had recently delivered to Hamburg. Hannover and Nuremberg were probably in his mind for early treatment; then, as soon as the longer nights of winter were available, a sustained attack on Germany's capital would finish it all. In November, he would make a famous statement: 'We can wreck Berlin from end to end if the U.S.A.A.F. will come in on it. It will cost between us 400 and 500 bombers. It will cost Germany the war.'[2] Harris was not prepared, at this time, to do anything at all which might divert one bomber for one night from his main aim. There would be no further experimentation with new techniques. No effort would be devoted to small targets.

Thus were many of the R.A.F. crews who returned from Peenemünde committed to what became known as the Battle of Berlin. The first raid on the capital took place just six nights after Peenemünde. This time, the German fighters were not sent to Berlin in vain; fifty-six bombers from the 789 dispatched did not return. Two follow-up raids, on 31 August and 3 September, also suffered severe loss. There was a pause until the main series of winter raids on Berlin commenced with the longer nights in November. The outcome can be quickly described. Peenemünde was destined to be Bomber Command's last big success for a long time. Between November and the end of March 1944, there were sixteen further major attacks on Berlin as well as nineteen raids on other German cities. In this main Battle of Berlin the R.A.F. lost 1,047 bombers, a destruction rate of 5.2 per cent.

The results gained did not warrant these severe losses. Neither

Berlin nor any other German city attacked in this period suffered damage in any degree approaching that inflicted on Hamburg the previous summer. Berlin was certainly not 'wrecked from end to end'. The will to carry on the war was not broken. Industrial capacity was not critically weakened. The German survival owes much to two factors: poor weather, usually too severe for the Pathfinders to provide reliable marking – in particular, Berlin proved disappointing for the use of H2S radar – and the resurgence of the Luftwaffe night-fighter force from the Window setback. The wide-ranging, freelancing tactics recently introduced and tried out at full scale for the first time on the night of the Peenemünde operation came into their own. The Germans soon introduced a new airborne radar set, the *SN-2*, which was not affected by Window. The controllers' skill at forecasting future moves and their 'running commentary' improved enormously. Major Herrmann's single-engined Wild Boar force continued to gain success over the targets – though often at heavy loss to themselves – and this element of the night-fighter defence trebled in strength. In what became known as the *Zahme Sau* (Tame Boar) tactic, the operations of the twin-engined fighters were extended further and further out along the bombers' routes to and from the target cities. A Bomber Command raid often became a grim, pitched battle extending many hundreds of miles. The climax was reached on the night of 30/31 March 1944 when ninety-six bombers were lost in the ill-fated raid on Nuremberg.

The Bomber Command men killed in the Peenemünde operation were soon joined by a sadly high proportion of their comrades who did not survive the Berlin raids. The reader may remember Flight Lieutenant Brian Slade, the twenty-one-year-old Pathfinder captain whose markers were the first to go down on Peenemünde, Wing Commander John White, the Deputy Master Bomber whose timely release of markers transformed the Peenemünde operation at a difficult point, and Flying Officer George Ross, the bomb aimer in the Master Bomber's crew who helped Group Captain Searby so much. Brian Slade and all but one man in his crew died when shot down on their marking run at Berlin only six nights after Peenemünde while flying their fifty-eighth or fifty-ninth operation. John White and two of his crew died on 18 November. George Ross finished his tour but went on 'one more raid' when a friend was short of a bomb aimer. He died at Berlin on 20 January 1944. There were many more. (Group Captain Searby survived a successful tour in command of 83 Squadron and, with the remainder of his crew, survived the rest of the war. Wing Commander Johnny Fauquier, the gifted Canadian who was the other deputy to Searby, went on to command 617 (Dambuster) Squadron and also survived.)

Throughout all these operations, Sir Arthur Harris continued with the same basic pre-Peenemünde tactics. They did not stand the test of the Battle of Berlin. He used the Master Bomber technique three times in the next month, but then discontinued it until the following spring. The important ball-bearing town of Schweinfurt, which the Americans had attacked at such heavy cost a few hours before Peenemünde, many of them expecting a British follow-up, was not raided by the R.A.F. until 25 February 1944, and then only after a firm, direct order from an impatient Air Ministry. For the remainder of the war, the greater part of Bomber Command continued to use standard Pathfinder marking techniques and Area Bombing methods, although Air Vice-Marshal Cochrane was allowed to develop 5 Group as a precision force with its own Pathfinder squadrons from the spring of 1944. I cannot conceal my personal opinion that this brilliant commander should have been given his head much earlier and on a wider scale.

Peenemünde's days of greatness were nearly over. Once they had cleared up after the raid, the foreign labourers were dispersed to many places in Germany. Little new construction work took place and the wrecked areas were deliberately left as they were so that R.A.F. reconnaissance aircraft would believe that Peenemünde had ceased to be important. In this way, the housing estate became a ghost town, and the happy community spirit never revived. But some important experimental work and the building of small numbers of V-2s for test firings continued to be carried out, and the Americans undertook three raids in July and August 1944, dropping 3,000 tons of bombs in approximately 1,200 B-17 Fortress sorties. One of the main objects was the destruction of the liquid oxygen plant which supplied fuel for German rockets. The bombing was very accurate on each occasion, but the death roll on the ground was probably not high; there was plenty of spare shelter capacity by then.

Most of the remaining Germans left Peenemünde early in 1945 when threatened by the advance of Russian forces; the few that were left stayed on in the vain hope that British or American troops would arrive before the Russians. A further evacuation, by sea to Kiel, took place at the end of April, and only a handful of civilians and a few troops from an S.S. unit were left to face the Russians when they arrived on 5 May. There was little fighting. The unit which occupied Peenemünde, commanded by Major Anatoli Vavilov, was part of the Second White Russian Army.[3] They approached from the south-west, via Wolgast, just beating a unit from the Kosciuszko Army, a free Polish force fighting with the Russians and advancing along the coast from Swinemünde. I found three people who were at Peenemünde at that time, a Polish girl labourer on a nearby farm and a German man and his wife at Karlshagen. They were reluctant to talk of what happened. The Polish lady says that the Russians went looking for 'the usual things – women and watches'. The German lady wrote, '*Der Mensch wird in seinem Siegestaumel zur Bestie.*' ('In the ecstasy of victory, man becomes a wild beast.')

The Russians tried to get the few technical men remaining to build a V-2 rocket from spare parts. Two were then killed, for reasons not known, and most of the others were taken to Russia. None had been among the leading figures at Peenemünde, but the Russians were taking anyone who knew anything about rockets. They then systematically removed every piece of salvageable machinery and it, too, was taken to Russia. Thus ended the life of Peenemünde as a scientific establishment.

In the meantime, however, the fruits of Peenemünde's earlier work had been put to operational use. Three important decisions concerning the production side of the rocket programme had been taken in Berlin soon after the R.A.F. raid. The overall control was to pass from the Wehrmacht into the hands of the S.S. This would ensure both greater security and a more 'determined' attitude. The major production centre was not to be at Peenemünde – now clearly known to the R.A.F. and vulnerable to further bombing – but at an underground site elsewhere. Finally, the manual labour force at the new site was to be provided almost exclusively by concentration-camp men, again for reasons of security; for they had no links at all with the outside world and the leaks from Peenemünde would not be repeated. This aspect of the scheme was successful, and it would take the Allies a further year to discover where the rockets were being made.

A new firm, *Mittelwerk*, formed to oversee and implement the new plan, though a commercial organization, was firmly under S.S. control. A suitable site for production was soon found in a complex of huge tunnels, previously used for various commercial purposes, under a mountain near the town of Nordhausen in the Harz region. (There are three Nordhausens in West Germany and at least three more in East Germany; this one is now just inside East Germany, approximately midway between Kassel and Leipzig.) Within two weeks of the R.A.F. raid on Peenemünde, the first 107 concentration-camp men and their S.S. guards were dispatched from Buchenwald, fifty miles away, to establish the Dora sub-camp. In little over a year, this grim place would house more than 13,000 such unfortunates.

A smaller part of the workforce was composed of forced foreign civilians and some Italian ex-soldiers. All were imprisoned below ground in harsh living and working conditions. Their mortality rate was high.[4]

Another grand production plan was announced on 1 October 1943: 1,800 rockets per month were to be manufactured in the underground factory – almost double the target for Peenemünde and its satellite factories before the Allied bombing! Fortunately for England the new figure was never achieved, although approximately 6,000 were built at Nordhausen between January 1944 and March 1945. So the rockets designed at Peenemünde were eventually built by a labour force of what can truly be described as slaves, deep underneath a mountain in central Germany.

The V-2 attacks on London and other places have been described many times and a brief summary will suffice here. The first operational rockets were fired on 8 September 1944 from a site in Holland, but for some time the bombardment was slow, intermittent and erratic. There were many other targets besides London: V-2s fell around Norwich and Ipswich, and many towns in northern France, Belgium and southern Holland were also attacked because they contained units of the Allied invasion armies. The most serious assault began in December, concentrating on London and on Antwerp, now the main port supplying the Allied armies in Europe. It continued until March 1945, when the rocket units were finally driven from their firing sites.

Approximately 2,500 rockets were launched during the seven months of the campaign. More than half – 1,265 – fell on Antwerp; London was hit by 517, and several hundred more landed in the surrounding counties. London suffered the heaviest casualties: 2,700 people were killed. There were some very serious individual incidents, the worst on 16 December 1944 when 271 people died at the Rex Cinema in Antwerp. London's worst incidents were 160 deaths in and around Woolworth's store in Deptford on 25 November 1944, 110 at Smithfield Meat Market on 8 March 1945, and 130 in a block of flats at Stepney on 27 March – the very last day of German rocket operations.

For much of this time, the V-2s had run alongside the V-1s, which had only a minor connection with Peenemünde. The first flying bombs arrived on 13 June 1944, eleven weeks before the first rocket. The Germans fired more than 10,000 of them at London, but mechanical failures and a successful effort by fighters, anti-aircraft guns and balloon defences resulted in only 2,419 reaching their destination. They killed a total of 5,500 people in England; the worst incident was at East Barnet, where 211 died on 23 August 1944. Poor, battered Antwerp received 2,448 flying bombs; its combined V-1 and V-2 deaths were 2,900 civilians and 743 military personnel. At Liège, 221 civilians and 92 military personnel were killed.[5]

The two weapons certainly caused much damage and severe casualties as well as anxiety for the Allied leaders. I do not feel qualified to comment in detail, but it should be mentioned that at one stage, more than half the Allied air effort was devoted to V-weapon targets – mostly the launching sites – thereby relieving the German armies and, particularly, their cities of air attack. On the other hand, the Germans might have secured a greater military advantage if they had devoted the massive resources required by the V-1 and V-2 programme to more conventional weapons. The main purpose of the rocket and the flying bomb – so to terrorize the English civilian population that the war against Germany could not be continued – failed completely.

Finally we come to the cost of these technically brilliant new weapons. The Luftwaffe's flying bomb, conceived several years after the Wehrmacht began their rocket programme, proved to be far more economical in its demands on Germany's scarce resources and effective in operational use. I am again obliged to David Irving for the information that the cost of each rocket fired operationally was approximately £12,000, that of a flying bomb – carrying a greater weight of explosive but, admittedly, more vulnerable to attack – a mere £125![6]

It was the American Army which captured the underground rocket factory in the Harz Mountains at the end of the war. They held on to this area for three months before handing it over to the Russians, removing a hundred completed V-2s and a multitude of useful documents. A few of the rockets were given to the British and French; the Americans carried out trials on the rest for possible use in the continuing war against Japan. Although few realized it at the time, this was the next step in the process by which a man would one day stand on the moon. Most of the rocket scientists fled west, into the arms of the Americans, or south, into what might have become Hitler's 'Last Redoubt'. Here, in Bavaria, the Americans captured General Dornberger, von Braun, and what one Peenemünde man calls 'the cream of the cream' of the old Peenemünde team which had remained together till the end of the war.

The Americans quickly realized that they held a pool of unique scientific ability and experience. They eventually had to release Dornberger to the British, who wanted to try him as a war criminal for the indiscriminate bombardment of civilians by rocket, but most of the remainder, under von Braun's leadership, were offered contracts to go to America and continue their experiments. There were few refusals; there was little prospect of such work being carried out in post-war Germany and the Americans seemed friendly and had plenty of money. Of the few Germans who accepted British or French offers, a small group came to the British Government's rocket research centre near Aylesbury and about fifty more went to the French centre at Vernon; these later worked on the modest joint European rocket programme. The Russians tried very hard to assemble a team but they were never able to match the collection of talent which went to the United States.

The Americans eventually employed 492 German rocket scientists and technicians; all went to the United States voluntarily and with proper contracts. For more than twenty years the core was formed by von Braun and 126 other men of the old Peenemünde team. They began with the further development of the old A-4 rocket (the V-2) at Fort Bliss, in Texas, moving later to Huntsville, Alabama, to build the new U.S. Army Redstone rocket. It was at Huntsville that most of the Germans settled with their families. The work so far had all been of a military nature; von Braun wanted to use the Redstone rocket for space research, but he had to wait until President Kennedy decided, for purposes of national prestige, to put a man on the moon before the Russians. Von Braun and his team were given a leading place in the ensuing space programme, and thus found that they had access to money and facilities undreamed of in the early years of their researches. They put their man on the moon in 1969.

Wernher von Braun, who married his cousin in 1947, lived only eight more years after seeing his greatest ambition fulfilled; he died of cancer at Alexandria, just outside Washington, in June 1977. His old chief, General Dornberger, had not been so lucky in his post-war career. The British wisely decided not to try him as a war criminal – their own bombing campaign against German cities would inevitably have been compared with Dornberger's 'crimes' – but he was not released for several years. He then followed other Peenemünde colleagues to the United States and was given lucrative work by the United States Air Force and by various civilian contractors, but he did not take part in the space programme and never received the acclaim and respect accorded to the Germans who did. He retired to Mexico in 1966, returning to Germany to die in a small town in the Black Forest in June 1980.

Most of the men who built rockets at Peenemünde are now retired. There is still a sizeable community at Huntsville; the rest are mostly scattered across the United States or have returned to

Germany. There is an active association based in Germany. As I said earlier, it was an interesting experience to attend one of their reunions. Some of the members are embarrassed, as so many Germans who served their country through the years of the Nazi dictatorship are embarrassed, at the part they played in the war. They talk willingly and proudly of their scientific achievements, less happily of the reliance of the rocket programme on suffering slave labour and of the effects of the V-2 on London, although the Allied bombing of German cities easily settles that score. They spoke of 'Doktor Dornberger', never 'General Dornberger'. The memory of von Braun is held in the greatest reverence.

I would like to pay tribute to the genuine friendship and help I received from many of the old Peenemünde team. They need not be too concerned about their image. Their original work was undoubtedly purely scientific, and the wartime interlude was forced upon them by events well beyond their control. Their part in mankind's exploration of space will never be forgotten.

Peenemünde itself is now in East Germany. I always like to inspect the scenes of the battles I describe, so I wrote to the G.D.R.'s Defence Attaché in London, asking for permission and advice for a visit to Peenemünde, and offering to submit to the close escort of the local police in case there are defence installations in that area which I should not see; the old Peenemünde West airfield is now a modern Warsaw Pact base. My letter was not answered and I did not care to make the journey without official approval. Polish people who have taken holidays in the area in recent years report that Zinnowitz is a thriving seaside resort again, but Karlshagen is a much quieter place. All the brick buildings in the old research establishment were demolished after the war and the bricks re-used. Concrete buildings remain, either barred to entry or in ruins. Part of the area of the old establishment is a prohibited zone. No trace remains of the old Trassenheide workers' camp; new forest growth covers the site. There is believed to be a memorial to the Polish men who died at Trassenheide, and in the Hauptstrasse at Karlshagen there is certainly a monument to the concentration-camp men of several nations who died at Peenemünde. It would be fitting if international tensions could one day be relaxed sufficiently to allow a memorial to be erected marking that place's achievement in the history of space exploration. In future years, Test Stand VII may be restored as a place of pilgrimage for devotees of such human endeavour.

The R.A.F. men who died on that night in 1943 also have their memorials. The sixty-nine bodies recovered from wrecked bombers around Peenemünde or from the coasts where they had drifted ashore are now in the keeping of that marvellous organization, the Commonwealth War Graves Commission; they lie in a British military cemetery in Berlin, in a sandy woodland setting probably similar to that around Peenemünde, alongside many of their friends who returned safely from Peenemünde but who died in the Battle of Berlin. The bodies of twelve more men who drifted further east in the Baltic lie in Poland; one, which was washed ashore 300 miles away on the Swedish island of Gotland, is buried at Göteborg. The aircrew shot down over or near Denmark are buried either at Aabenraa in Denmark or at Kiel.

But more than half of the R.A.F. dead were never found, and the Runnymede Memorial for the Missing, overlooking the river Thames, bears the names of 125 men whose graves are the wreckage of their bombers at the bottom of the Baltic or in the sand dunes of Peenemünde.

The surviving Bomber Command men who flew to Peenemünde will never forget that night.

I remember the Peenemünde raid so well, much more clearly than the Hamburg or Berlin raids. Even the Pathfinder operations in which I later took part did not produce the tension that the Peenemünde raid did. Even after thirty-seven years, the memory of the Lancasters going down still remains very vivid. It was a night out for the German night fighters. (Sergeant J. E. Hudson, 49 Squadron)

In looking through my log book, it is of interest to note that, of thirty operational entries, including three on Berlin, the Peenemünde raid is the only one with the notation 'HOT'. (Flying Officer F. T. Judah, 419 Squadron)

As a final footnote to my account, may I stress that I was very proud to have taken part in the Peenemünde raid. There is no doubt that, at the time, it was considered to be an operation of quite critical significance and no subsequent reassessment, of which, with Bomber Command activity, there have been so many, can diminish the sense of achievement that we felt about it. (Sergeant O. E. Burger, 77 Squadron)

NOTES

1. *The Nuremberg Raid* deals with the period between the Peenemünde operation and the end of the Battle of Berlin in greater detail than is possible here.

2. Official History, vol. II, p. 9.
3. The details are from *The Rocket Team* by Ordway and Sharpe, 1979.
4. These details are from *Hitler's Last Weapons* by Jozef Garlinski, pp. 106–9.
5. Most of these details come from pp. 285–95 of *The Mare's Nest* by David Irving; the Antwerp and Liège casualty figures are from Peter G. Cooksley's *Flying Bomb*, p. 185.
6. *The Mare's Nest*, p. 314.

The Original Bomber Command Operation Order

'R.D.F.', in paragraph 1, is 'Radio Direction Finding', the original cover name for radar, which was still being used. It was employed here so as to conceal from bomber crews that the Germans were making rockets at Peenemünde.

Several aspects of this original plan, such as the order of Aiming Points, the allocation of groups to Aiming Points, and part of the route, were later changed, and the Master Bomber feature was obviously added afterwards.

The following abbreviations are used for different types of bomb: H.E. – High Explosive, H.C. – High Capacity, M.C. – Medium Capacity, G.P. – General Purpose, T.D. – Time Delay.

This document was not released to the Public Record Office; it was loaned privately.

BOMBER COMMAND OPERATION ORDER No. 176

9th July, 1943.

Information

1. Heavy and successful bombing of Germany has forced the enemy to concentrate his energies on increasing the production of countermeasures against our night bombers. It is known that among these countermeasures a new form of highly specialized R.D.F. equipment, which promises to improve greatly the German night air defence organization, is being developed and made at Peenemünde.

2. The experimental establishment at Peenemünde is situated on a tongue of land on the Baltic Coast, about 60 miles north-west of Stettin. The whole complex, which covers an area of some 8,000 yards by 2,000 yards, includes the experimental station, assembly plant and living quarters housing the scientific and technical experts. The destruction of this experimental station, the large factory workshops and the killing of the scientific and technical experts would retard the production of this new equipment and contribute largely to increasing the effectiveness of the bomber offensive.

3. In view of the importance of this target, it is essential that it should be effectively damaged. It is clearly advantageous to do so in one attack, otherwise the enemy is likely considerably to increase the existing defences, but if necessary the attack will have to be repeated until the requisite degree of destruction has been achieved.

4. *Regarding our own Forces.* – The importance of striking a really heavy blow

at Peenemünde makes it necessary to employ the largest possible force for attack. Therefore GOODWOOD figures of Halifaxes, Stirlings and Lancasters will be called for from all Operational Groups.

Intention

5. To attack and destroy the Experimental R.D.F. Establishment at Peenemünde.

Execution

6. *Date of Attack*. – This attack is to take place on the first suitable occasion when either there is sufficient cloud cover over Denmark to enable a dusk attack to be made or on the first suitable night which offers sufficient hours of darkness to enable the flight over enemy territory to be completed between evening and morning nautical twilights.

7. *Aiming Points*. – The aiming points referred to in the under-mentioned paragraphs are taken from the annotated plan of the target dossier, copies of which are being forwarded to Groups by the Intelligence Branch of this headquarters.

8. *Nos. 3 and 5 Groups*. – All available Stirlings and Lancasters of Nos. 3 and 5 Groups are to attack the Experimental Station (E), the destruction of which will interfere with the research work being carried out on the development of the special apparatus.

9. *No. 1 Group*. – All available Lancasters of No. 1 Group are to attack and destroy the two large factory workshops (B) where it is believed that the special equipment is being finally assembled.

10. *Nos. 4 and 6 Groups*. – All available Halifaxes from Nos. 4 and 6 Groups are to attack the living and sleeping quarters (F) in order to kill or incapacitate as many of the scientific and technical personnel as possible.

11. *Path Finder Group*. – No. 8 (PFF) Group is to supply aircraft for marking the island of Rügen and other suitable points *en route*. Each aiming point at the target is also to be marked. Full details of the method to be employed in marking the aiming points are to be passed to Groups by No. 8 (PFF) Group on the day when the operation is ordered. The remaining Pathfinder forces are to attack the Workshops 'B' in conjunction with No. 1 Group.

12. Seventy-five per cent. of all Lancasters are to carry 100 per cent. H.E. bomb loads made up as follows:—

    (a) Twenty-five per cent. of the total available lift of H.E. carrying aircraft to be made up with 4,000-lb. H.C. and M.C. bombs.

    (b) The remaining 75 per cent. of the total lift to be made up with 1,000-lb. M.C. or G.P. and 500-lb. M.C. bombs.

    (c) The remaining 25 per cent of Lancasters are to carry maximum economic incendiary loads.

13. Seventy-five per cent. of all Stirlings and Halifaxes are to carry the maximum H.E. bomb loads, made up with large H.C. bombs and 1,000-lb.

and 500-lb. M.C. and G.P. bombs. The remaining 25 per cent. of aircraft are to carry 100 per cent. incendiary bomb loads.

14. *Bomb Fuzing.* – All 4,000-lb. M.C. bombs and all H.E. bombs carried by aircraft attacking Aiming Point 'F' are to be fuzed tail inst. Of the remaining 1,000-lb. and 500-lb. bombs, 95 per cent. are to be fuzed TD .025 and 5 per cent. are to be fuzed long delay with No. 37 pistol. Long delay fuzes will be varied up to the maximum delays available.

15. *Route.* – The route is to be as follows:—
> Base.
> 55° 20′ N., 8° 29′ E.
> 54° 24′ N., 13° 40′ E.
> Island of Rügen.
> Target.
> Mando.
> Base.

The total distance from the Danish coast to the target and return to the Danish coast by this route is 464 miles.

16. The attack is to commence at Z hours and is to last 40 minutes. The timing on individual aiming points is subject to slight alteration on the day on which the operation is ordered, this being dependent on the wind direction over the target which may necessitate the aiming points down-wind being attacked first. Air Officers Commanding Groups are, subject to this proviso, to ensure that their forces are evenly distributed throughout this period, paying particular care to ensure that their forces are led by the most experienced crews available. Aircraft carrying incendiaries are to attack at the end of each wave.

17. *Bombing Tactics.* – The extreme importance of this target and the necessity of achieving its destruction with one attack is to be impressed on all crews at briefing. If the attack fails to achieve the object it will have to be repeated the next night and on ensuing nights regardless, within practicable limits, of casualties. Special care is to be exercised to ensure that bomb aimers are fully conversant with the technique to be adopted by the Pathfinders in marking their individual points. Ground markers only are to be bombed. On no account are crews to attempt to bomb their respective aiming points by visual means. Bombing is to be carried out at the best tactical height for accuracy, i.e. about 8,000 ft. No aircraft are to attack below 4,000 ft.

18. *Security.* – It is of utmost importance that knowledge of this operation is confined to as few individuals as possible. At present, this knowledge is to be confined to Air Officers Commanding and their Senior Air Staff Officers only.

19. *Executive.* – This operation will be known by a code name which will be issued separately. The Executive, together with the number of aircraft

taking part, and any modifications to the route, will be passed to Groups in the normal manner on the morning preceding the attack.

20. ACKNOWLEDGE BY TELEPRINTER.

for Air Vice-Marshal,
Senior Air Staff Officer,
Bomber Command.

BC/S.30314/Ops.

R.A.F. Operational Performance and Roll of Honour

The purpose of this appendix is to list every R.A.F. unit taking part in the Peenemünde raid and in the supporting operations of that night, to catalogue the number of sorties dispatched and successfully completed, and to provide details of the casualties. The opportunity is taken to list the name of every Allied airman who died.

The aircraft which became total losses are identified by the factory serial number and the captain's name, whether he was killed or not. The number 'down' allocated to each aircraft, e.g. '35th down' for the first entry, in 12 Squadron, corresponds to the number on the map of 'R.A.F. Losses' on the following pages. These numbers correspond to the order in which the bombers are believed to have been destroyed. The locations of crashes of which no trace was ever found have been estimated from Luftwaffe pilots' claims, German ground observations, the reports of returning R.A.F. crews, and assumptions made about a lost aircraft's probable position in a wave and the time due over the target. This should provide reasonably reliable details in most cases, but the word 'probably' indicates that the location cannot be completely confirmed. In the case of four aircraft, there is no way of narrowing down the crash locations further than two possible sites for each; this is indicated by notes at the relevant points.

The cause of loss can be assumed to be 'shot down by German night fighter' unless otherwise stated. In earlier books, I have been able to supply the names of the German fighter crews, but the air battle near Peenemünde was so concentrated that no reliable identifications can be made; in shooting-down incidents away from the target area, the identity of the German crew has already been mentioned in the relevant chapter.

The operational experience of each lost crew has been added where known; where there was a mixed crew, the details represent the best estimate of the crew's average record. The dead are listed by crews in alphabetical order, except the captain; if the full crew is not named, the rest were not fatal casualties. The locations of the homes of the dead are given with as much accuracy as possible.

Although the 'rank on sleeves' actually held at the time of the Peenemünde raid has been used in the text, the appendix quotes any higher posthumous rank. The following abbreviations are employed:
Wing Commander – W/Cdr, Squadron Leader – S/Ldr, Flight Lieutenant – F/Lt, Flying Officer – F/O, Pilot Officer – P/O, Warrant Officer – W.O., Flight Sergeant – F/Sgt, Sergeant – Sgt. Prisoners of war are 'P.O.W.s.'.

NO. 1 GROUP

113 Lancasters dispatched, 106 bombed (2 on secondary targets), 3 missing; 21 men killed, no P.O.W.s.

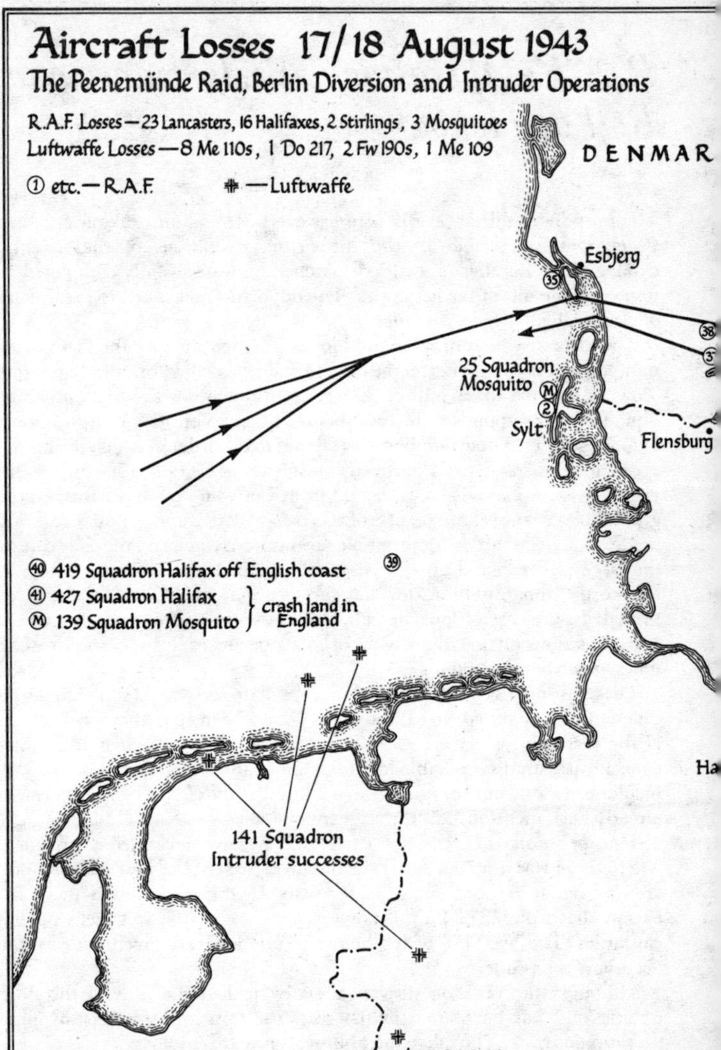

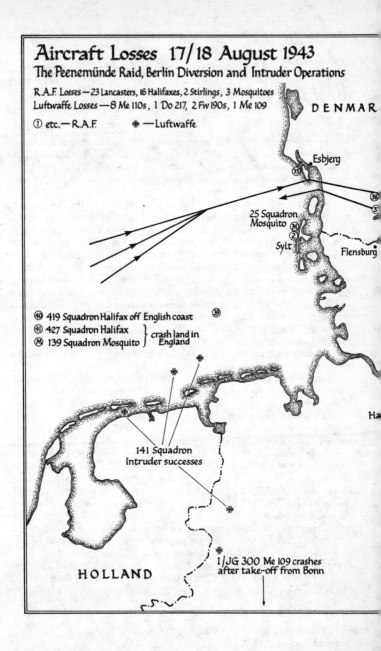

Aircraft Losses 17/18 August 1943
The Peenemünde Raid, Berlin Diversion and Intruder Operations
R.A.F. Losses — 23 Lancasters, 16 Halifaxes, 2 Stirlings, 3 Mosquitoes
Luftwaffe Losses — 8 Me 110s, 1 Do 217, 2 Fw 190s, 1 Me 109
① etc. — R.A.F.
✠ — Luftwaffe
DENMAR
Esbjerg
35
38
25 Squadron Mosquito
M
2
Sylt
Flensburg
40 419 Squadron Halifax off English coast
41 427 Squadron Halifax
M 139 Squadron Mosquito
crash land in England
39
141 Squadron Intruder successes
I/JG 300 Me 109 crashes after take-off from Bonn
HOLLAND
Ha

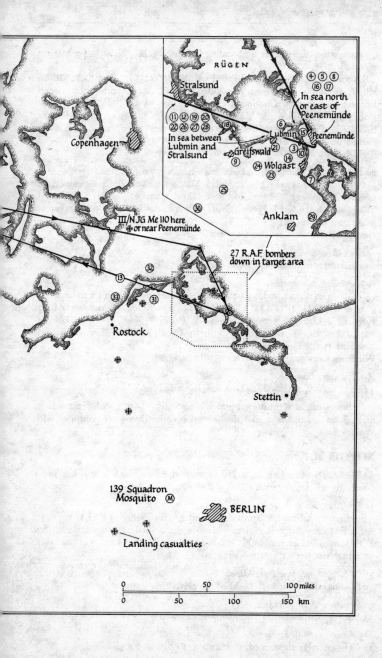

RÜGEN

Stralsund

④ ⑤ ⑧
⑯ ⑰
In sea north
or east of
Peenemünde

⑪ ⑫ ⑲ ⑳
㉒ ㉖ ㉗ ㉘   ⑱

⑥
Lubmin ⑮ Peenemünde
In sea between   ③
Lubmin and   Greifswald ㉑   ⑩
Stralsund   ⑨   ⑭
          ㉔ Wolgast
          ㉓   ⑦

Copenhagen

㉕

III/NJG Me 110 here
✠ or near Peenemünde

㉚   Anklam ㉙

27 R.A.F. bombers
down in target area

㉜
⑬
㉝   ㉛

Rostock

Stettin •

139 Squadron
Mosquito Ⓜ   BERLIN

Landing casualties

0   50   100 miles
0   50   100   150 km

12 Squadron, Wickenby
25 Lancasters dispatched, 25 bombed (1 on secondary target), 1 missing; 7 men killed.

Lancaster DV168 (Pilot: S/Ldr F. B. Slade D.S.O., Tavistock, Devon, killed), probably 35th down. Also killed: F/O G. R. Carpenter, Hall Green, Birmingham; Sgt S. Chapman, Sutton, Surrey; P/O J. F. B. McIntyre, Edinburgh; P/O C. W. A. Manning, London; Sgt L. Myers, Wigan, Lancs: F/O P. H. Phillips, Glen Iris, Victoria. Crew on 12th operation; pilot and some others of 2nd tour.

100 Squadron, Grimsby
20 Lancasters dispatched, 19 bombed, 1 missing; 7 men killed.

Lancaster ED647 (F/O H. I. Spiers, Masterton, New Zealand, killed), 5th down. Killed: Sgt O. M. Atkins, Ammanford, Carmarthen; Sgt S. J. Cassell, St Helens, Lancs; Sgt J. Francis, Northampton; Sgt K. F. Goode, Chepstow, Monmouthshire; Sgt C. W. Torbett, Welling, Kent; P/O J. Weaver, Newfound, Hants. Crew on 1st operation.

101 Squadron, Ludford Magna
20 Lancasters dispatched, 17 bombed, no casualties.

103 Squadron, Elsham Wolds
24 Lancasters dispatched, 24 bombed (1 on secondary target), 1 missing.

Lancaster ED725 (P/O P. O'Donnell, London, killed), 34th down. Killed: F/Sgt E. R. Biggs, Petersham, New South Wales; F/Sgt P. J. Capon, Gillingham, Kent; Sgt W. H. Greaves, Oldham, Lancs; Sgt C. N. Lee, Doncaster, Yorks; F/Sgt M. G. Medhurst, East Brisbane, Queensland; Sgt C. P. Williams, Copnor, Hants. Crew on 3rd operation.

460 Squadron, Binbrook
24 Lancasters dispatched, 23 bombed, no casualties.

(166 Squadron at Kirmington and 300 and 305 – both Polish – Squadrons at Ingham did not take part in the raid because they were equipped with Wellingtons.)

NO. 3 GROUP

54 Stirlings and 12 Lancaster IIs dispatched, 61 bombed, 2 Stirlings and 1 Lancaster missing; 13 men killed, 9 P.O.W.s.

15 Squadron, Mildenhall
5 Stirlings dispatched, 4 bombed, 1 missing; 3 men killed, 4 P.O.W.s.

Stirling EE908 (Sgt R. Grundy, Birmingham, killed), 7th down. Killed: Sgt E. Honeybill, Levenshulme, Manchester; Sgt C. F. Hudson, Bournville, Birmingham. Crew on 12th operation.

75 (New Zealand) Squadron, Mepal
12 Stirlings dispatched, 11 bombed, no casualties.

90 Squadron, West Wickham
15 Stirlings dispatched, 15 bombed, no casualties.

115 Squadron, Little Snoring
12 Lancaster IIs dispatched, 12 bombed, 1 missing; 7 men killed.

Lancaster DS630 (F/O F. R. C. Pusey, Wotton-under-Edge, Glos., killed), 13th down. Killed: F/O C. G. Bruton, Orono, Ontario; P/O J.D.S. Cable, Radlett, Herts; Sgt J. T. Corbett, South Lopham, Norfolk; Sgt L. P. Howard, Tue Brook, Liverpool; Sgt T. M. Leonard, Prudhoe, Northumberland; Sgt M. G. McKibbon, Toronto. Crew on 3rd operation.

149 Squadron, Lakenheath
2 Stirlings dispatched, 2 bombed, no casualties.

199 Squadron, Lakenheath
2 Stirlings dispatched, 2 bombed, no casualties.

214 Squadron, Chedburgh
7 Stirlings dispatched, 6 bombed, no casualties.

218 Squadron, Downham Market
5 Stirlings dispatched, 4 bombed, no casualties.

620 Squadron, Chedburgh
5 Stirlings dispatched, 4 bombed, 1 missing; 3 men killed, 5 P.O.W.s.
  Stirling EE457 (S/Ldr A. D. Lambert, P.O.W.), 6th down. Killed: Sgt D. J. Carrington, Cosham, Hants; F/O L. G. Kennett, East Dean, Sussex; Sgt R. E. Thompson, Sturminster Newton, Dorset. Crew on 13th operation; pilot on 2nd tour.

622 Squadron, Mildenhall
1 Stirling dispatched, 1 bombed, no casualties.

138 Squadron, Tempsford
8 Halifaxes dispatched on supply-dropping operations to Occupied Europe, no casualties.

(161 Squadron, Tempsford, and 196 Squadron, Witchford – both special duty squadrons – and 192 Squadron, Feltwell, converting from Wellingtons to Stirlings, took no part in operations.)

NO. 4 GROUP

145 Halifaxes dispatched, 137 bombed, 3 missing; 20 killed, 2 P.O.W.s.

10 Squadron, Melbourne
18 Halifaxes dispatched, 15 bombed, 1 missing; 8 men killed.
  Halifax JD200 (P/O A. J. E. Long, Downend, Bristol, killed), probably 39th down but possibly 4th down by Flak in sea near Peenemünde (see also 77 Squadron aircraft loss). Killed: F/O C. L. Barbezat, Latimer, Bucks; Sgt J. Cooper, Enfield, Middx; Sgt D. A. Galloway, Denny, Stirlingshire; Sgt D. Goulden, North Shields, Northumberland; Sgt J. J. V. Heal, Winchester, Hants; Sgt L. H. Sefton, Ferndale, Glamorgan; Sgt F. Willets, Handsworth, Birmingham. Crew on 9th operation.

51 Squadron, Snaith
24 Halifaxes dispatched, 24 bombed, no casualties.

76 Squadron, Holme-on-Spalding-Moor
20 Halifaxes dispatched, 20 bombed, no casualties.

77 Squadron, Elvington
21 Halifaxes dispatched, 19 bombed, 1 missing; 7 men killed.

Halifax JD 324 (Sgt F. E. Shefford, Hull, Yorks, killed), probably 4th down by Flak in sea near Peenemünde but possibly 39th down (see also 10 Squadron aircraft loss). Killed: Sgt F. J. Lane, Grantham, Lincs; Sgt A. W. Ready, Newport, Monmouth; Sgt H. F. Roza, Liverpool; Sgt J. B. L. Smith, Crail, Fifeshire; Sgt J. R. Vint, Cleland, Lanarks; Sgt G. Wood, Newton-le-Willows, Lancs. Crew on 3rd operation.

78 Squadron, Breighton
21 Halifaxes dispatched, 19 bombed plus 1 which reached target but could not operate its bomb release, no casualties.

102 Squadron, Pocklington
17 Halifaxes dispatched, 17 bombed, no casualties.

158 Squadron, Lissett
24 Halifaxes dispatched, 23 bombed, 1 missing; 5 men killed, 2 P.O.W.s

Halifax JD 260 (P/O W. D. Caldwell, Lyall Bay, Wellington, New Zealand, killed), 3rd down by Flak at Peenemünde. Killed: F/Sgt M. Czajkowski, Millet, Alberta; Sgt R. H. Reay, Gateshead, Co. Durham; Sgt J. C. D. Riddell, Wishaw, Lanarks; Sgt A. Tice, Standish, Lancs. Crew on 7th operation.

(466 Squadron, Leconfield, not on raid because equipped with Wellingtons.)

NO. 5 GROUP

117 Lancasters dispatched, 109 bombed, 17 missing; 111 men killed, 13 P.O.W.s.

9 Squadron, Bardney
12 Lancasters dispatched, 12 bombed, no casualties.

44 (Rhodesia) Squadron, Dunholme Lodge
13 Lancasters dispatched, 13 bombed, 3 missing; 20 men killed, 1 P.O.W.

Lancaster DV202 (P/O R. C. Harding, Kirkland Lake, Ontario, killed), 15th down. Killed: Sgt L. F. McDermott, Oxhey, Herts; F/Sgt P. Prendergast, Liverpool; F/Sgt P. Pynisky, Sydney, Nova Scotia; Sgt W. H. Quance, Leicester; F/Sgt S. Shaw, Stapleford, Notts; Sgt T. N. Weston, Northendon, Lancs. Crew on 8th operation.

Lancaster W4935 (P/O R. M. Campbell, Fauldhouse, West Lothian, killed), 19th down. Killed: Sgt J. Graham, Glasgow; Sgt H. C. MacAninch, Glasgow; Sgt W. Philip, Galashiels, Selkirkshire; F/O L. G. Popperwell, Devonport, Devon; P/O A. H. Thompson, Dublin; Sgt J. G. Watkins, Coleshill, Warwicks. Crew on 5th operation.

Lancaster JA897 (P/O W. J. Drew, Woking, Surrey, killed), 24th down. Killed: Sgt J. H. Bassett, Lewisham, London; Sgt T. H. R. James, Gatooma, Southern Rhodesia; F/Sgt J. J. Jopling, New Eltham, London; Sgt J. D. M. Reid, Ayr; P/O S. I. Rudkin, Leicester. Crew on 7th operation.

49 Squadron, Fiskerton
12 Lancasters dispatched, 11 bombed, 4 missing; 23 men killed, 5 P.O.W.s.

Lancaster JA892 (Sgt C. Robinson, P.O.W.), 14th down. Killed: Sgt D. Parkin, Grasscroft, Yorks; F/Sgt J. I. Wallner, Hanover, Ontario. Crew on 13th operation.

Lancaster ED805 (S/Ldr R. G. Todd-White, Woodford Wells, Essex, killed), 16th down. Killed: F/O A. Batchelor, Streatham, London; Sgt T. Brocklehurst, Huddersfield, Yorks; Sgt G. Humble, Newcastle-upon-Tyne; F/O B. James, Rhondda, Glamorgan; F/O F. Plant, Hyde, Cheshire; Sgt A. Purrington, Portsmouth. Crew on 2nd operation of 2nd tour.

Lancaster JA851 (P/O T. E. Tomlin, D.F.C., Mutley, Plymouth, killed), 36th down. Killed: F/Sgt W. A. Davies, Shrewsbury; P/O W. J. Rooke, Blachall, Queensland; F/Sgt G. B. Silvester, D.F.M., Binfield, Berks; Sgt C. Stancliffe, Norton, Nr Malton, Yorks; P/O T. Tonkin, D.F.M., Rose Green, Sussex; Sgt K. E. Watson, Southgate, London. Crew on 24th operation.

Lancaster JA691 (F/O H. J. Randall, Fulham, London, killed), 37th down. Killed: Sgt N. W. Buchanan, Barcaldine, Queensland; Sgt R. Fowlston, Skegby, Notts; Sgt L. F. Freeman, Smethwick, Staffs; Sgt L. J. Henley, Sparkbrook, Birmingham; Sgt R. W. Slaughter, Guildford, Surrey; Sgt W. J. Stiles, Wolverton, Warwicks. Crew on 8th operation.

50 Squadron, Skellingthorpe
11 Lancasters dispatched, 11 bombed, no casualties.

57 Squadron, Scampton
16 Lancasters dispatched, 14 bombed, 1 missing; 8 men killed.

Lancaster ED989 (W/Cdr W. R. Haskill, D.F.C., Verwood, Dorset, killed), probably 32nd or 33rd down. Killed: F/Sgt C. Butterworth, Heaton Mersey, Lancs; Sgt J. F. Harkness, Glasgow; Sgt J. E. John, Swansea; F/O J. Jones, Lewisham, London; F/Sgt J. L. Lamb, Montreal; Sgt D. E. Nye, Keston, Kent; Sgt R. A. C. M. Stringer, Twickenham, Middx. Crew on 5th operation.

61 Squadron, Syerston
13 Lancasters dispatched, 10 bombed, 4 missing; 28 men killed, 2 P.O.W.s.

Lancaster W4766 (F/Lt T. A. Stewart, D.F.M., P.O.W.), 10th down. Killed: Sgt J. C. Bradey, Edmonton, Alberta; P/O R. K. Buxton, D.F.M., Bristol; Sgt N. W. H. Clark, Cartcosh; Sgt T. A. Harris, Faversham, Kent; F/Sgt L. H. Thompson, Winchester Springs, Ontario; F/Sgt J. F. Trotter, D.F.M., Doncaster, Yorks. Crew on 18th operation, most on 2nd tour.

Lancaster ED661 (P/O H. R. Madgett, D.F.M., Sidcup, Kent, killed), 11th down. Killed: P/O R. Bradley, Toronto; P/O J. M. Lewis, Gurneyville, Alberta; F/O F. D. Norton, D.F.C., Bridgend, Glamorgan; P/O S. G. Palk, Merton, Surrey; P/O H. Robinson, Oxspring, Yorks; P/O A. W. A. Souter, Beckenham, Kent; P/O J. J. Wakefield, Bracknell, Berks. Crew on 26th operation.

Lancaster JA900 (F/Sgt R. J. R. Docker, Liverpool, killed), 12th down. Killed: Sgt E. G. Francis, Aveley, Essex; Sgt S. W. James, Portsmouth; Sgt R. Laughton, Hucknall, Notts; Sgt L. Lucas, Alfreton, Derbys; Sgt P. W. Mitchell, Battersea, London; F/Sgt R. Urquhart, Spanish, Ontario; P/O A. N. Vidler, Blayney, New South Wales. Crew on 16th operation.

Lancaster W4934 (F/O W. Hughes, Leadgate, Co. Durham, killed), 17th down. Killed: Sgt B. J. W. Brown, Middleton, Suffolk; Sgt D. Easton, Dundee; Sgt T. Graham, Braco, Perthshire; Sgt W. B. Ness; Sgt L. H. Scholey,

Batley Carr, Yorks; Sgt R. C. Walton, Poynton, Cheshire. Crew on 1st operation.

106 Squadron, Syerston
9 Lancasters dispatched, 9 bombed, no casualties.

207 Squadron, Langar
9 Lancasters dispatched, 9 bombed, no casualties.

467 (R.A.A.F.) Squadron, Bottesford
10 Lancasters dispatched, 9 bombed, 2 missing; 10 men killed, 5 P.O.W.s.
    Lancaster LM 342 (S/Ldr A. S. Raphael, D.F.C., Maida Vale, London, killed), 8th down. Killed: Sgt A. C. Brand, Alva, Clackmannanshire; F/O R. G. Carter, D.F.C., Toronto; P/O D. Fielden, St Albans, Herts; F/Sgt F. B. Garrett, Clifton, Oxfordshire; Sgt F. Grey, Newbridge, Monmouthshire; F/Lt M. H. Parry, Bristol; Sgt V. Smith, Stanmore, Middx. Crew on 19th operation. S/Ldr Raphael was the acting squadron commander, F/Lt Parry the Squadron Bombing Leader flying as an observer.
    Lancaster ED 764 (P/O F. W.Dixon, D.F.M., P.O.W.), 18th down. Killed: Sgt L. C. Hayward, Tottenham, London; Sgt P. Lowe, Dukinfield, Cheshire. Crew on 21st operation.

619 Squadron, Woodhall Spa
12 Lancasters dispatched, 11 bombed, 3 missing; 22 men killed.
    Lancaster ED 982 (P/O A. J. Pearce, Penarth, Glamorgan, killed), 26th down. Killed: Sgt T. B. Barrie, Forfar, Angus; F/O L. G. Davis, D.F.M., Bow, London; Sgt R. D. Deugard, Downderry, Cornwall; Sgt C. B. Francis, Eastleigh, Hants; Sgt W. H. Humphrey, Birmingham; F/O J. M. Warren, Edgware, Middx. Crew on 10th operation.
    Lancaster EE 147 (P/O O. A. O'Leary, Ottawa, killed), 29th down. Killed: Sgt D. G. Cox, West Bromwich, Staffs; F/Sgt R. Crossley, Barnsley, Yorks; F/Sgt L. F. English, Auckland, New Zealand; Sgt J. T. Hubbard, Gateshead, Co. Durham; Sgt J. H. Shaw, Bingley, Yorks; Sgt T. Underdown, Middlesbrough. Crew on 9th operation.
    Lancaster EE 117 (W/Cdr I. J. McGhie, D.F.C., Aberfan, Glamorgan, killed), 38th down. Killed: Sgt A. C. R. Chapman, Kettering, Northants; P/O P. M. Goldsmith, Prospect, South Australia; F/Sgt P. J. Horsham, Oxford; F/O E. G. Prest, Upper Stewiacke, Nova Scotia; Sgt W. A. Mitchell, Crewkerne, Somerset; P/O V. G. Stabell, Hillston, New South Wales; W. O. F. A. Thompson, Cornwall, Ontario. Crew on 7th operation, some of 2nd tour.

(617 Squadron, Scampton, took no part in the operation.)

NO. 6 (CANADIAN) GROUP

52 Halifaxes and 9 Lancaster IIs dispatched, 57 bombed, 10 Halifaxes and 2 Lancasters missing, 1 further Halifax written off; 66 men killed, 19 P.O.W.s.

419 (Moose) Squadron, Middleton St George
17 Halifaxes dispatched, 17 bombed, 3 missing; 22 men killed.
    Halifax JD 158 (F/Lt S. M. Heard, Regina, Saskatchewan, killed), 27th down. Killed: Sgt G. Blyth, Dundee, Scotland; W.O. J. W. Dally, New Toronto, Ontario; F/Sgt D. M. MacPherson, Brighton, South Australia; P/O

P. O. McSween, New Waterford, Nova Scotia; Sgt J. J. Newbon, Manchester; F/Sgt D. Thornton, Toronto; F/Sgt G. S. Walter, Vancouver. Crew on 14th operation.

Halifax JD458 (F/Sgt S. T. Pekin, Vite Vite, Victoria, Australia, killed), 28th down. Killed: Sgt H. C. Baker, Newport, Monmouthshire; Sgt F. P. Davis, Penarth, Glamorgan; Sgt J. K. Gilvary, Bray, Co. Wicklow, Ireland; Sgt H. Price, Palmer's Green, London; F/O P. J. Sparkes, Acton, London; Sgt E. C. Ramm, Hackney, London. Crew on 6th operation.

Halifax JD163 (F/Sgt J. M. Batterton, Welland, Ontario, killed), 40th down, in North Sea. Killed: Sgt A. Dixon, Lancaster, Lancs; F/Sgt J. O. Jerome, Hamilton, Ontario; Sgt D. A. Lloyd, Wrexham, Denbighshire; Sgt H. U. Morris, Welland, Ontario; F/Sgt G. F. Parker, York Township, Ontario; Sgt L. F. Power, Mulgrave, Nova Scotia. Crew on 7th operation.

426 (Thunderbird) Squadron, Linton-on-Ouse

9 Lancaster IIs dispatched, 8 bombed, 2 missing; 13 men killed, 1 P.O.W.

Lancaster DS681 (W/Cdr L. Crooks, D.S.O., D.F.C., Peterborough, Northants, killed), 25th down. Killed: P/O T. Dos Santos, Trinidad; Sgt J. C. Hislop, Glasgow; F/Sgt A. J. Howes, Shepherd's Bush, London; F/Lt F. P. Marsh, D.F.C.; P/O H. M. Smith, Toronto. Mixed crew varying between 1st operation for two members to 6th and 8th operations in 2nd tour for others.

Lancaster DS674 (F/Lt D. D. Shuttleworth, D.F.C., Regina, Saskatchewan, killed), probably 32nd or 33rd down. Killed: Sgt S. Barnes, Little Hulton, Lancs; Sgt G. W. Bentley, Southampton; P/O J. M. L. Bouvier, D.F.M., Montreal; P/O K. C. Gawthorp, Cypress River, Manitoba; F/O G. C. Robinson, Regina, Saskatchewan; F/O G. W. Scammel, D.F.C., London. Crew on 16/22nd operations, F/O Scammell of 2nd tour.

427 (Lion) Squadron, Leeming

12 Halifaxes dispatched, 11 bombed, 1 missing, 1 written off; 5 men killed, 2 P.O.W.s.

Halifax DK243 (P/O F. J. D. Brady, Quebec City, killed), 21st down. Killed: Sgt J. L. Fletcher, North Battleford, Saskatchewan; Sgt O. M. McIntyre, New Norway, Alberta; Sgt I. W. Pugh, Bontddu, Merionethshire; W.O. J. L. Troman, Vancouver. Crew on 2nd operation.

Halifax DK227 (Sgt W. H. Schmitt), 41st down, written off after combat damage and crash-landing at Mildenhall; no casualties.

428 (Ghost) Squadron, Middleton St George

14 Halifaxes dispatched, 14 bombed, 3 missing; 16 men killed, 5 P.O.W.s.

Halifax EB211 (F/Sgt J. Sheridan, London, Ontario, killed), 20th down. Killed: W.O. W. L. Cogger, Prince Albert, Saskatchewan; Sgt D. Kennedy, Enfield, Middx; F/Sgt T. B. Lifman, Arborg, Manitoba; W.O. E. R. Marks; Sgt N. R. Mitchell, Dundee, Scotland; F/Sgt M. B. Murphy, Paynton, Saskatchewan. Crew on 14th operation.

Halifax DK230 (F/Lt G. W. N. Fanson, Winnipeg, killed), 22nd down. Killed: F/Sgt L. M. Banks, Brantford, Ontario; F/Sgt J. A. Leighton, Prince Rupert, British Columbia; Sgt R. A. Lewis, Buckhurst Hill, Essex; Sgt R. G. McCallum, Glasgow; P/O D. J. McNeill, Toronto; F/O D. H. Orr, Moose Jaw, Saskatchewan. Crew on 20th operation.

Halifax DK238 (F/Sgt W. W. Blackmore, Cardston, Alberta, killed), 31st down. Killed: F/Sgt F. S. Williams, Swinton, Lancs. Crew on 20th operation.

434 (Bluenose) Squadron, Tholthorpe
9 Halifaxes dispatched, 7 bombed, 3 missing; 10 men killed, 11 P.O.W.s.

Halifax EB258 (P/O F. J. Piper, Tuxford, Saskatchewan, killed), 2nd down by Flak at Sylt. Killed: F/Sgt C. A. Brown, New Westminster, British Columbia; F/Sgt G. R. Connor, Hanover, Ontario; F/Sgt R. C. Jordan, Glen Rose, Texas, U.S.A.; F/Sgt J. I. R. R. Renaud, Knowlton, Quebec. Crew on 2nd operation.

Halifax DK260 (F/Lt I. L. Colquhoun, Edmonton, Alberta, killed), 23rd down. Killed: W.O. C. P. Fitzpatrick, Toronto; F/Sgt J. P. C. Lapointe, Montreal; Sgt D. A. Young, Gosport, Hants. Crew on 5th operation, pilot on 2nd tour.

Halifax EB276 (P/O G. M. Johnston, Moose Jaw, Saskatchewan, killed), 30th down, rest of crew all P.O.W.s. Crew on 14th operation.

(408 (Goose) Squadron, Leeming – all crews on leave; 429 (Bison) Squadron, East Moor, and 432 (Leaside) Squadron, Skipton-on-Swale – both equipped with Wellingtons – and 431 (Iroquois) Squadron, Tholthorpe – converting from Wellingtons to Halifaxes – took no part in the raid.)

NO. 8 (PATHFINDER) GROUP

73 Lancasters and 21 Halifaxes dispatched to Peenemünde, 8 Mosquitoes dispatched to Berlin; 90 aircraft bombed at Peenemünde, 7 or 8 at Berlin; 2 Halifaxes and 1 Mosquito missing, 1 Mosquito written off; 14 men killed, 2 P.O.W.s.

7 Squadron, Oakington
17 Lancasters dispatched, 17 bombed, no casualties.

35 Squadron, Graveley
10 Halifaxes dispatched, 10 bombed, 1 missing; 5 men killed, 2 P.O.W.s.

Halifax HR862 (P/O P. R. Raggett, Herne Bay, Kent, killed), 9th down, probably by Peenemünde Flak. Killed: F/O S. A. Baldwin, Shepherd's Bush, London; F/O A. J. Perkins, Marston Green, Warwicks; Sgt V. Webster, Totley, Yorks; F/Sgt D. S. Woods, Manor Park, Essex. Crew on 21st operation.

83 Squadron, Wyton
15 Lancasters dispatched, 14 bombed, no casualties.

97 Squadron, Bourn
18 Lancasters dispatched, 17 bombed, no casualties.

139 Squadron, Wyton
8 Mosquitoes dispatched, 7 or 8 bombed, 1 missing, 1 written off; 2 men killed.

Mosquito DZ379 (F/O A. S. Cooke, Wichita Falls, Texas, U.S.A., killed), shot down by night fighter, crashed at Berge, near Nauen, 35 kilometres west of Berlin. Also killed, Sgt D. A. H. Dixon, Glasgow. Crew on 3rd operation with this squadron.

Mosquito DZ465 (F/Lt R. A. V. Crampton), written off after crash-landing at Swanton Morley; crew slightly injured.

156 Squadron, Warboys
22 Lancasters dispatched, 21 bombed, no casualties.

405 (Vancouver) Squadron, Gransden Lodge
11 Halifaxes and 1 Lancaster dispatched, 11 bombed, 1 Halifax missing; 7 men killed.

Halifax HR817 (F/O H. S. McIntyre, Copper Cliff, Ontario, killed), 1st down by Flensburg Flak. Killed: F/Sgt D. C. B. Angus, Quebec City; P/O T. J. Bowling, Milehouse, Plymouth; Sgt H. W. Cooke, Watton, Norfolk; F/Sgt W. E. Gimby, Saulte Ste Marie, Ontario; F/Sgt W. M. Haugen, Strongfield, Saskatchewan; Sgt T. A. Pargeter, Sanderstead, Surrey. Crew on 6th operation.

1409 (Meteorological) Flight, Oakington
1 Mosquito dispatched on weather reconnaissance in daylight hours before the Peenemünde raid; operation successfully carried out.

(105 and 109 Squadrons at Marham, equipped with Oboe Mosquitoes, took no part in the raid.)

LONG RANGE INTRUDER OPERATIONS, FIGHTER COMMAND

28 Mosquitoes and 10 Beaufighters dispatched; 4 German fighters destroyed plus two more claimed but with no German documentary evidence to confirm, 10 airfields bombed. 1 Mosquito missing, 2 men P.O.W.s.

25 Squadron, Church Fenton
4 Mosquitoes dispatched, 1 missing.

Mosquito HX826 (S/Ldr F. N. Brinsden). Shot down by Flak near Westerland airfield, crew taken prisoner.

141 Squadron, Wittering
10 Beaufighters dispatched, 4 German fighters destroyed, no casualties.

157 Squadron, Hunsdon
2 Mosquitoes dispatched, no casualties.

410 (R.C.A.F.) Squadron, Coleby Grange.
2 Mosquitoes dispatched, no casualties.

418 (R.C.A.F.) Squadron, Ford
9 Mosquitoes dispatched, no casualties.

605 (County of Warwick) Squadron, Castle Camps
11 Mosquitoes dispatched, 2 German fighters attacked with unconfirmable results, no casualties.

Luftwaffe Night-Fighter Unit Performances

This appendix cannot be quite as comprehensive as the previous one because so few Luftwaffe unit records survived the war, but it is believed that the general picture provided is accurate. More fighters may have been lost than are recorded here – on past experience, the number would not have exceeded another 10–15 per cent.

The German night-fighter units were organized into *Staffel*, *Gruppe* (normally three *Staffeln*), and *Geschwader* (three or four *Gruppen*). The *Staffel* was roughly the equivalent of an R.A.F. flight or a small U.S.A.A.F. squadron, the *Gruppe* of an R.A.F. squadron or a small U.S.A.A.F. group, and the nearest equivalent of *Geschwader* is 'wing'. Abbreviations were normally used; e.g. 3/NJG1 was the 3rd *Staffel* of the 1st Night-Fighter *Geschwader* and III/NJG1 was the 3rd *Gruppe* of that *Geschwader*. The specialist Wild Boar unit was JG300. All these units were part of a divisional and corps organization, but as these had little significance on the night of the Peenemünde operation they have been omitted.

The following abbreviations are used for aircraft makes: Me – Messerschmitt, Ju – Junkers, Do – Dornier, Fw – Focke-Wulf. The German abbreviation for the Messerschmitt 109 and 110 was Bf (Bayerische Flugzeugwerke), but the common English form 'Me' will be used here. German ranks are abbreviated as follows: Hauptmann – Hptm., Oberleutnant – Oblt, Leutnant – Lt, Oberfeldwebel – Ofw., Feldwebel – Fw., Unteroffizier – Uffz.

I/NJG1, Venlo
Approximately 9 Me 110s dispatched on the Wild Boar operation without success or loss. (This unit had been badly handled by Allied fighter escorts in the U.S.A.A.F. operation to Schweinfurt a few hours earlier.)

II/NJG1, St Trond
12 Me 110s and 1 Do 217 dispatched on Wild Boar operation. 13 bombers claimed shot down, actual success possibly 10; 3 of own aircraft lost, no fatal casualties.

Me 110 G-4 5363 (Lt Musset). Shot down by bomber, crashed south of Rostock.

Me 110 G-4 5572 (Oblt Henseler). Crew baled out after mechanical failure, crashed east of Parchim.

Do 217 —— (Lt Mitzke). Shot down by bomber, crashed south of Barth.

III/NJG1, Twenthe
Me 110s dispatched on Wild Boar operation; some kept back for local box duty. 3 bombers claimed; 1 of own aircraft lost with one man killed.

Me 110 G-4 6228 (Hptm. Dormann, wounded). Shot down by 141 Squadron Beaufighter, crashed north-east of Lingen. Radar operator, Ofw. Friedrich Schmalscheidt, killed.

IV/NJG1, Leeuwarden

Possibly not on Wild Boar operation; some Me 110s used on local duties. 1 bomber claimed but difficult to confirm. 3 Me 110s lost, all to 141 Squadron Beaufighters; 5 men killed.

Me 110 G-4 4874 (Fw. Vinke). Crashed into North Sea; Fw. Karl Schödel and Uffz. Johann Gaa killed.

Me 110 G-4 5469 (Fw. Georg Kraft, killed). Crashed into North Sea.

Me 110 G-4—— (Lt Gerhard Dittmann, killed). Crashed near Holwerd, Holland; Uffz. Theophil Bundschu also killed.

Parts of NJG2, recently returned from Italy, were refitting at Gilze Rijen in Holland; at least one Me 110 from the *Ergänzungsstaffel* (replacement flight) reached the Peenemünde area and claimed one bomber.

I/NJG3, Vechta, Wittmundhafen and Kastrup

Me 110s, Ju 88s and Do 217s dispatched on Wild Boar operation, possibly some on local box duty. 2 bombers claimed; none of own aircraft lost.

II/NJG3, Schleswig and Westerland

Me 110s, Ju 88s and Do 217s dispatched on Wild Boar operation and on local box operations. 5 bombers claimed; none of own aircraft lost.

III/NJG3, Lüneburg and Stade

Me 110s dispatched on Wild Boar operation; no successes or losses.

IV/NJG3, Grove and Aalborg

Ju 88s and Do 217s probably used only for local box operations. 3 bombers claimed; none of own aircraft lost.

Some aircraft of NJG4, from airfields in southern Belgium and northern France, were sent north with the intention of taking part in Wild Boar operations in case an attack developed in the Ruhr or central Germany, but they saw no action and suffered no loss.

I/NJG5, Stendal and Volkenrode

Me 110s dispatched on Wild Boar operation; no successes or losses.

II/NJG5, Parchim and Greifswald

Me 110s dispatched on Wild Boar operation. 7 bombers claimed (6 by *schräge Musik*); 1 of own aircraft lost, 3 men killed.

Me 110 G-4 5443 (Stabsfw. Saevert). Shot down by bomber, crashed south of Stettin. Gefreiter Heinrich Bauer was killed.

Uffz. Otwin Sparer and Uffz. Werner Zahl were killed when they baled out over the sea from a damaged aircraft which later landed safely.

III/NJG5, Kolberg, Werneuchen and Greifswald

12 Me 110s dispatched on Wild Boar operation. 1 bomber claimed; 1 of own aircraft lost, two men killed. This was the first operation for this new *Gruppe*.

Me 110 G-4 —— (Lt Karl Gerber, the *Gruppe* adjutant, killed). Presumed shot down by a bomber over the sea. Uffz. Wenzel Matschiner was also killed.

NJG6, based at various airfields in Germany and Romania, took no part in operations on this night.

Stab and I/JG300, Hangelar (Bonn)
Fw 190s and Me 109s dispatched on Wild Boar operation. 3 bombers claimed, 1 of own aircraft lost.

Me 109 G-6 18570 (pilot's name not known). Crashed near Siegen after engine fire.

II/JG300, Rheine
Fw 190s dispatched on Wild Boar operation. No claims known; 2 of own aircraft lost, 1 man killed.

Fw 190 410254 (Fw. Walther Schu, killed). Crashed while landing at Briest airfield, near Brandenburg.

Fw 190 530371 (Lt Max Kräwinkel, wounded). Destroyed in crash-landing at Burg, near Magdeburg.

III/JG300, Oldenburg
Me 109s assumed to have been dispatched on Wild Boar operation; no record of performance.

(Fw. Hakenjos, pilot in an unknown *Gruppe* of JG300, shot down a Mosquito near Berlin.)

Acknowledgements

Part 1   Participants

The following men and women were all involved in the Peenemünde Raid and I am particularly grateful to them for their willing and generous help.

BOMBER COMMAND AIRCREW

(All ranks are those held on 17 August 1943. Abbreviations not used earlier: Air Commodore – Air Cdre, Group Captain – Gp Capt.)*7 Squadron:* S/Ldr S. Baker, F/Lt P. H. Cutchey, F/O K. McIntyre, W.O. C. Thornhill, F/O O. J. Wells. *10 Squadron:* F/Sgt D. E. Girardau, Sgt E. A. Jones, F/Sgt F. R. Stuart, Sgt T. L. Thackray, Sgt J. D. Whiteman. *12 Squadron:* Sgt F. A. Attwood, Sgt R. Burr, Sgt J. A. L. Currie, Sgt A. C. Farmer, Sgt H. H. Hoey, Sgt T. Matthews, Sgt P. R. Milton, F/Lt J. N. Rowland, F/O W. F. Snell, Sgt D. R. Tattersall, Sgt F. Wadsworth, F/Lt V. Wood. *15 Squadron:* Sgt C. S. Carter, F/Sgt W. L. Combs, Sgt R. A. Scandrett, Sgt L. C. Wood. *35 Squadron:* F/Lt J. Annetts, F/Lt A. J. F. Davidson, F/Lt S. R. Green, F/Sgt A. V. Hardy, F/O C. A. Hewlett, P/O L. E. N. Lahey, F/Sgt N. J. Matich, Sgt P. H. Palmer, Sgt W. E. Sutton, F/Lt G. R. Whitten. *44 Squadron:* Sgt F. G. Abel, P/O D. R. Aldridge, Sgt K. R. Blundell, W/Cdr R. L. Bowes, Sgt J. A. Dellow, Sgt T. S. Holmes, F/Sgt H. E. Palmer, P/O H. Rogers, Sgt W. Sparkes. *49 Squadron:* Sgt A. F. Anderson, Sgt W. Boyd, F/O P. F. Duckham, Sgt J. E. Hudson (died 1981), F/Sgt B. W. Kirton, P/O W. J. Lowe, Sgt C. Robinson, F/O B. L. Schauenberg. *50 Squadron:* P/O D. A. Duncan, Sgt E. Poulter, F/Sgt W. C. B. Smith. *51 Squadron:* Sgt K. S. Batten, F/Sgt M. C. Foster, Sgt A. R. Jordan, Sgt H. G. Phillips, Sgt W. Twort. *57 Squadron:* F/Sgt H. S. Gifford, Sgt A. G. Harrison, F/O E. Hodgkinson, Sgt J. Sheriff. *61 Squadron:* Sgt G. E. Moffitt, Sgt H. Pritchard Roberts, F/Sgt A. E. Wilson. *75 Squadron:* F/Sgt W. H. Batger, Sgt W. A. Kirk. *76 Squadron:* Sgt A. H. L. Atkinson, Sgt L. I. Brown, Sgt R. Clough, Sgt A. W. Davis, P/O K. Hewson, Sgt T. Isaacs, Sgt A. Kirkham, F/O R. G. McCadden, Sgt M. A. Manser, Sgt F. A. Newton, Sgt K. R. Parry, F/Lt E. A. Strange, Sgt G. W. R. Taylor, Sgt V. A. Thomson, Sgt G. G. A. Whitehead. *77 Squadron:* Sgt O. E. Burger, S/Ldr D. H. Duder, Sgt A. G. S. McCulloch, F/Lt F. G. Shaw. *78 Squadron:* Sgt A. E. Beswick, Sgt E. H. Burgess, Sgt E. A. Gosling, Sgt J. Greet. *83 Squadron:* F/Sgt F. J. Chadwick, F/Lt S. J. Coleman, Sgt H. Coles (died 1980), Sgt P. L. T. Lewis, S/Ldr N. H. Scrivener, Gp Capt. J. H. Searby, Sgt J. W. Slaughter, F/Lt R. F. W. Turner. *90 Squadron:* P/O E. G. Appleby, P/O D. A. Beaton, Sgt A. R. Clarke, F/O W. S. Day, Sgt J. H. Fenn, Sgt T. Fitzsimmons, Sgt P. Foolkes, Sgt K. G. Forester, Sgt T. D. Gregory, Sgt S. Guyan, F/O G. W. Ingram, Sgt R. A. James, Sgt J. G. Morris. *97 Squadron:*

F/Sgt W. H. Layne, F/Sgt G. Pearce, S/Ldr E. E. Rodley. *100 Squadron:* W.O. J. R. Clark, Sgt G. W. Cooke, Sgt S. N. Cunnington, Sgt L. Y. Easby, W.O. D. G. Edwards, Sgt W. G. Green, P/O W. K. Hynam, Sgt J. J. McAnaney. *101 Squadron:* Sgt G. R. Fawcett, F/Sgt L. H. King, F/Lt R. L. L. McCulloch, Sgt J.-J. Minguy, Sgt R. Schofield. *102 Squadron:* Sgt E. L. Dutton, Sgt K. Mountney, Sgt R. G. Pharo, F/Sgt W. A. Rice, F/O J. W. Ward, Sgt H. Williams. *103 Squadron:* F/Sgt C. W. Annis, P/O R. Atkinson, P/O J. T. Birbeck, Sgt G. F. Brice, F/O J. A. Day, P/O E. J. Densley, W.O. S. F. Gage, Sgt P. W. Lees, Sgt R. J. H. Littleton, Sgt C. K. Maun, P/O N. Olsberg. *106 Squadron:* Sgt L. G. Berry. *115 Squadron:* Sgt D. W. N. Franklin, Sgt G. R. Mooney, Sgt H. Smith. *139 Squadron:* F/Lt R. A. V. Crampton, F/Lt G. F. Hodder, W.O. V. J. C. Miles (died 1981), Sgt C. R. T. Mottershead, F/Sgt E. R. Perry. *156 Squadron:* Sgt G. D. Aitken, P/O P. A. Coldham, F/O A. S. Drew, Sgt D. H. Evans, W.O. A. P. Fast, F/Sgt J. E. Foley, Sgt G. Forbes, F/O C. R. Johnson, Sgt H. G. Murly, F/O C. R. Norton, P/O F. J. Wilkin, P/O H. J. Wright, F/O R. P. Wright. *158 Squadron:* Sgt G. S. Almond, Sgt J. Cotter, P/O H. Frisby, Sgt A. M. Glendenning, Sgt E. Grace, Sgt T. Kennedy, Sgt J. E. T. Pearson, Sgt E. Sanderson, F/O T. Smart, P/O A. K. Young. *199 Squadron:* Sgt R. Taylor. *207 Squadron:* S/Ldr D. M. Balme, Sgt A. Cordon, Sgt. L. W. Mitchell. *214 Squadron:* F/Sgt A. Boyd, Sgt R. Conolly, F/O K. E. W. Evans, Sgt R. Foggin, F/O G. H. Hart, Sgt C. Houlgrave, F/Sgt H. Triplow. *218 Squadron:* Sgt A. W. D. King, F/O M. J. Morel, W/Cdr W. G. Oldbury. *405 Squadron:* P/O H. Gowan, Sgt J. G. McLaughlan, S/Ldr P. G. Powell, P/O G. J. South. *419 Squadron:* F/Lt J. D. Corcoran, Sgt W. F. Griffiths, P/O S. E. James, F/O F. T. Judah, Sgt E. R. Kirkham, Sgt J. McIntosh, Sgt E. S. Mulholland, F/O J. A. Westland. *427 Squadron:* Sgt G. J. A. Chaput, P/O R. W. Charman, Sgt R. T. Johnson, Sgt R. McNamara, P/O G. S. Schellenberg, F/Sgt R. L. Skillen, P/O G. L. Vogan. *428 Squadron:* Sgt S. A. Baldwin, P/O N. M. Bush, W.O. A. Harrison, Sgt G. F. Hodson, Sgt R. G. Seaborn. *434 Squadron:* F/Sgt L. G. Christmas, Sgt P. S. Crees, Sgt J. R. Dobie, Sgt G. N. Irving, Sgt J. Pollard, Sgt K. W. Rowe. *460 Squadron:* F/Sgt H. L. Britton, Sgt G. Cairns, F/Sgt R. C. Coveny, F/Sgt A. G. Elwing, F/O A. Flett, Sgt H. Gorell, Sgt E. F. Groom, Sgt I. C. Heath, F/Sgt F. H. Magnus, W/Cdr C. E. Martin, Sgt W. L. Miller, P/O D. B. Moodie, F/Sgt G. J. Oakshott, P/O T. E. Osborn, F/O J. E. C. Radcliffe, F/Sgt G. J. Sharpe, F/O K. L. Shephard, F/Sgt B. Treacy, F/Sgt J. Venning. *467 Squadron:* Sgt P. G. Barry, Sgt C. A. Bicknell, Sgt C. A. Cawthorne, Sgt R. Garnett, Sgt F. G. Miller, Sgt G. W. Oliver, F/Sgt G. F. Tillotson, P/O J. H. Whiting. *619 Squadron:* F/Sgt J. Simkin, F/O A. H. Tomlin (died 1981). *620 Squadron:* F/Sgt J. L. Elliott, S/Ldr A. D. Lambert, Sgt C. C. Leeming, Sgt W. H. Sonnenstein.

Gp Capt. C. D. C. Boyce, of 8 Group H.Q., flew on the raid with a 97 Squadron crew.

FIGHTER COMMAND INTRUDERS

25 Squadron: Sgt C. E. Booth, F/O V. Bridges (died 1980), S/Ldr F. N. Brinsden. *141 Squadron:* F/O M. S. Allen, S/Ldr C. V. Winn. *157 Squadron:* F/O G. V. Carcasson. *605 Squadron:* F/Lt D.H. Blomeley, F/O A. G. Woods.

COMMANDERS AND STAFFS

Air Ministry: Air Cdre S. O. Bufton, Director of Bomber Operations.
Bomber Command H.Q.: Air Chief Marshal Sir Arthur Harris, Gp Capt. N. W.
D. Marwood- Elton, W/Cdr W. I. C. Inness, S/Ldr F. A. B. Fawssett.
5 Group H.Q.: S/Ldr T. J. Beach, Air Cdre H. V. Satterley (died 1982).
8 Group H.Q.: S/Ldr H. W. Lees.
540 Squadron: F/O W. M. Hodsman, Intelligence.

THE COMMUNITY OF PEENEMÜNDE
(including servicemen and civilians in nearby villages)

German: Franz Atenhan, Otto Beisswenger, Lisa Berghof, Herbert Bick, Prof.
F. W. Bornscheuer, Regina Boy, Walter Bracher, Wilhelm Buckesfeld, Karl
Bührer, Franz Czekalla, Erich Dänicke, Max Donaubauer, Wilhelm
Ebenau, Dr Willy A. Fiedler, Werner K. Gengelbach, Pfarrer Helmut
Graeber, Helmuth Hagenström, Edgar Heym, Inge Holz (now Faren-
burg), Horst Huber, Karl Huber, Gerhard Hufer, Dieter K. Huzel, Dora
John (now Freytag), Matthias Kempkens, Dorette Kersten (now Schlidt),
Liesl Kielhorn (now Reichel), Rudolf Klaes, Alfred Klein, Erika Klein,
Prof. A. H. Knothe, Horst Köpke, Otto Kraehe, Dieter Krölls, Werner
Küsters, Gisela Lichtenberg, Otto Lippert, Dr Werner Magirius, Anna
Maissen-Nagel, Herbert Maronde, Dr Siegfried Marquardt, Heinz Menschel,
Irmgard Mühlenbeck, Gerda Naujoks (now Sallar), Ernst Palm, Gertrud
Pawehls (now Hölge), Kurt Peiss, Kurt Peters, Karl-Heinz Pfeffer, Lotti
Priem, Axel Roth, Arthur Rudolph, Gerhard Rühr, Karl Schreiner, Ernst
E. Seiler, Günter Spalding, Hermann Steinmetz, Edmund J. Stollenwerk,
Georg Stork, Franz Treib, Christel Voss (now Clemens), Herbert
Wawretschek, Hildegard Weiß, Prof. Dr Siegfried Winter.

Polish: Jakub Bajurski, Marian Balt, Tomasz Baranski, Waclaw Barszcz,
Czeslaw Bloch, Stanislaw Bogolodczyk, Ignacy Bryl, Zdzislaw Chorosz,
Robert Czech, Mieczyslaw Dabrowski, Wladyslaw Dabrowski, Eryk Dobiecki,
Zenon Drozdowski, Stefan Flis, Zenon Gara, Antoni Geborys, Jozef Geborys,
Franciszek Gontarz, Kazimierz Haber, Stefan Hildebrandt, Stefan Janowski,
Kasimierz Kierzkowski, Jan Maliglowka, Stanislaw Marchewka, Jan
Marzynski, Jozef Mlynarski, Kazimierz Mszanowski, Walerian Nowaczyk,
Jozef Nowak, Irena Ocipka (now Piotrowska), Jan Pasenik, Franciszek
Poniecki, Stanislaw Prawucki, Aleksander Rzepkowski, Jan Skwarek,
Stanislaw Smolak, Jan Tomanek, Antoni Wasiak, Feliks Wereszczynski.

Luxembourgers: Alois Schiltz, Henri Steffen.

French: Jean Degert.

Ukrainian: Major Peter N. Paley.

LUFTWAFFE AIRCREW

I/NJG1: Uffz. Helmut Fischer. *II/NJG1:* Oblt Walter Barte, Hptm. Eckart
von Bonin, Obergefreiter Helmut Hafner, Lt Johannes Hager, Ofw. Rudolf

Lüdeke. *III/NJG1:* Hptm. Wilhelm Dormann. *I/NJG3:* Uffz. Eberhard Scheve; Oblt Paul Zorner. *II/NJG3:* Uffz. Josef Krinner. *III/NJG3:* Lt Hans Raum. *IV/NJG3:* Uffz. Benno Gramlich. *II/NJG5:* Uffz. Walter Hölker, Lt Peter Spoden, Lt Rudolf Thun. *JG300:* Major Hajo Herrmann, Oblt Friedrich-Karl Müller.

General Josef Kammhuber, commander XII Fliegerkorps, also helped.

Part 2   Personal Acknowledgements

Once again it is my pleasure to record thanks to the many people in different countries who provided such valuable help in the preparation of this book.

Pride of place must go to Chris Everitt, of Eton Wick, who has carried out the entire Public Record Office search of documents for this book as well as other research. I cannot stress too much how useful this help has been.

Close behind Mr Everitt must come Janet Mountain, my regular typist, who, for the sixth time, has coped so diligently with the extensive correspondence of the research and the typing of two drafts of the manuscript. The third in this group of leading helpers is my wife, Mary, who drew the preliminary maps and also carried out the tedious but all-important work of checking the typescript.

The following individuals also gave generous voluntary assistance. The listing by countries and sometimes in alphabetical order does not imply any order of merit. I am extremely grateful to them all. *England:* Alan Cooper of Orpington, Tom Cushing of Little Snoring, Elizabeth and Malcolm Downie, Dr Stanislaw Sobolewski, Ted Sylvester, Annie Taverner and Alan Taylor, all of Boston, Mike Hodgson of Mareham-le-Fen and Peter Pountney of Grimsby. *Germany:* Arno Abendroth of Berlin, Hans-Martin Flender of Siegen, Gus Lerch of Frankfurt, Norbert Krüger of Essen and Emil Nonnenmacher of Eppstein/Taunus. *Denmark:* Anders Bjørnvad of Rude, Major Flemming B. Muus of Virum and Niels Chr. Rasmussen of Nykøbing. *Luxembourg:* Henri Koch-Kent. *Switzerland:* Paul Spitzer, Zug. *Australia:* Godfrey Ball, Greenslopes, Brisbane. *New Zealand:* John Barton, Auckland.

I am also most grateful to the following voluntary bodies and their secretaries for placing appeals on my behalf in their magazines or newsletters: Air Crew Association (John Williams), Air Gunners' Association (F. N. Gill), The Pathfinder Association, The Royal Air Forces Association, R.A.F. Ex-Prisoner-of-War Association (Dan London), The Wickenby Register (Arthur Lee), R.C.A.F. Association, Royal Canadian Military Institute, Pathfinder Association of Queensland (Allan Vial), Ehemaliger Peenemünder (Heinz Grösser and Frau Sallar), La Fédération des Travailleurs Déportés et Refractaires of Brussels, Les Déportés du Travail of Paris, La Fédération des Victimes du Nazisme Enrôlées de Force of Luxembourg, and ZBoWiD (Polish Association for Fighters for Liberty and Democracy) – particularly Mr Stanislaw Cybulski of the Warsaw Railway Workers' Branch.

As ever, helpful people at many official establishments have responded willingly to my requests for information, and I am pleased to record my thanks to them: the Ministry of Defence (Depts AR8b, AR9, the Air Historical Branch and the Personnel Management Centre), the Records Sections of the Australian, Canadian and New Zealand Defence Ministries, the Imperial War Museum, the Boston Branch of Lincolnshire Libraries, the Cranwell College Library, the Boroughs of Chelsea, Hounslow and Norwich, the Parish Council of Woodhall Spa, the Town Archives at Arnhem in Holland and the Deutsche Dienststelle in Berlin.

I acknowledge the Controller of H.M. Stationery Office for permission to quote from Crown Copyright documents in the Public Record Office.

I would like to express my thanks to the editors of the following newspapers and magazines for publishing my appeals for participants in the Peenemünde raid.

United Kingdom: *Birmingham Post, Bucks Herald, Central Somerset Gazette, Crowle Advertiser, Daily Telegraph, Eastern Daily Press, Grimsby Evening Telegraph, Leicester Mercury, Lincolnshire Echo, Lincolnshire Standard, Liverpool Post, London Evening News, Manchester Evening News, Newcastle Evening Chronicle, Nottingham Evening Post, The Times Literary Supplement, Western Morning News, Yorkshire Post; Air Mail, Air Pictorial, R.A.F. News, Spaceflight, R.U.S.I. Journal, Ukrainian Press.*

Germany: *Der Abend*, Berlin, and *Berliner Morgenpost, Darmstädter Tagblatt, Flensburger Tagblatt, Hannoversche Allgemeine Zeitung, Nordsee Zeitung, Rheinische Post, Saarbrücker Zeitung; Stuttgarter Zeitung, Allgemeine Judische Wochenzeitung, Europäische Wehrkunde, Jägerblatt; Luftwaffen Revue, Marine Rundschau, Wehrwissenschaftliche Rundschau.*

Poland: *Express Wieczorny, Glos Szczecinski, Przekroj, Slowo Powszechne, Zycie Czestochowy, Zycie Warszawy.*

Canada: *Hamilton Spectator, Regina Leader Post, Victoria Colonist, Winnipeg Free Press, Czas* (Polish Times of Winnipeg), *Sentinel* and *Sentinelle.*

Australia: *Melbourne Sun, Queensland Courier Mail, Sydney Sunday Telegraph; Wings.*

New Zealand: *Christchurch Press, Dunedin Evening Star.*

U.S.A.: *Aviation Week and Space Technology, Huntsville Times, Jewish Veteran, National Jewish Monthly, Chicago Sonntagpost, Torchlight.*

Denmark: *Frihedskampens Veteraner.*

Luxembourg: *Luxemburger Wort.*

Bibliography

OFFICIAL HISTORIES

Craven, W. F., and Cate, J. L., *The Army Air Forces in World War II*, University of Chicago Press, 1948–58.
Foot, M. R. D., *S. O. E. in France*, H.M.S.O., 1966.
Webster, Sir Charles, and Frankland, Noble, *The Strategic Air Offensive against Germany, 1939–1945*, H.M.S.O., 1961.

OTHER WORKS

Braham, J. R. D., *Scramble*, Muller, 1961.
Cooksley, Peter G., *Flying Bomb*, R. Hale, 1979.
Dornberger, Walter, *V-2*, Viking, 1954 (original German is *V-2, Der Schuss ins Weltall*, Bechtle Verlag, Esslingen, 1952).
Garlinski, Jozef, *Hitler's Last Weapons*, J. Friedmann, 1978.
Harris, Sir Arthur, *Bomber Offensive*, Collins, 1947.
Irving, David, *The Mare's Nest*, Kimber, 1964.
Jones, R. V., *Most Secret War*, Hamish Hamilton, 1978.
Lawrence, W. J., *No. 5 Bomber Group R.A.F.*, Faber, 1951.
Ordway, Frederick I., and Sharpe, Mitchell R., *The Rocket Team*, Heinemann, 1979.
Searby, Air Commodore John H., *The Great Raids: Peenemünde*, Nutshell Press, 1978.
Verity, Hugh, *We Landed by Moonlight*, Ian Allen, 1978.

Index

READ MORE IN PENGUIN

In every corner of the world, on every subject under the sun, Penguin represents quality and variety – the very best in publishing today.

For complete information about books available from Penguin – including Puffins, Penguin Classics and Arkana – and how to order them, write to us at the appropriate address below. Please note that for copyright reasons the selection of books varies from country to country.

In the United Kingdom: Please write to *Dept. JC, Penguin Books Ltd, FREEPOST, West Drayton, Middlesex UB7 0BR*

If you have any difficulty in obtaining a title, please send your order with the correct money, plus ten per cent for postage and packaging, to *PO Box No. 11, West Drayton, Middlesex UB7 0BR*

In the United States: Please write to *Penguin USA Inc., 375 Hudson Street, New York, NY 10014*

In Canada: Please write to *Penguin Books Canada Ltd, 10 Alcorn Avenue, Suite 300, Toronto, Ontario M4V 3B2*

In Australia: Please write to *Penguin Books Australia Ltd, 487 Maroondah Highway, Ringwood, Victoria 3134*

In New Zealand: Please write to *Penguin Books (NZ) Ltd,182–190 Wairau Road, Private Bag, Takapuna, Auckland 9*

In India: Please write to *Penguin Books India Pvt Ltd, 706 Eros Apartments, 56 Nehru Place, New Delhi 110 019*

In the Netherlands: Please write to *Penguin Books Netherlands B.V., Keizersgracht 231 NL–1016 DV Amsterdam*

In Germany: Please write to *Penguin Books Deutschland GmbH, Friedrichstrasse 10–12, W–6000 Frankfurt/Main 1*

In Spain: Please write to *Penguin Books S. A., C. San Bernardo 117–6° E–28015 Madrid*

In Italy: Please write to *Penguin Italia s.r.l., Via Felice Casati 20, I–20124 Milano*

In France: Please write to *Penguin France S. A., 17 rue Lejeune, F–31000 Toulouse*

In Japan: Please write to *Penguin Books Japan, Ishikiribashi Building, 2–5–4, Suido, Tokyo 112*

In Greece: Please write to *Penguin Hellas Ltd, Dimocritou 3, GR–106 71 Athens*

In South Africa: Please write to *Longman Penguin Southern Africa (Pty) Ltd, Private Bag X08, Bertsham 2013*

READ MORE IN PENGUIN

HISTORY

The Guillotine and the Terror Daniel Arasse

'A brilliant and imaginative account of the punitive mentality of the revolution that restores to its cultural history its most forbidding and powerful symbol' – Simon Schama.

The Second World War A J P Taylor

A brilliant and detailed illustrated history, enlivened by all Professor Taylor's customary iconoclasm and wit.

Daily Life in Ancient Rome Jerome Carcopino

This classic study, which includes a bibliography and notes by Professor Rowell, describes the streets, houses and multi-storeyed apartments of the city of over a million inhabitants, the social classes from senators to slaves, and the Roman family and the position of women, causing *The Times Literary Supplement* to hail it as a 'thorough, lively and readable book'.

The Anglo-Saxons Edited by James Campbell

'For anyone who wishes to understand the broad sweep of English history, Anglo-Saxon society is an important and fascinating subject. And Campbell's is an important and fascinating book. It is also a finely produced and, at times, a very beautiful book' – *London Review of Books*

The Making of the English Working Class E. P. Thompson

Probably the most imaginative – and the most famous – post-war work of English social history. 'A magnificent, lucid, angry historian … E. P. Thompson has performed a revolution of historical perspective' – *The Times*

The Habsburg Monarchy 1809 –1918 A J P Taylor

Dissolved in 1918, the Habsburg Empire 'had a unique character, out of time and out of place'. Scholarly and vividly accessible, this 'very good book indeed' (*Spectator*) elucidates the problems always inherent in the attempt to give peace, stability and a common loyalty to a heterogeneous population.

BY THE SAME AUTHOR

The Berlin Raids   R.A.F. Bomber Command 1943–44

This fascinating and meticulous study draws on eyewitness accounts from both sides and previously unreleased documents to re-create the most sustained – and controversial – bombing offensive of the Second World War.

Task Force   The Falklands War, 1982

Martin Middlebrook has sought out all the available evidence from documentary and personal sources on both sides, and draws some controversial conclusions about the conflict. 'A first rate book' – *British Book News*

The Nuremberg Raid   30–31 March 1944

What should have been a routine raid on the city turned into a major disaster, with Bomber Command suffering its heaviest losses of the war. 'Martin Middlebrook's skill at description and reporting lift this book above the many memories that were written shortly after the war' – *The Times*

The First Day of the Somme   1st July 1916

It was the blackest day of slaughter in the history of the British Army, with 60,000 casualties – one for every eighteen inches of the front. 'A particularly vivid and personal narrative' – *The Times Literary Supplement*

Convoy   The Battle for Convoys SC. 122 and HX. 229

In March 1943, two convoys set off from New York across the Atlantic with supplies for the United Kingdom. But this was at the height of the Battle of the Atlantic – 'the only thing that really frightened me,' as Churchill said. Martin Middlebrook portrays the climax of that hard, drawn-out struggle with grim accuracy.

BY THE SAME AUTHOR

The Battle of Hamburg

Operation Gomorrah was Bomber Command's code name for the devastating fire raids on Hamburg in July 1943. 'Controversy will persist for generations; Mr Middlebrook's book will provide useful raw material to feed the fires of debate' – Max Hastings

The Schweinfurt-Regensburg Mission

On 17 August 1943, the entire strength of the American heavy bomber forces in England struck deep into southern Germany for the first time. The outcome was the American air forces' worst defeat of World War Two. 'As always Martin Middlebrook brings a clear eye, a clear mind and a clear pen to his meticulously detailed description and analysis' – *Economist*

The Kaiser's Battle

The last great battle of the First World War began in March 1918 when the German armies struck a massive blow against the weakened British troops. 'The clever blending of written and oral accounts makes the book an extremely convincing reconstruction' – *Sunday Times*

The Fight for the 'Malvinas'

The first full account in English of the Falklands War as the Argentinians saw it. 'The most fascinating of the hundreds of literary endeavours on that episode' – *Daily Telegraph*